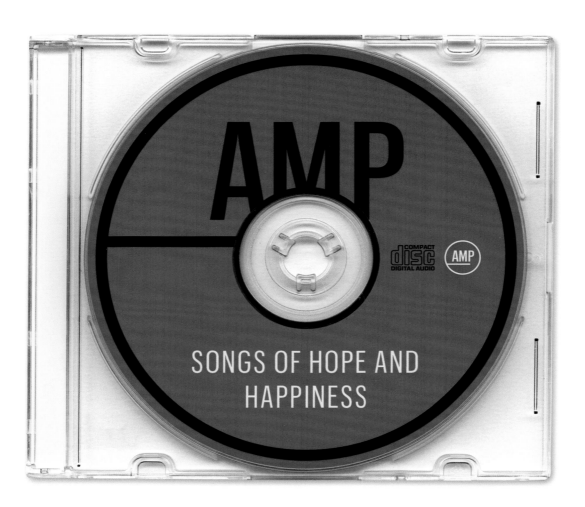

THE AWESOME MUSIC PROJECT CANADA

Produced by Terry Stuart · AMP CURATOR
Engineered by Robert Carli · AMP CURATOR
Arranged by Scott Steedman · AMP EDITOR
Remixed by Peter Cocking · AMP DESIGNER

PAGE
TWO
BOOKS

"I'VE ALWAYS BEEN A MUSICIAN. I THINK WE ALL ARE, IT'S JUST THAT ONLY SOME OF US LEARN TO PLAY INSTRUMENTS."

CHRIS HADFIELD

contents

SIDE 3
MUSIC & EXPERIENCE

SIDE 4
MUSIC & COMMUNITY

HOW CAN MUSIC SHIFT OUR MOOD IN A HEARTBEAT?

A **couple of** summers ago, my neighbour Terry Stuart asked me if I wanted to help him create a collection of stories about songs that make people happy and hopeful. I didn't have to think twice about my answer. This was a no-brainer.

Not a chance.

Terry is full of crazy ideas, like . . . all the time. This was one of them.

Terry was obsessed with trying to figure out why music changes the way we feel, and he was convinced that there was some magic playlist or song that could soothe the most turbulent mind or heart. He asked everyone he met if there was a piece of music that made them happy, searching for a formula that I simply did not believe existed. I didn't doubt the transformative power of music; anyone who has rocked a baby, heard a children's choir, been to a rock concert, or attended a funeral knows what music can do to us. But I believed there was no such thing as a universal "happy" song or perfect playlist. And I still believe that. To put it bluntly, a song that makes one person happy can make another person cringe.

Then I read the stories.

Reading the stories, I realized it wasn't about the song; it was about the story behind the song. It was through the stories that I was reminded of the unspeakable power of music to shape our experience, transport us to a different time and place, and move our hearts. Music can change us. It can change everything.

The same quality that makes music such a highly subjective and personal experience is also what makes stories about music so unique and compelling. The stories you will read in this book are as diverse as the people who tell them. Some are about loss. Some are about hope. Some are just memories of good times that will make you smile. Others will make you cry. While you may not like the song that someone else cherishes, the real treasure is what's *behind* it. These stories remind us that music isn't just something we listen to or dance to. It's something we feel.

introduction

ROBERT CARLI

And why do we feel something when we hear music? Why do we want to dance? Why do we cry when we hear a melody unravel, or get chills at the sound of a voice from our past? How can music shift our mood in a heartbeat?

Turns out, Terry was obsessed with these questions, too. In addition to being a man with crazy ideas, he also possesses one of the most curious minds I know, and he was driven to learn more about the science behind the music. That led him to the Centre for Addiction and Mental Health, Canada's largest mental health teaching hospital and one of the world's leading research centres. And that turned The Awesome Music Project into much more than just a book of stories about music. It has become a campaign to help raise awareness and funds to drive research that explores the links between music and mental health.

We hope that when you read these stories you will be reminded of the healing power of music. We hope that you see yourself in some of them. Or see someone you know. Or maybe just enjoy a good story. And discover some new music along the way.

Everyone has a music story. In this book you'll find 111 of them.

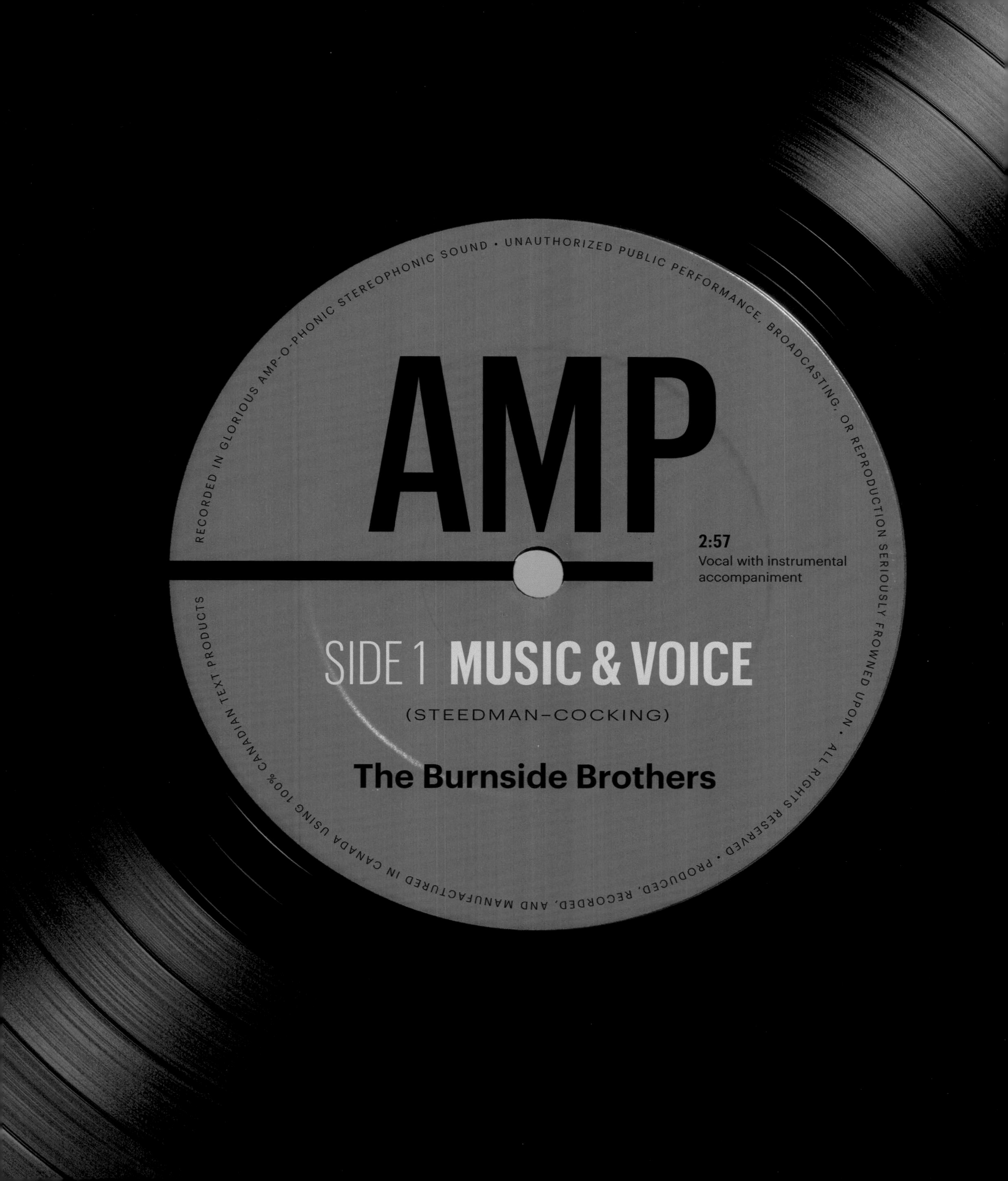
RECORDED IN GLORIOUS AMP-O-PHONIC STEREOPHONIC SOUND • UNAUTHORIZED PUBLIC PERFORMANCE, BROADCASTING, OR REPRODUCTION SERIOUSLY FROWNED UPON • ALL RIGHTS RESERVED • PRODUCED, RECORDED, AND MANUFACTURED IN CANADA USING 100% CANADIAN TEXT PRODUCTS
AMP
2:57
Vocal with instrumental accompaniment
SIDE 1 MUSIC & VOICE
(STEEDMAN–COCKING)
The Burnside Brothers

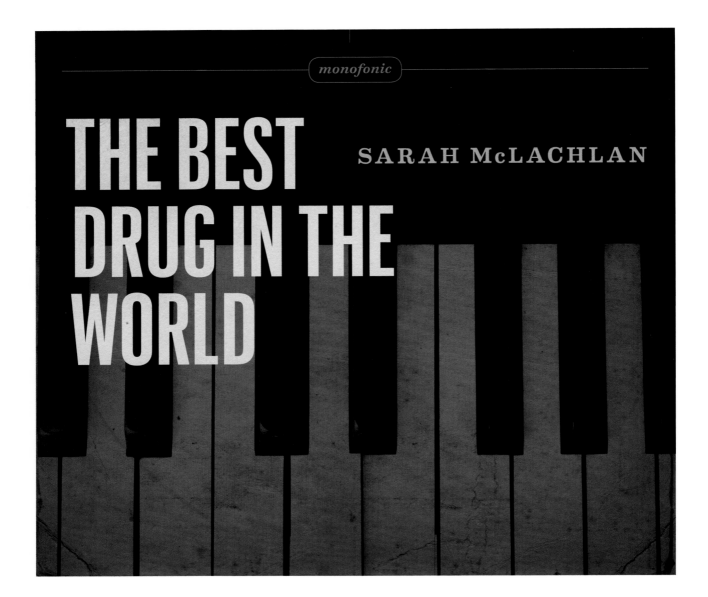

THE BEST DRUG IN THE WORLD

SARAH McLACHLAN

I have been a musician for as far back as I can remember. Music flows through my veins like blood. It is the salve I apply to soothe the harshness of the real world. It has been a steadfast friend, always there, always offering comfort.

I grew up the third child and only daughter of a loveless marriage. My mother was a distant, often angry woman. She did her best but there wasn't much mothering going on. I was a lighthearted, happy kid in my early years, but everything changed when I hit junior high. I had practiced kissing with a girlfriend over the summer, as we were excited at the thought of having a boyfriend and discovering the mysteries of love and romance. In the first week of school, the story that I was a lesbian spread like wildfire. I became a target of constant bullying and abuse by a small group of tough girls.

My elementary school friends quickly fell away and I found myself very much alone. I went to my mother but she told me I was being ridiculous and

> **Singing and playing made me feel free, unburdened, and joyful. Music released me from my loneliness by connecting me to something bigger.**

oversensitive, so I was left to figure it out on my own. The attacks felt relentless. One time I was leaning under my desk to pick up my pencil and, as the whole class watched, Laura (my nemesis) started kicking me repeatedly. I looked up imploringly at my English teacher, who saw it all but just turned his back. I felt terribly betrayed, and distrusted most adults from that day on.

Through all this, thankfully, I had music. The girls never discovered me in the wings of the gymnasium, where I had found an old upright piano. I hid there at recess and lunch, playing that ancient instrument, consoling and healing myself. With music, I didn't feel alone. My mother couldn't love me the way I needed her to, but she did support and provide for years of guitar and piano lessons, for which I am deeply thankful. They not only taught me about melody, chord structure, and harmony, but, more importantly, they also opened up a whole new vista of emotional understanding, a lens through which I could make sense of the world and see my own worth. I didn't know if I was any good but I knew how singing and playing made me feel: free, unburdened, joyful. Music released me from my loneliness by connecting me to something bigger.

I joined a band in grade 11 and the first gig we ever played was at Dalhousie University, to four hundred people. After practicing in a friend's basement once a week, we were standing on a stage in front of all those people, drawing them in with the sounds we were creating. It was a magic I'd never experienced, a spiritual awakening. Music became my church that night—*this,* I thought, *is what I want to do for the rest of my life.* This visceral connection, this shared joy, is the best drug in the world.

From that first raw gig, amazingly enough, I was offered a deal to join a small independent label called Nettwerk Records. I quickly accepted and, after a year of art college, moved from Halifax across the country to Vancouver. I had been given the golden ticket and never looked back. I started writing my own songs and telling my stories, and, in doing so, began to heal. I figured out who I was and what I had to offer through music.

In 2002 I started a free music program for at-risk and underserved children and youth in Vancouver. Public schools were cutting music programs so a lot of kids had little or no access to music education. With the help of the non-profit school Arts Umbrella, we launched a pilot project, which soon became the Sarah McLachlan School of Music. We now serve more than a thousand kids a year between our three schools, in Vancouver, Surrey, and Edmonton. We provide a safe, nurturing environment where everyone has a voice and is heard, seen, and valued.

What I would have done for a place like this when I was growing up. Hearing the kids' stories and seeing their pride in their songs brings me so much joy. I am thankful for everything that has brought me to where I am today. My struggle gave me a deeper empathy and sense of purpose and music gave me a voice to do something about it.

Sarah McLachlan has sold more than forty million albums worldwide since 1989. She has received three Grammy and twelve Juno awards and was recently inducted into the Canadian Music Hall of Fame.

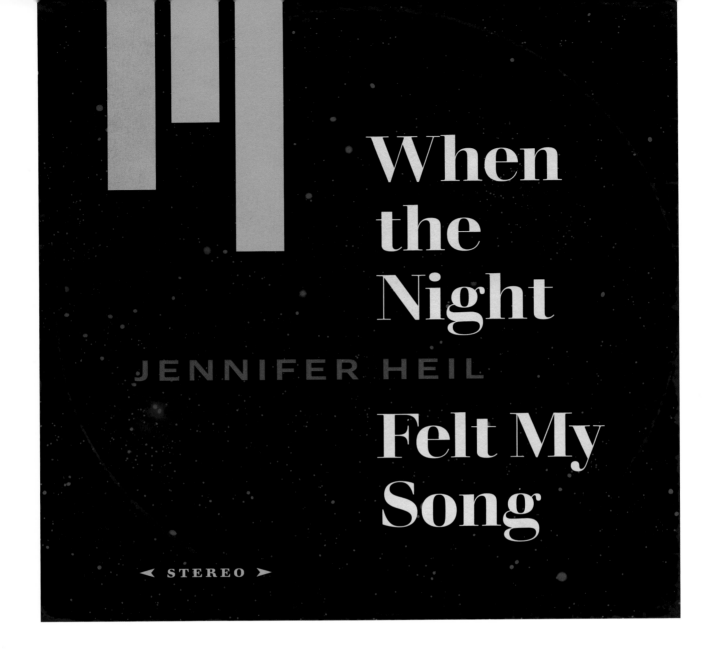

When the Night

JENNIFER HEIL

Felt My Song

◄ STEREO ►

I was an Olympic mogul skier at age eighteen. At that level, the little things are the difference between success and failure—and one of the things that turned me from a fourth-place finisher into a gold-medal winner was music.

As a child I loved to dance. I couldn't stop moving whenever music came on. I grew up in Spruce Grove, Alberta. I remember making the family pilgrimage to the mountains, listening to my dad's music in the car. My favourite was the Fine Young Cannibals,

especially "She Drives Me Crazy." Just singing it now, I can see myself in a fluorescent fanny pack and suit, rocking those slopes. I'm a really bad singer—I shouldn't even sing in the shower. My love of music comes from rhythm and beat, which plays into my love of sport and movement.

When I reached the national ski team and started working with a sports psychologist, we began using music as a tool to help me perform. Even if I had slept badly or was feeling performance anxiety,

I could tap into a place of freedom and joy with the right song. There wasn't a single day when I didn't compete with big nerves, but the music helped me channel that anxiety.

At the 2006 Olympics in Torino, Italy, I had different playlists for different moments. I'd listen to a few beats in the ski lodge; I'm not a morning person, I needed that to get me going. Then I'd start my ski day with a slower, deeper bass beat, to tap into the grittiness, focus, determination. I wanted to stay steady, not get too excited too quickly. That beat was great for going up the chairlift, doing the first inspection of the course.

Then came the morning qualification, the first run. It's super gutsy—if you don't make it into the top sixteen on that one run, you don't even get the chance to compete for a medal. I warmed up with a song I always liked; for years it was an Alicia Keys one.

Between runs I would try to nap in the lodge. I'd be over-amped and would put on classical music to calm myself down. People found it funny that I was able to nap in the middle of a competition day.

The ski events in Torino were held in the Dolomite Mountains, in the evening. Being out on the mountain with a beautiful, pink-orange sunset night after night was an experience I'll never forget. I remember standing in the start gate, thinking, *Wow, the show is starting.*

My special song for the final medal run was "When the Night Feels My Song" by Bedouin Soundclash. It's kind of reggae, ska, a bit slower, but it's uplifting, and so aligned with where I was as an athlete. I was a favourite who was tipped to win a medal, so there was a lot of pressure, but I felt really grounded. I was grateful for all the support, and that song and beat were so positive that they really elevated my energy.

It has a marching beat in it, like I was marching toward this big moment. And the lyrics talk about

It was my special song for the final medal run on the day I won gold at the 2006 Winter Olympics.

what a beautiful day it is. There's one line that describes being all alone as the day turns to night—there can be fear in that moment, but excitement, too, and the song kept even that high-pressure instant positive.

I was up in the staging area ten or fifteen minutes before the race, doing leg swings and quick feet drills to get into the moment. The music tapped into that rhythm and joy, and I gave myself a few moments to dance—which isn't easy in ski boots! Then I took off the earbuds about two minutes before the race and went through my ritual: run up the hill, knock the snow off my boots, put my bindings on, then move on deck, tapping into the power of my breath and making sure I'm totally aware of my environment. Then into the start gate.

I never skied with music. When I was skiing I was listening to the sound of my breath, the scrape of my skis on the snow. And the roar of the crowd; that day I won gold, and the night felt my song.

Jennifer Heil is a mogul skier who won gold at the Torino Olympics in 2006 and silver in Vancouver in 2010. She works with several charities, including Because I Am a Girl and Right to Play, and helped create B2ten, which raises funds to support amateur Canadian athletes.

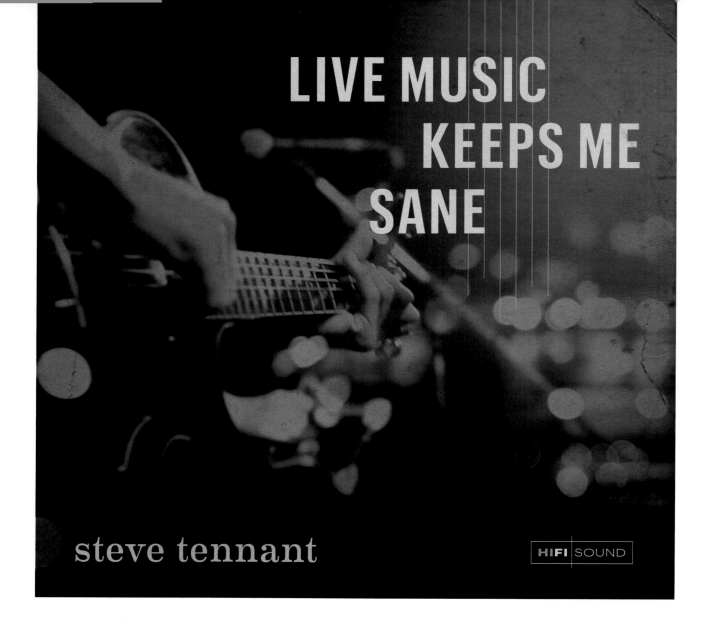

LIVE MUSIC KEEPS ME SANE

steve tennant

There is no doubt. Live music—aided by old-timer hockey and a loving, supportive spouse—has kept me sane. I spent forty years as an advocate for adults with developmental disabilities, mostly in and around wee Perth, Ontario, and loved it, but it was stressful work. Add raising three children and helping out local charities, and live music really made the difference.

I've been a music lover all my life. I grew up in Toronto in its 1960s heyday, when you could sneak into downtown clubs (when the legal drinking age was still twenty-one) and hear greats like Stan Getz, T-Bone Walker, Moe Koffman, Brian Browne, the Downchild Blues Band, and B.B. King. It meant a bus, streetcar, and subway trek to and from my Etobicoke 'burb but it was worth it. Music has always allowed me to step away from the stresses of the day and recharge.

I moved out of "Tranna" in '74 and had to search harder for my live music fix. Luckily, I was often on provincial committees through work or charitable groups and attended meetings and conferences

SOMEONE HAS TO BE A LISTENER. I DON'T PLAY, SO THAT'S ALWAYS BEEN ME.

back in the big smoke. The Colonial and Albert's Hall in the Brunswick House became my go-to haunts. In the evenings, while most of my meeting cronies were sitting in their hotel rooms watching TV, I'd be out scouring the nightclubs for my music fix till the wee hours.

The stars aligned when we moved to Perth, Ontario. Though it's rural and small, the town is home to many wonderful musicians who often play for the love of it. Imagine my joy when a I found a local pub named Tinkers that brought in top talent weekly: Jackie Washington, Colleen Peterson, Willie P. Bennett, and Georgette Fry, as well as quality locals. Later, the same pub, now called the Crown & Thistle, started hosting open mic nights every week, with players driving out from Ottawa or Kingston to join in. These impromptu jams were incredible. Keith Glass (Prairie Oyster) had moved to Perth and his visiting musical friends would often come and join in. I'd go home recharged, the frustrations of the day forgotten, my hope for the future restored.

When I became chair of a provincial committee, I started arranging meetings in Toronto for Tuesdays so I could get the train down on Monday and attend the shows of a terrific group that a high school friend, organ player Rob Gusevs, was in. Called Sisters Euclid, they played at the Orbit Room, an upstairs hole-in-the-wall on College Street. They were an instrumental band, with Rob on organ, Gary Taylor on drums, Ian DeSouza on bass, and one of Canada's top session players, Kevin Breit, on guitar.

Guitarists came from all over to be amazed by Breit. There was something about his playing that was so rejuvenating. He would start a song, mix it up with Gusevs's organ, then head off on one of his eclectic solos. It would get "way out there" for many, but he totally took me with him, soaring throughout the stratosphere and somehow always bringing me safely back long after I thought that was even possible. It was the ultimate re-energizer, my fix.

About fifteen years ago, my partner and I started organizing monthly concerts in our home, hosting singer-songwriters from around the world. Being able to listen to fabulous musicians in our intimate living room with forty of our friends was a great way to satisfy my musical needs, and being able to offer others the experience of listening to top-class players who wouldn't normally play a tiny place like Perth made it even more special. We've since moved the concerts to a restaurant because I'm too old to move furniture—and we can share with far more people.

Someone has to be a listener. I don't play, so that's always been me. I'm thankful for all the opportunities I've had to listen to live music. Through tough times, depression, supporting aging parents, and now retirement, it's been my saviour.

May the music continue . . . for my mind's sake.

Steve Tennant is a retired caregiver who lives in Perth, Ontario.

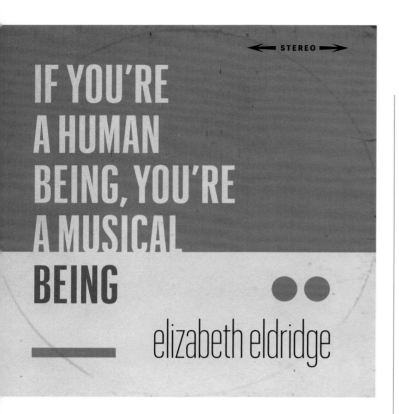

IF YOU'RE A HUMAN BEING, YOU'RE A MUSICAL BEING

elizabeth eldridge

How to begin to describe one's relationship with music? It's an intimate, personal connection. A person's musical tastes are the rawest representation of all that makes them who they are. The soundtrack of my life is a veritable hodge-podge of everything from the Rolling Stones and Rachmaninoff to Ray Charles and Radiohead.

Even at a young age I can remember feeling like I was at the top of a roller coaster when I listened to a piece of music I liked. It was more than just a boost in mood. It was a deep emotional connection. It invigorated. It evoked. It was magic.

As a high school student contemplating what I wanted to be when I grew up, I was drawn to helping fields, like teaching and nursing. The planets aligned when my piano teacher happened to mention a program she'd recently heard about: music therapy. I did a bit of research and learned that music therapists are trained to harness the healing properties of music to help people in many different ways.

I read about music therapists helping patients who'd suffered strokes to talk again; supporting kids on the autism spectrum in connecting with their parents and peers through music; creating calm, meaningful moments through song with individuals in the late stages of dementia. I knew this was the perfect career for me—and I was right.

In my clinical practice as a music therapist, I have learned that being musical means being human. If I had a nickel for every time I've heard someone say, "I couldn't carry a tune in a bucket," "I have absolutely no rhythm," or "I'm the least musical person you'll ever meet," I'd have a very shiny baby grand piano in my living room.

Don't believe the hype—music isn't "perfection" or "divine." Music that connects to the core of our emotions is wholly imperfect, and is most beautiful in its natural state: a mother gently rocking her child, singing a lullaby; kids shriek-singing their favourite song at the top of their lungs; you, singing in the shower or waltzing about the kitchen, which unfortunately adults often do only while home alone. Some of the most meaningful moments I've experienced through music have packed that punch because of a genuine connection to the music and to other people, not because of technical accuracy.

Don't let self-consciousness hold you back from fully experiencing the awesomeness of music. If you have vocal cords, you can sing. If you have muscles in any part of your body, you can feel and express rhythm.

If you're a human being, you're a musical being.

Elizabeth Eldridge is a professional speaker, music therapist, and music teacher. She is the founder and director of Arpeggio Music Therapy and Arpeggio Health Services, both based in her home of Charlotte County, New Brunswick.

We artists do something unusual—we produce something that isn't useful. I don't build houses, create wealth, administer institutions. I make classical music, music that can make people feel better or worse, or, if I'm lucky, maybe mend a broken heart. Every day I put myself out there on the stage and hope people will like what I do. It's very difficult. You have to be very strong and never quit, and hope for the dream to come true and stay true.

I have had lots of moments in my life when I've thought I was losing it, not getting where I wanted to be. But you can't just quit and decide to do something else. What would that be? Music is all I have. Without it, I couldn't survive. When I'm not playing the violin I don't feel healthy.

One song that says it all is "The Show Must Go On" by Queen. That particular song is so important to me that I arranged a special version for violin and orchestra with my friend Bobby Cyr and have started playing it at all my concerts. The arrangement actually dates back to 2003, but I recently recorded it with the Vienna Symphony Orchestra. I've just been touring all over Canada and Europe, ending every show with that piece.

Whenever I play "The Show Must Go On" I feel empowered, like I'm living life on my own terms. I feel like I'm capable of doing anything. Powerful music can create that feeling. The words are simple; the singer keeps wearing a smile, despite a breaking heart and flaking makeup. The combination of the lyrics, the harmony, and the rhythm makes it very simple for the brain and the heart to relate and go forth.

When Freddie Mercury, Queen's singer, says "the show," of course he doesn't just mean the concert or the event. The show is life, and it must go on whatever happens, and it will, whether you are participating or not. It's a reminder that everything is temporary, that people love you one moment and

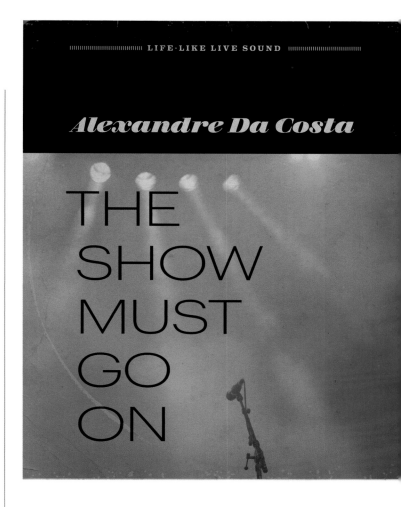

||||||||||||||||||| **LIFE-LIKE LIVE SOUND** |||||||||||||||||||

Alexandre Da Costa

THE SHOW MUST GO ON

hate you the next. That's the beauty of it. A simple statement hides a more profound reflection. The show must go on.

It helps that Mercury was pretty much the best live performer ever. He really was the best of the best. To have a guy like that saying those words with such passion and energy says it all.

Alexandre Da Costa is a virtuoso concert violinist and conductor from Montreal who has played with many of the greatest orchestras in the world. His latest release, *Stradivarius at the Opera*, recorded with the Vienna Symphony Orchestra, was a global bestseller and became a multimedia concert that toured the world.

The music both inspired and healed me. A new career had begun.

When I was thirteen my mother took me to a concert that would determine the course of my life. The performer was an Englishman, Julian Bream, a virtuoso of what I knew then and there was the most beautiful instrument in the world: the Spanish-style classical guitar. I loved everything about it: the crystalline sounds created by the plucked strings, the beauty of its curved shape, the smell of cedar and rosewood, the way Bream cradled the instrument close to his body, and, of course, the unique and romantic music that he somehow conjured from it.

My father had been born in Spain, and my parents happened to have given me an inexpensive Spanish guitar the previous Christmas. All through my teenage years, learning how to play it was my passion and my obsession. I went on to study with the best teachers in the world, including Bream and the Spanish maestro Andrés Segovia, and I spent two years in Paris as the private student of the French guitarist Alexandre Lagoya.

For the next three decades I toured the globe, releasing twenty-some albums and earning the moniker "The First Lady of the Guitar." I was a virtuoso and a superstar, appearing three times on the *Tonight Show Starring Johnny Carson* and hosting my own TV specials. My life was a romance novel, a fairy tale complete with a handsome husband in Beverly Hills.

Then, in 2002, I performed my last classical concert. For the past two years I had been struggling with diminished coordination in the middle finger of my right hand. I was diagnosed with musician's focal dystonia, a little-understood condition that causes a very specific map in the brain to lose its definition. It seemed that forty years of playing the same notes millions of times had caused one finger to rebel and no longer obey my brain's commands. There was absolutely nothing physically wrong with my hand, and no pain whatsoever, except in my heart. But it felt like a personal tragedy.

I had to quit performing in 2003, and would not return to the stage until 2009. My marriage ended in divorce and I moved all alone to Miami, where, still struggling to retrain my disobedient finger, I fell in love again—this time with the beautiful melodies on an album by a Croatian singer and guitarist named Srdjan Givoje. I must have played that album two hundred times. The music both inspired and healed me. A new career had begun.

The first song I recorded with Srdjan was "Little Seabird," my lyrics an allegory for the struggles of life. I had always written poetry and songs, but had never dared to sing them. I now realized that I was a natural songwriter and reinvented myself as a singer, while still playing my beloved guitar with a simplified technique. I wrote English lyrics to some of the

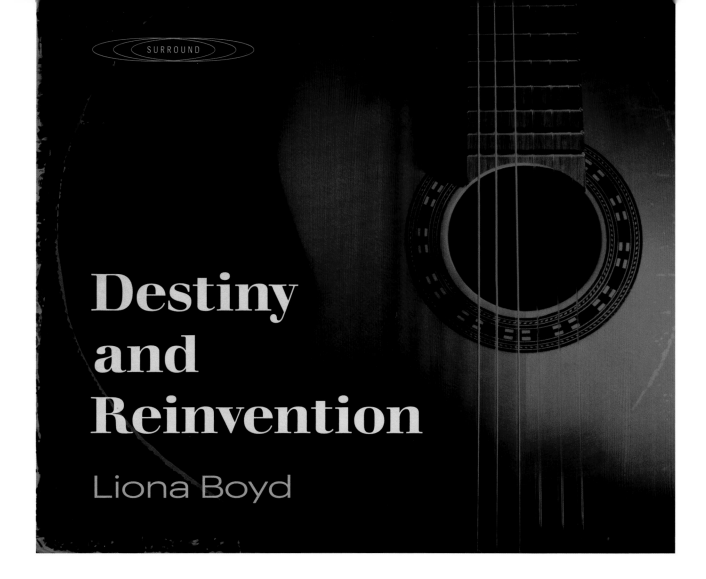

Destiny and Reinvention

Liona Boyd

beautiful Croatian melodies and wrote many original songs myself, then recorded an album of love songs with Srdjan. The creative upwelling helped soothe the emotional agonies I had endured over the last six years, when I'd feared my performing days were over forever. Playing and singing at the same time felt so natural, as if it had been my destiny all along.

I have since recorded six new albums, the latest to be released this fall, all produced by the brilliant Peter Bond. After my concerts, when people tell me how my music has touched them, I can only give thanks to the universe for bringing three extraordinary men—Julian Bream, Srdjan Givoje, and Peter Bond—into my life and taking me on unexpected journeys of musical creativity. In return for these blessings I have been able to share, comfort, heal, and inspire others around the world through my music.

Little did my dear mother know as she bought tickets to hear Julian Bream all those years ago how much she was about to change both of our lives.

Liona Boyd was born in London, UK, and grew up in Toronto. A classical guitarist, singer, and composer, she has released twenty-eight albums and won many awards, including the Order of Canada. She has written two memoirs, *In My Own Key* (1998) and *No Remedy for Love* (2017).

A TATTOO

DAVE ON BIDINI

MY HEART

I WINNOWED IT DOWN, AND TATTOOED IT ON MY HEART. BE YOURSELF. YOU'RE BEAUTIFUL.

It was fun that time I saw the Ramones. Well, maybe *fun* doesn't quite describe it. It was during the World Music Festival at the CNE, on the Old Ex grounds in Toronto. Ted Nugent played in a loincloth, although it was maybe more of a loin pelt. Aerosmith was there. Goddo, too.

This was 1979. It was a hard rock festival and the Ramones were wrong-booked the way they were wrong-booked lots in their career because they were so singular. Nobody really knew what to do with them. Nobody except their hardcore fans, but you could count them on two hands, at least in Toronto.

I'd never heard of the Ramones before. They were just a name on a bill beside Johnny Winter and Moxy and Nazareth, who also played. The Ramones went on fourth, maybe fifth, just as the crowd was getting pretty stoned and hammered, although not me. I was fifteen.

They played and people hated them. Pretty soon, the skies filled with stuff: shoes, plastic flasks, transistor radios, cookies, other food. It was raining garbage. The Ramones played five or six songs and then gave the crowd the finger and unplugged— brzzzzzzz—and left. Later, Joey Ramone told me that someone threw a bag of sandwiches on stage, and they ended up eating them for lunch.

To my left were maybe ten or twelve kids—punks, the kind I'd seen on the news. In front of me, and everywhere else, were stoners, and they surrounded the punks, who were telling the long, greasy-haired heads to fuck off. The heads went at them and the punks took them on. They took them on and they didn't care. I'd never seen anything like it in my life.

The whole crazy, primeval scene made me ask a very fundamental question of myself: Who would I want to be part of? Would I wanna be with the stoners who'd thrown shit at musicians the way drunks had thrown shit at Daniel Lanois opening

for the Hip on Canada Day at Molson Park in 1994? ("This song's for assholes who throw shit at musicians," Gord had said.)

Or would I wanna be with the punks, who cared so much about this band that they were willing to take on dozens of meatheads who hated them for what they looked like and for the band they loved? There was shouting, then cops on horseback, who came in through a gate near the back of the field.

That day, I knew what direction my life would take, and why. I was pointed like a vector against all I'd been taught: be like everyone else, fit in, make art that sounds like other art, don't worry people, don't alarm them, don't make strong flavours, play the game. Instead, I took my advice from something Johnny Ramone told the *Village Voice* a few years later when asked about the simplicity of the band's music (even though it isn't simple): "Just being yourself is being intelligent."

I winnowed it down, and tattooed it on my heart. Be yourself.

Be you.

You're beautiful.

Dave Bidini sang and played guitar for the Rheostatics for twenty-seven years, releasing eleven albums. He has also written two plays and twelve books, including the classic *On a Cold Road,* shortlisted for 2011 CBC Canada Reads. He now performs with Bidiniband.

BRUCE SELLERY

One Day More

ORIGINAL BROADWAY CAST

I **grew up** in London, Ontario, in the '80s. Those were the days of big hair, Benetton rugby shirts, and a whole lot of homophobia.

I wasn't an unpopular kid, but did get teased pretty regularly for being effeminate, "talking like a girl," and being "so gay." I shed a lot of tears over the insults. But what was more upsetting was the thought of how horrible my life would most certainly be once my terrible secret was revealed.

Once we hit high school and puberty kicked in, my peers ramped up their attacks. For the first time ever, I felt unsafe. It was a cold, snowy February night in grade 10 and I was at home alone. All of a sudden I heard loud noises—bang, bang, bang—and realized the house was being pelted with snowballs. The shouting started almost immediately: "Bruce is a faggot. Bruce is a faggot." I was terrified.

So I did what many closeted gay kids of that era would have done: I reached into my records and

pulled out a Broadway musical. As the massive headphones slid down over my ears, the slurs disappeared and Jean Valjean took over, singing "One Day More," from the musical *Les Misérables*.

"One Day More" is a beautiful, soaring anthem. It features all the main characters in the show, backed up by the entire chorus, and brings act one to a thunderous conclusion. My simple interpretation of it at that moment was "bear with it just one day more, and everything will be fine."

Musical theatre was a real refuge for me growing up, and not just on the record player. When my mom started working outside the home after raising five kids, she used her first paycheque to take the whole family to see *A Chorus Line* in Toronto. It was not the most age-appropriate choice, given that I was maybe nine years old, but I was riveted nonetheless. Later, my dad took me to the O'Keefe Centre to go see *Dreamgirls*, and then to New York City with my twin sisters to see *42nd Street*. My oldest sister was a big theatre fan, too, so I had a lot of exposure to the Broadway cast albums of the day: *Evita*, *Annie*, *Godspell*. And when she went into the theatre business a few years later, I got to visit her backstage.

I have now seen *Les Misérables* on stage many times; in England the first time, then in Australia, Toronto, Montreal, and New York. And that song, "One Day More," gets me every single time. The optimism it stirred up in me three decades ago, that everything will be fine, was fulfilled. Everything *is* fine.

Bruce Sellery is a business journalist, TV host, and keynote speaker. He is the money columnist for *Cityline* and CBC Radio, hosted *Million Dollar Neighbourhood* on the Oprah Winfrey Network, and was one of the founding staff members of BNN Bloomberg. His first book, *Moolala*, was a national bestseller. He lives with his husband and daughter in Toronto.

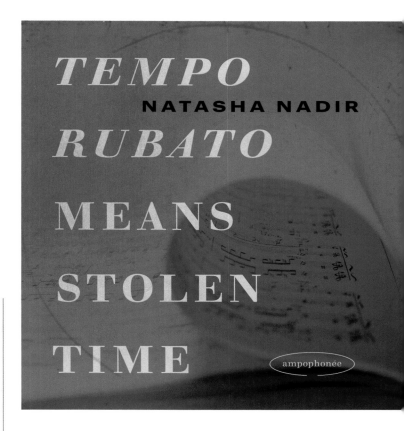

TEMPO
RUBATO
MEANS
STOLEN
TIME

NATASHA NADIR

ampophonée

Music escapes from the dance hall across the street and enters an apartment window, where a girl can be seen dancing with a boy. She is falling in love with him. He might be falling in love with her. If he does, her future is secured; if not, there is very little hope for her. The stage is set for one of the most compelling love scenes in the modern American theatre. As the scene plays out, the girl, who has a slight limp, stumbles, and the couple knocks over her glass unicorn, breaking the horn. Even though it's her favourite piece of glass, she realizes that without a horn, it's just like all the other horses. This is how the "Gentleman Caller" makes her feel—just like any girl, dancing with a boy at a dance. This is the penultimate scene in Tennessee Williams's *The Glass Menagerie*.

The music that is playing is Chopin's *Nocturne in E flat Major*; at least that's what I imagined when I directed this exquisite play for my thesis production at UBC. It has a waltz-time signature that you can just barely dance to because the tempo changes so much over the duration of the piece. It sounds exactly like the first dance between a couple who are trying to find their rhythm. The music moves from halting waltz to ethereal trills, tracking the moments when they are in step and flying, and when they falter.

When I first read the Gentleman Caller scene, I was captivated by how much is revealed and exchanged between these two characters. It plays like an intricate dance. But when I paired the scene with this beautiful piece of music, both the scene and the piece took on a new life. Like the characters waltzing around the tiny apartment, the music and words danced in step, elevating the beauty in each other. They transform one another, just for a moment.

I don't know what it is about Chopin's *Nocturne in E flat Major* that feels so . . . minor, almost as if it can't quite get to major and just hovers on the brink. It lives in nostalgia, mourning something that will never be, but maybe could have been.

Natasha Nadir is a Vancouver-based director, playwright, and dramaturg. She has an MFA in directing from the University of British Columbia and was artistic associate at Gateway Theatre. She is a member of the Wet Ink Collective.

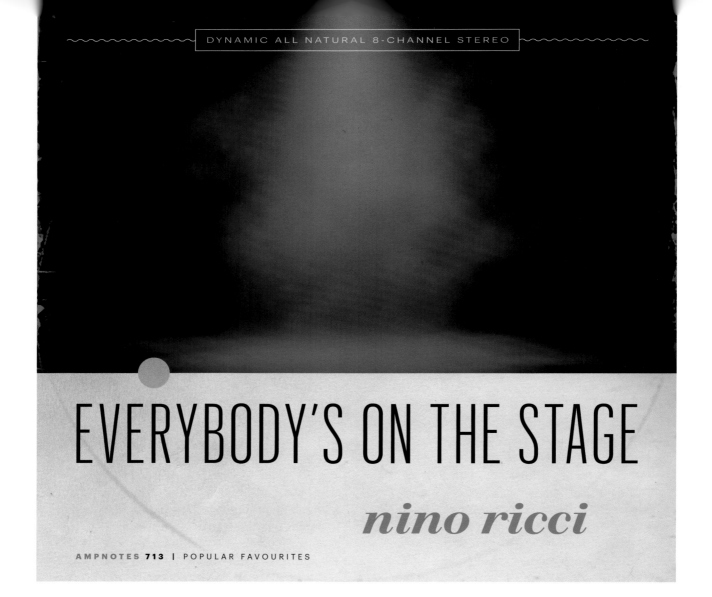

EVERYBODY'S ON THE STAGE

nino ricci

AMPNOTES **713** | POPULAR FAVOURITES

Growing up I had a conflictual relationship with music. Conflictual because I had to play third or fourth fiddle to the musical tastes of my older siblings, who had already claimed for themselves such coveted territory as Led Zeppelin and *Dark Side of the Moon* before I'd had a chance to develop tastes of my own. Conflictual because even among my peers I was always hopelessly belated, with friends who were die-hard fans of Iggy Pop and David Bowie before I'd even heard of them. Conflictual because in my early teens I'd become addicted to cheesy Italian pop tunes like "Mamma"

and "La Prima Cosa Bella" that branded me as hopelessly square, lip-syncing to the latter at a high school talent show wearing a rhinestone-studded Gino shirt in my one, failed attempt at musical glory.

Not that I didn't have my musical moments. Necking for the first time in my brother's Pontiac while Bread's "If" played on the 8-track. Finding the strength to carry on during the darkest days of teenage despond after stumbling on Jethro Tull's "Skating Away (on the Thin Ice of the New Day)." It wasn't that music didn't move me; if anything, it moved me too much, arousing emotions that often

Music moved me too much, arousing emotions that often felt just this side of the bearable, every unnameable fear and hope and longing somehow bound up in them.

felt just this side of the bearable, every unnameable fear and hope and longing somehow bound up in them. Yet like Jethro Tull's skater, I never quite managed to shake the sense that I was the perpetual outsider, sitting alone in the dark in the bleachers while everyone else was jamming on the stage.

All of my musical insecurities rose to the surface again when I became friends with fellow novelist Paul Quarrington. Paul had actually cut his artistic chops not as a writer but as a musician, penning his first books to kill time on the road touring as a bass player for Joe Hall. Despite having racked up an impressive heap of writing awards since then, he had continued to think of himself less as a writer than as a musician who happened to write, always keeping a guitar close at hand and occasionally taking to the road with his blues/roots ensemble Porkbelly Futures. The monthly poker games Paul held at his house were like courses in musical history: Django Reinhardt might make an appearance, and Woody Guthrie, with the night usually closing out with the unsung hero behind such Quarrington favourites as "Galveston," "MacArthur Park," Jimmy Webb.

I was ready at first to dismiss Paul's musical inclinations as just a holdover from adolescence. The more I got to know him, though, the more I saw how music indeed went to his core. He had a gift for bringing people together from across the bounds of his creative selves, a skill that seemed to derive from the musician in him, from his sense of the creative act as an ensemble one. It was at musical events that Paul came into his own, all the inevitable armouring that has to happen in any roomful of writers, who spend far too much time working alone, giving way to an openness and generosity that seemed his truest self. At musical events you could spot some fellow musician in the audience and invite them on stage to share the limelight, something that never happened at

literary events; you could pay tribute to someone you admired without the slightest bit of irony or subtext. If writing was where Paul earned his living and made his name, music was where he turned to recharge from all that earning and name-making.

It was to music that Paul turned when he was diagnosed with terminal lung cancer in 2009. Over the next eight months he completed a final tour with Porkbelly Futures; recorded two final albums, one solo and one with the band; and finished a memoir about his relationship to music. He recorded his last song, "Are You Ready," featuring his childhood friend Dan Hill on backup vocals, just ten days before his death. Less than two weeks before that he had attended my family's annual New Year's Eve bash, where he was a fixture, and where he had played some Jimmy Webb on his beat-up Gibson still looking as if he might live forever.

These days I'm usually still the musical misfit in the room. Thanks to Paul, though, at least I feel like I'm up on the stage now with everyone else, even if all I can do is hum along.

***

Nino Ricci is a Toronto-based writer who has published six novels and two works of non-fiction. His many accolades include two Governor General's Awards and the Order of Canada.

LEARNING HOW TO MOVE

celia moase

I used to wish I could dance freely, but something held me back. After I moved to Halifax from PEI for school, I gradually learned that I was suffering from depression and anxiety. While navigating my mental health, I met some wonderful people who introduced me to the reggae scene, and who also happened to attend great dance parties. I finally lost my inhibitions about dancing. Where before I had wanted to move my body but had felt too anxious to let go, now I was surrounded by musicians, DJs, and music lovers who were all so positive, accepting, and empowering. After seven years in Halifax, I finally felt safe to express myself and dance.

For the next year, whenever reggae came on, I knew how to move to it. I felt empowered, accepted, loved. It was a freeing time. Aside from knowing who Bob Marley was, I hadn't listened to reggae before. For the first time, I could sense my body naturally knowing how to move—and there was so much reggae to discover! It was very liberating. Ever since, I've been able to dance whenever I want to, without needing drinks or a certain song anymore. Once you know how to dance—how to not care—it stays with you.

The next year I decided to move to Toronto, to pursue photography. I felt like I was going against the grain, leaving the East Coast for the big city. I listened a lot to "Soul Rebel" by the Gladiators, dancing in my apartment while I was packing up and driving around the city I knew I was leaving. I felt like a rebel, and the music gave me motivation.

In Toronto, I found people didn't dance as much. I kept thinking, *Why aren't you moving your body?* But it felt good doing my own thing, knowing I had already tapped into my freedom. I was still involved in the music scene, and went out often to shoot gigs.

One night I went to see a band my co-worker was in. I was taking photos and dancing when I happened to meet the man who is now my partner. Although I missed his set—now forever part of our story—he had played right before I arrived.

The next day, over lunch, he mentioned his Jamaican roots: his father and both grandmothers are from the island. Reggae is in his blood; he grew up with it. He asked me what music I liked. I knew it would be a surprise to him, but I replied, smiling, "Reggae." He laughed—and we've been together ever since.

Celia Moase is a photo-based artist. Born and raised in PEI, she now lives in Toronto with her partner, Dason, and their son, Naro.

suzanne

TIM WYNNE-JONES

I failed high school English. I was going to be an architect, anyway, so they passed me . . . what would I need with English in the drafting room? When I was being interviewed for architecture school, in order to see if I was generally informed, they asked me, among other things, whether I'd heard of *The Spice-Box of Earth*. And sure, I'd read about it in *Time* magazine. I hadn't actually read the book; hadn't heard of Leonard Cohen other than through that article. Certainly, didn't know he wrote songs. Still, I passed the test.

Then at the University of Waterloo, in a rooming house of boy engineers and—mercifully—one English major, I heard "Suzanne." The English major made us listen to it. He thought of us all as heathens and had taken upon himself the gruelling task of introducing us to the arts.

"Suzanne" was the first poem I ever truly got. Got in the gut. Got in the blood. Got deep. I don't mean understand; don't mean write a test on; don't mean could analyze within an inch of its precious life. Those were the things I hated about high school English, the things that got in the way.

Architecture fell by the wayside. I was thrown out after three years. I think they were afraid that if I designed buildings, people would die. So I did the only thing that made any sense to me at the time: I joined a rock band, sang in a Spadina bar in striped bell bottoms, a leather vest, and with my face painted paisley. It was there I first started writing songs myself. And songs led to stories and stories to books. Thirty-five titles later, two Governor General's Awards and the Order of Canada, I still vividly remember that wet fall day, sitting cross-legged on the musty carpet of a student rooming house, letting Leonard's words wash over me and sink in, knowing *this* was what I wanted: to build stuff with words.

They say we are completely new every seven years. It's been fifty-one since I first heard "Suzanne"—I'm working on my eighth new life. I've listened to other versions of "Suzanne," but none touches me the way Leonard's does. There is a residue of that first time with her, Suzanne, on the shore of every cell in my body. The tides of time don't seem to wash her away.

Tim Wynne-Jones's latest book, *The Ruinous Sweep*, is a thriller, and his fourteenth novel. His books have been translated into a dozen languages. He lives with his wife, the writer Amanda Lewis, on seventy-six acres of bushland near Perth, Ontario.

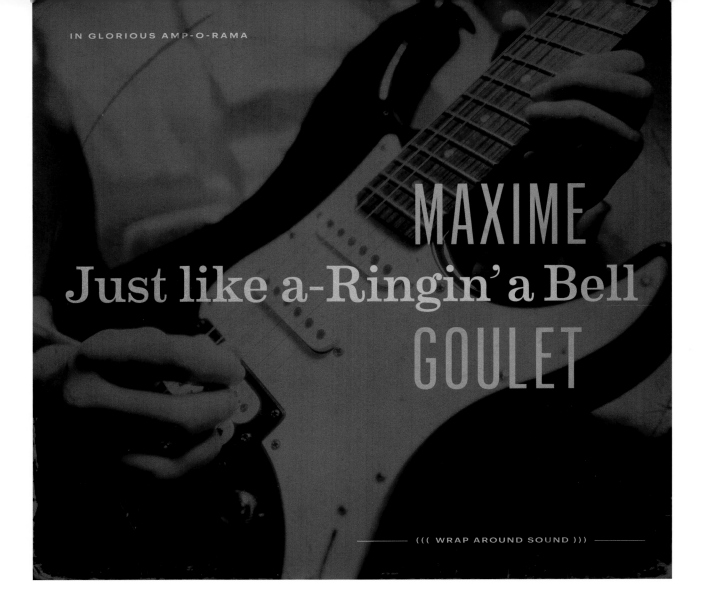

Just like a-Ringin' a Bell

MAXIME GOULET

(((WRAP AROUND SOUND)))

In high school I was a long-haired, slightly introverted, hippie-like boy. Like most teenagers, I felt I didn't "fit in." My Fender Telecaster electric guitar was my escape, my wonderland, the shoulder I cried on. I spent so much time bent over that magical piece of wood!

One of my adult role models was my English teacher, Michael Lewis. He was smart, sensitive, caring, curious, and open-minded. Plus, he sang and played guitar. He always dressed well, in a bowtie, which made me feel as if teaching us was a special event worth dressing up for.

To encourage students to write in English, Mr. Lewis required every student to keep a journal. We could write about anything we wanted: our thoughts, our feelings, our struggles, our daily life, our discoveries. We gave him the journal every week. Mr. Lewis wouldn't simply correct our spelling mistakes; he'd also write back.

I recently moved to a new apartment. While packing, I found my journal. I felt embarrassed by what I had written. Such clichéd teenage emotional whining! But his replies were always touching, and always made me feel he understood me. His writing made me feel special, like my emotions were important.

Each year, before the Christmas holidays, my school would organize a show. Any student could audition to present a little performance: music, theatre, dance, comedy, whatever. The only restriction was that it had to be in French, since it was a francophone school. Back then (in grade 11, in 1997, age seventeen), all the music I was interested in was American and British pop-rock from the '60s and '70s. I thought if I put together a band and the singer was my English teacher, maybe the school would let us perform a song in English. I asked Mr. Lewis if he'd be willing to join our band for the show. He accepted and asked me to choose a song.

I suggested "Johnny B. Goode," the hit single by rock 'n' roll icon Chuck Berry. I loved the energy of that song. It was rock at its most pure and raw. It opened with a catchy guitar solo and had a simple chord progression, which made it easy to improvise more guitar solos along the way. What more could I ask from a song in order to shine in front of my classmates?

Mr. Lewis also liked my choice, but mostly for the lyrics. The song talks about a little country boy playing his guitar by the railway tracks, and how everyone who hears him says he will be a great musician when he becomes a man. "You are Johnny B. Goode!" Mr. Lewis told me. This made me feel he really believed in me and my potential. I also liked how the song described a boy who couldn't read or write so well, but who played the guitar like he was "a-ringin' a bell." I have dyslexia and reading and writing was always a challenge, so I bonded with that lyric.

At the concert, I went on stage with a flower-power shirt and bell-bottom pants. Mr. Lewis, who usually

The performance was a huge success, and after my split-jump ending, we got a standing ovation.

dressed up, was wearing jeans, sunglasses, and a leather coat with a huge American flag on the back. The stage backdrop was filled with Christmas decorations. The crowd went wild.

Looking back at a video of the show, I wince when I see that my guitar solo was way too long, and Mr. Lewis's guitar was completely out of tune. Nevertheless it was a huge success, and after my split-jump ending, we got a standing ovation. The whole experience helped me believe in myself.

Fast-forward twenty-one years. I still get chills when I hear "Johnny B. Goode" on the radio. Unlike Johnny, I didn't become "the leader of a big old band"; and, to the surprise of my old high school classmates, I don't play guitar anymore. But I did make it in music, as a classical music and video game composer. Who would've guessed? Probably Mr. Lewis.

Maxime Goulet is a classical music composer who was born in Montreal and teaches composition at the University of Sherbrooke. His orchestral works, including *Symphonic Chocolates*, have been performed by leading orchestras on four continents. He has also scored more than twenty-five video games, including *Warhammer 40,000: Eternal Crusade*.

MICHAEL KISSINGER

Skating to the Oldies

I'm comfortable enough to admit that I have some deficiencies as a human being. I can be emotionally distant. I have problems saying no to free alcohol. I do not possess cash experience. But probably the most glaring black hole in my ruggedly handsome universe is my lack of ice-skating skills.

Growing up on the mean streets and bird-themed cul-de-sacs of Nanaimo during the feather-haired 1980s, I learned at an early age that when it came to organized sports you either played soccer or hockey, and never the twain shall meet. The same went for musical allegiances. In my experience,

devotees of the Smiths tended to keep a healthy, celibate distance from Van Halen and their partying ilk, though I'm sure there's a mash-up out there of "Girlfriend in a Coma" and "Hot for Teacher" that kicks major ass.

Since soccer was cheaper than hockey and didn't involve 5 a.m. practices or pubic-hair-related hazing rituals, my parents enrolled all of their kids in the beautiful game, which we interpreted as the mildly attractive game.

And while I believe twelve years of soccer made me a gentler, less bar-fight-prone person, my on-ice

If there is an upside to being a grown man gingerly orbiting an ice rink while overly emotive hits of the '80s waft through the air, it's this: I'm improving.

inexperience has haunted me more than picking Eric Staal in the second round of two hockey pools I'm suffering through this year.

So I enrolled in adult skating lessons.

For the past four months, my friends Jeff and Paul and I have carpooled every Saturday to the Britannia Community Centre in Vancouver for our weekly episode of dudes on ice. As a high school math teacher, a registered nurse on the Downtown Eastside, and an editor at a community newspaper, respectively, we make an unlikely bunch of skaters-in-training, especially considering that our class shares the ice with several groups of five- to ten-year-olds.

So far we've learned to stop properly, skate backward, glide on one foot, and transition between skating forward and backward to the point that I think I could have made the 1973–74 Vancouver Canucks. Mind you, I usually fall every other lesson, but I attribute that to my pugnacity, testosterone, truculence, and belligerence.

The most humbling part of my ongoing transformation from wobbly, Bambi-like fawn-on-frozen-pond to beer league superstar is the adult open skate we attend Tuesday nights to practice what we've learned on the weekend.

Surrounded by young couples in love, groups of giggly friends and one flamboyant fifty-something male figure skater who possesses a striking resemblance to Gowan in the video for "Moonlight Desires," the three of us sequester ourselves to a coned-off area of the rink. That's where we work on an array of suggestively named skating skills such as crossovers, c-pushes, and double-sculling, all to a poorly amplified soundtrack of Top 40 hits from Katy Perry to Journey's "Don't Stop Believin'" interpreted by the cast of Glee. Then, without fail, usually as I take

a solo flight around the rink to stretch out my tired, soccer-scarred limbs, it comes on: "Forever Young," by German synth-pop band Alphaville.

Rife with cheesy 1984 production values, which have somehow come back in fashion, and penetrating lyrics that basically repeat the phrase "forever young" over and over, the song has the exact opposite effect its lyrics try to convey. Never at any point do I feel forever young nor want to be forever young when I hear Alphaville's sad-sack vocalist bleat his way through what can only be described as the sonic equivalent of a vasectomy.

If there is an upside to being a grown man gingerly orbiting a community centre ice rink while overly emotive hits of the '80s waft through the air like Drakkar Noir cologne, it's this: I'm improving. Every week I get a little better, which is something most of us experience less and less as we get older. Apart from learning a dance move called "the floss" from a YouTube video last year and memorizing the lyrics to Billy Joel's "Sleeping with the Television On," I can't remember the last time I acquired a new skill or practiced something unfamiliar until I became competent at it.

Maybe it has something to do with time and energy and the lack thereof the older I get. Or maybe I've become what I've always feared—stuck in my ways. Or perhaps, as former Vancouver Canuck Todd Bertuzzi once said after sucker-punching a fellow skater, promptly ending his career, "It is what it is."

Michael Kissinger is the city editor for the *Vancouver Courier*. He grew up in Nanaimo, BC, and has an MFA in creative writing from the University of British Columbia.

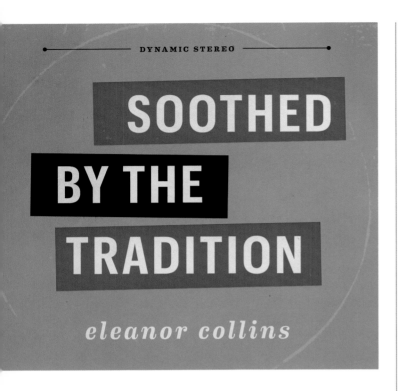

SOOTHED BY THE TRADITION

eleanor collins

Music is and always has been my language. I think in music speak. Somehow, much of life is answered in a composer's lyric or phrase. This is especially true at this stage of my life, when as a performer I have sung so many songs and vocally danced with so many composers.

Now that I'm in my nineties, I no longer wish to sing about romantic love. I am more interested in exploring universal love, healing love, or investigating life script lyrics that express this moment in time or my belief system or unexpressed emotions, like Joe Raposo's "Bein' Green" or Artie Butler's "Here's to Life."

My earliest connection to music was as a young girl joining in the singing of old-time songs or African American spirituals at church or with my Uncle Bert's family band. A tradition was in place that whenever the cousins got together, as children and then in later life, we would begin to harmonize. That was how we connected with each other; it helped us express our shared background, affirmed us a family. The harmonizing just felt good physically and emotionally. It's such a pity that later generations have lost this tradition.

We were all living separate lives of survival and despair as we tried to navigate an often-hostile world. Coming together to create a harmonic blend brought us much joy and allowed us to forget the challenges and stresses of our lives. It felt like fun! We didn't need to articulate the various roadblocks in our lives; we just needed to create some music. In an instant we would feel soothed and supported by each other and by the very tradition itself.

I recently went to see the a cappella vocal group Take 6 at the Queen Elizabeth Theatre in Vancouver. The music and the performers had a profound effect on me. It was very healing to physically engage in that call-and-response type of music. "Mary Don't You Weep" reminded me of songs we sang as children in Sunday school, like "This Little Light of Mine." But here the songs were presented with fully orchestrated arrangements, so as an adult, I could employ what I was hearing to heal the child within. I found myself moved to express myself physically as a response to the call of the music. It became not just a song but an experience.

Nowadays I am very attuned to lyrics. We are never too old to learn or to be reminded of former life lessons; call it learning through song! I'm thinking of the lyric in "Here's to Life" that says that all you get from life is all that you give. I love riding along in my daughter's car and hearing great music on the radio or a tape. That really elevates my mood, even on a trip to the doctor's. It brings emotional relief! Yes, music I like can still ease my stress and give me an overall feeling of well-being.

Eleanor Collins was the first black artist in North America and the first woman singer in Canada to host her own national TV show; called *The Eleanor Show*, it debuted in 1955. Vancouver's "First Lady of Jazz" was a star on many other early CBC TV and radio shows. She was awarded the Order of Canada in 2014, on her ninety-fifth birthday.

The Birth of Poetry

AMPTONES 111

One spring Saturday—May or June—in 1972, in Halifax, my father took me, my brothers, and some neighbourhood friends—including a gal I was sweet on (shyly, secretly)—out for a drive. Dad helmed a station wagon that he'd spray-painted funkily in two shades of blue (lapis lazuli and sapphire), and he was having fun, speeding us up hills and cascading down the other side. For a split second, we seemed to float, to fly. He was sharing with us an element of his motorcycle pleasures, "B.F."—"Before Fatherhood"—as he motored us to Sunnyside, where ice cream and onion rings awaited.

Being the eldest son, a pecking-order post that I relished, I got to sit up front, near the dashboard radio, while my private crush was behind me on the back seat. Of course, I was sure that my feelings were unknown to all. Or, rather, so I hoped.

We were both twelve, and had been friends for two years. Our alliance began out of rivalry—we were both the "smartest" kids in our working-class, grade-school classes: white girl from down the block and brown (black) boy from up the street. But we were entering puberty, and our emotions were shifting as our bodies sprouted toward their adult forms.

But that day—that afternoon—was the moment when I realized, incontrovertibly, inklings of love, urged on, helplessly, by my sudden recognition that the songs spilling from the dashboard, AM, CJCH radio playlist—a mix of Golden Oldies (the Supremes and Bobby Vinton) and Top 40 (the Jackson 5 and Anne Murray)—were speaking to me, for me, somehow expressing my inchoate desires for that girl on the seat behind me.

Later that afternoon, after we'd all returned to our separate homes, I borrowed my father's portable radio, lay down on my bed, and tuned myself—attuned myself—to those songs of kisses, of close dances, of letters "sealed with a kiss," of brandy and starlight and candlelight and wine and sugar and "teardrops on my pillow" and that whole magic movement where the heart is suddenly sensitive, intelligent, and yearning to be wise.

George Elliott Clarke was born in Nova Scotia and has written eighteen books of poetry, five plays, and two novels about the black Canadian community there, which he calls "Africadia." He was Canadian Parliamentary Poet Laureate for 2016–17; his latest books of poetry are *Canticles I (MMXVI)* and *(MMXVII)*, two volumes attacking imperialism, racism, and slavery.

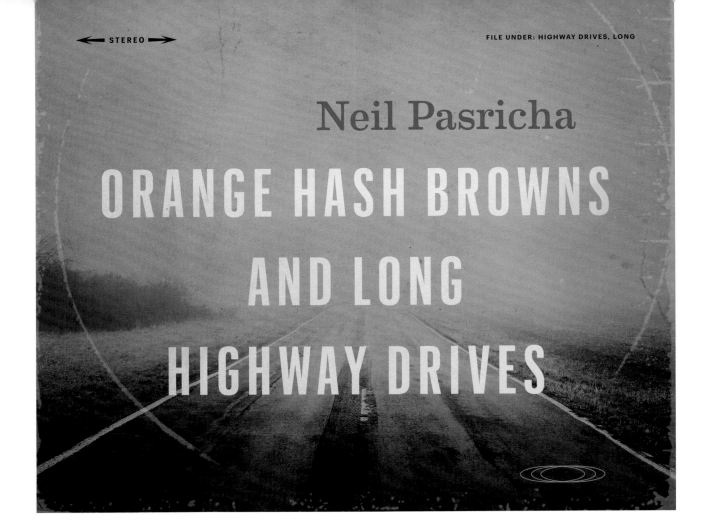

Neil Pasricha

ORANGE HASH BROWNS AND LONG HIGHWAY DRIVES

It was 1990.

I was ten years old and I asked for a mini-system for Christmas. My first! My parents went to Consumers Distributing and bought a bizarre five-in-one system that caught the front wave of the CD revolution before the back wave of the record-player revolution faded out. This Taiwanese knockoff actually had a record player on top, front-loading CD player underneath, an AM/FM radio, and two tape decks at the bottom, so you could perform the extremely rare feat of recording a record onto cassette.

I loved that mini-system. It was such a weird mutant that I think I saw part of my awkward outsider identity congealed and reflected back through the thing. I was the only brown kid in my school.

My house smelled like curry. I had thick Coke-bottle glasses. I never combed my hair. I never talked to girls.

Fast-forward to 1997. I was still listening to my first two CDs: *Forever Your Girl* by Paula Abdul and *Rhythm Nation* by Janet Jackson. Then something strange happened. A popular kid named Rob suddenly took an interest in me. I have no idea why. Rob wore his hair long, carried a guitar everywhere, dated the most popular girl at school, and was really kind and likeable, too. One of those all-round guys that everyone respected.

In our last semester of high school Rob and I began going to the local diner every day between classes. I found myself driving off every morning to philosophize over hash browns that I swirled in ketchup till they were onion-tinged smears of orange mush.

Rob was lead singer of his own band and was really into music, so all his favourite bands became my favourite bands. He first tipped me onto the Beatles and Led Zeppelin and Jeff Buckley and . . . the Tea Party.

The Tea Party?

Yes, they were a three-piece band from Windsor, Ontario, specializing in dense layered goth rock infused with Eastern influences like sitars and tablas and harmoniums. I had grown up hanging out in unfinished basements with my parents and sister while guys would play tablas and harmoniums and the pundit would lead people through prayers and songs to welcome a new baby or celebrate a new home. Hearing those instruments in a totally different and much cooler context blew my mind, especially with Jeff Martin's deep voice screaming about the grip of "temp-tation!"

I bought their latest CD, *Transmission*, and listened to it endlessly.

Near the end of the school year, Rob asked me if I wanted to go see a Tea Party concert in some giant field south of Belleville, Ontario, a couple of hours east of us. He said he'd drive, he'd bring a couple of girls, and I was welcome to join. I said yes right away.

When Saturday afternoon came he picked me up in his beat-up car with two girls I'd never met sitting in the back seat. He steered us onto the highway and proceeded to drive to Belleville like he was in a car chase. I tried to casually hang on for dear life while making idle chit-chat: "So, what do you think they'll play?" The sudden step up the social ladder was overwhelming. I should have been at home studying chemistry but instead I was in a car, on a highway, going to a concert, with Rob and two girls!

More than twenty years later I can still see the beautiful sunset falling over shimmering Lake Ontario while music blasted out of giant speakers on the stage. For the first time I really lost myself, in a tight sweaty mob jumping and singing and cheering while tablas were drummed and sitars wailed and darkness fell and stars slowly appeared in the sky.

The night wasn't about me, wasn't about Rob, wasn't about the girls. It was about the music. It was only about the music. Because the music is always only about the music. We fall out of ourselves, feel it together, stop our thinking, practice our feeling, forget our brains, and remember our bodies.

It would take many more years, but that was one of the first nights I started to see the thick, shellacked layers of self-judgment, self-criticism, and self-labelling I had coated myself with over the first couple of decades of my life. I started to feel that I could maybe put a little crack in that shellac if I aimed my mind a different way.

I got addicted to that feeling.

I left Rob and my hometown behind the next year to begin studies at Queen's University, and I reverted back to my natural resonant frequency of dutiful class attendance, hardcore studying, and trying to be as perfect as possible. Orange hash browns and long highway drives were long gone . . .

But I had a new release now.

Over the four years I was at Queen's I probably went to fifty concerts. I saw the Tea Party every time they came through town, along with bands like the Lowest of the Low, Sloan, Hawksley Workman, Wide Mouth Mason, and Our Lady Peace.

I fell in love with the shows because they took me out of my head, out of my brain, and out of my stress.

And because they were a place where weird mutants and awkward outsiders were always welcome.

Neil Pasricha is an author, podcaster, and public speaker whose international bestsellers include The Book of Awesome series and *The Happiness Equation*. He received a Canada's Top 40 under 40 award in 2018.

LIKE A KNIFE THROUGH MY HEART

SKYE WALLACE

When I was four years old, my grandpa had a Randy Travis album he played all the time, *Always & Forever*, his second album. I got hold of the tape and carried it around everywhere. I learned all the words, without knowing what they meant; I was obsessed with it.

I was a pretty passionate little kid, very dramatic and in tune with my emotions, and somehow those songs really lit a fire in me. I didn't understand a thing about music, but they got me from a raw emotional standpoint. "I Told You So" was the song that really grabbed me; it's so heartwrenchingly dramatic. The first line—about calling someone up for the first time to tell them you love them—kills me. It was like a knife through my heart.

As I've grown and become a musician, I've learned to appreciate what makes that album great. It's such a crisp and cohesive whole, the players are so in tune, the pedal steel soars. All the emotions are really well articulated; the arrangements are so well done. He's a Christian country singer, which is not my thing at all, but that album has subtly influenced all of my music. A little over two years ago I was going through a severe depression and *Always & Forever* was a saviour; listening to it calmed me down, made me feel that everything was going to be all right.

In my own songs I've tried to tap into that sort of emotion. As a woman, it's really important to me to tell stories that haven't been heard or are ignored. My latest single, "Swing Batter," is based on a true story: the 1911 trial of Angelina Napolitano in Sault Ste. Marie, Ontario. After years of domestic abuse at the hands of her husband, a pregnant Napolitano attacked and killed him with an axe. She was sentenced to death following the birth of her child, but

while she waited in prison for her baby to be born, there was an international outcry from early feminist groups arguing she had acted in self-defence. Her sentence was later lessened to life, and she was released after eleven years.

It really threw me when I heard that story; there's so much anger in it. I wanted to evoke that, give power to it in song. One of the first times I played "Swing Batter" was in Sault Ste. Marie, where the audience all knew the story (there was a movie made about it in 2005 called *Looking for Angelina*). It was really amazing to first bring it to a crowd of people who felt it personally, the way I did.

When I released the song, people told me how much it had touched them; a couple of women with a history of abuse even reached out to tell me they felt moved, empowered, and not alone. It felt so good to be able to help, to connect with someone in that way. The way Randy Travis connected with me when I was four years old.

Skye Wallace is a classically trained singer with East Coast roots who discovered punk rock in her youth. She released her second album, *Something Wicked*, in 2016 and is working on a new one that focuses on stories of women from across Canada; "Swing Batter" will be on it.

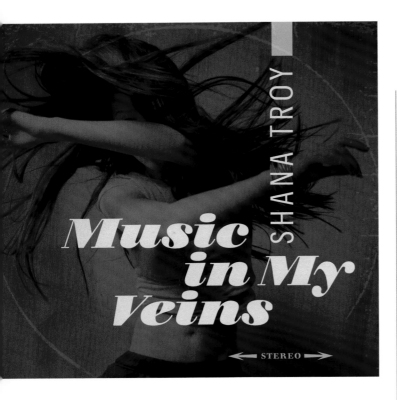

Music in My Veins

SHANA TROY

STEREO

One of my earliest memories of music was watching Paula Abdul performing on an awards show; I must have been ten years old. I was mesmerized by her dancing across the stage and singing at the same time. She was so cool; all I wanted was to be just like her. Paula could sing, dance, and perform like no one had before! In my eyes at least. I loved her catchy songs and danced to them every time they played on the radio.

But it was when I saw Paula perform live a few months later that my love affair with dancing became serious. I've never stopped dancing since. I had been taking ballet classes from the age of four, but when I was home I was choreographing pop shows with my sisters for anyone in the family who would watch; we'd dance to Madonna, New Kids on the Block, Boy George, and Paula, of course.

My love of dance led me through professional ballet school and eventually dancing for ballet companies. I understood classical music and loved ballet; they went hand in hand. I loved the nuances of classical music and could often visualize stories happening just by closing my eyes and letting the soft melodies transform me. But, ironically, when my father—who loved classical music and would often play it—put it on, it would drive me crazy. At home I found it boring and repetitive, but when I danced in ballet shows and worked on choreographies, classical music calmed me and kept me focused. I found a sense of security in this music, and a sense of purpose.

While I was dancing for a ballet company, I began to get restless. I craved some different musical stimulation, a new type of music to dance and express myself to. The answer came in the form of becoming a cheerleader for the Montreal Alouettes. I danced ballet all day long, then got sweaty in hip hop cheerleading classes by night, and loved the musical switch like never before. I was happy and learning new ways to express myself, and it felt great. The switch from one type of music to another kept my mind stimulated and challenged, and I was extremely thankful.

Flash forward eighteen years and that love of opposition in music and dance has opened all sorts of doors in my professional dance career. I've had the opportunity to perform in musicals, TV shows, and commercials, and toured the world dancing with singers.

I'll be forever grateful to my parents for exposing me to such varied music, and for always encouraging me to pursue my dreams. To this day, I listen to music all day long; the choice depends on how I'm feeling or how I'd like to feel on a particular day. I'm dancing for a different audience now: my one-year-old baby, who has the music in his veins as much as I do.

Shana Troy is a classically-trained-turned-commercial dancer who has performed on TV shows and live concerts and toured the world with singer Véronic DiCaire. She lives in Montreal, where she teaches barre classes and dances for her son.

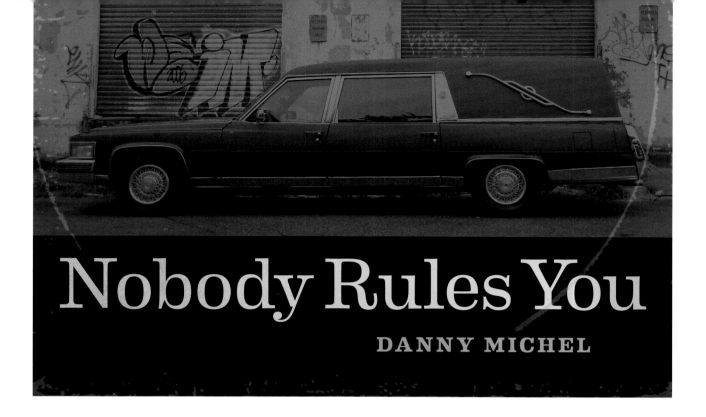

Nobody Rules You

DANNY MICHEL

When I was about thirteen or so I saw a movie called *Harold and Maude,* a comedy about a teenage boy who falls in love with a seventy-nine-year-old woman. To this day it's still my favourite film. It came along at the perfect time in my life and taught me so much. I too fell in love with the character Maude, played by Ruth Gordon. I still live by her rulebook, and probably wouldn't have had the courage to become a musician without her. Maude taught me to march to the beat of my own drum, to not to take things too seriously (but take the right things seriously), to live in the moment, to live and love as much as I could, to appreciate art and nature—and to always question authority. She was the perfect combination of hippy and rebel.

In my twenties I bought an old 1970 Cadillac hearse that my first bands used to haul our equipment around in. But secretly I wanted it because Harold and Maude drove one. Looking back I can't believe my parents let me park that "monstrosity" in the driveway.

The soundtrack of the movie was by Cat Stevens and the main song was called "If You Want to Sing Out, Sing Out." A perfect match to the sentiment of the film. I can't hear this song without feeling absolute joy and hope. No other song does that to me. I loved it so much that twenty-five years later I wrote a song, called "Nobody Rules You," in homage to the film and the song. My version seemed to strike a chord with lots of people and many schools across Canada started getting students to perform it. Hearing those kids sing my song is one of the most rewarding feelings I've ever had. I can only hope I'm passing on a little of Maude to them.

Danny Michel is a musician and producer. His albums include *Feather, Fur & Fin; Matadora; White & Gold;* and *Black Birds Are Dancing over Me,* recorded in Belize. His 2007 album, *Khlebnikov,* was written and recorded aboard a Russian icebreaker. When not performing, he's fighting for musicians' rights and the environment, making short films, hosting *Dan's Space Van,* and running his studio.

If I was feeling down, her magnificent voice would raise my spirits; if I was happy, listening to her would make me even happier.

When I was twenty-one years old, I was at a friend's party and heard this magnificent soprano voice singing opera. I asked who it was, and the answer was Leontyne Price. She had just released her first, self-titled album, which featured Puccini and Verdi arias. She had the most fabulous voice I had ever heard and I was hooked. I was never an opera fan, but rather a Leontyne Price fan.

After I graduated from UBC, Hugh Pickett, who owned Famous Artists Limited, the company that presented almost every attraction that came to Vancouver back then, asked me if I would like to take on the job of business manager. I accepted the offer, an offer that would change my life forever.

I first met Leontyne when Famous Artists presented her at the Queen Elizabeth Theatre on February 5, 1970. I went to the theatre that afternoon for the sound check and watched and listened, fascinated, as she stood on the stage vocalizing. I watched from the orchestra, then moved to the back of the upper orchestra, then up to the lower balcony and to the back of the upper balcony. She was singing without a microphone—no opera soloists were miked during their concerts back then—but everywhere I went I had no difficulty hearing her. Such was the power of her wonderful voice.

FAL presented her in concert six more times, the last on March 22, 1988. That concert was a bittersweet affair for me. I had seen all of her Vancouver performances, plus several in Seattle and Portland. I had also seen her at the Met in *Aida* and *Madama*

Butterfly, and in *Il Trovatore* and *Ariadne auf Naxos* at the San Francisco Opera. I was pretty choked up realizing this was going to be the last time I would see Leontyne on stage, and perhaps in person ever again.

To this day, I still feel that her voice is the greatest I have ever heard. When I listen to any other opera singer, I have a Leontyne Price Scale that they must compare to, and all of them fall just a little short, no matter how fabulous their voices are. There is just something so very special about Leontyne's voice that touches my heart.

A few years after I moved into my house in 1971, a couple of barn swallows made a nest inside my front porch. They raised their first two babies there, and in the fall they all took off for parts unknown. The following year and for every year up to 1994, a pair returned in the spring and took up residence in their spring-summer home, some years having a brood of three, four, or five.

On this particular day, I was out in the front yard cutting the lawn and listening on my headphones to one of my favourite Leontyne Price recordings, *Puccini Heroines.* Suddenly I was aware of a flock of birds flying in and out of my front porch; they were swallows. They started swooping over my head, perhaps eight to ten times, then flew away. Imagine listening to Leontyne's glorious voice singing Puccini's wonderful music with a flight of swallows swooping over your head over and over again. That was a truly spiritual experience.

Through the years I have always listened to Leontyne's recordings. If I was feeling down, her magnificent voice would raise my spirits; if I was happy, listening to her would make me even happier. Such was the power of this wonderful woman's voice and the effect her music has always had on me.

Ron McDougall worked his whole life in the theatre. He writes about music on his blog, *My Four Ladies*.

A Voice That Touches My Heart

RON McDOUGALL

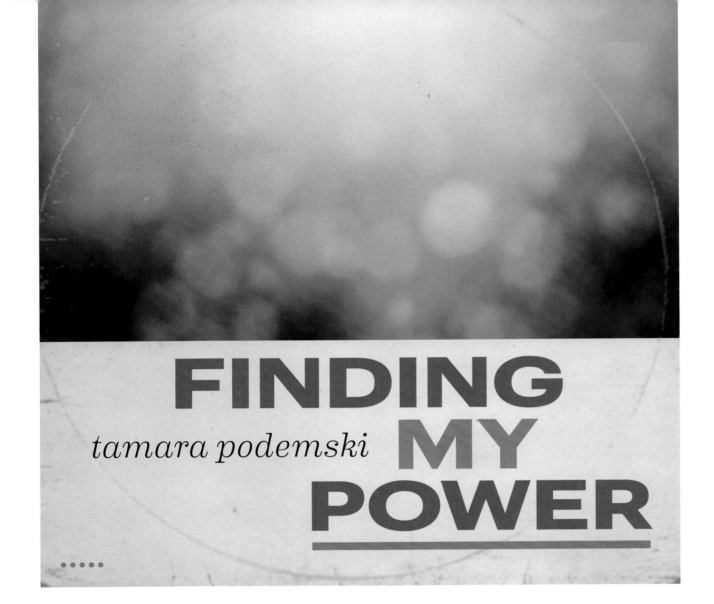

FINDING MY POWER

tamara podemski

I've always loved musicals. I love the torch songs, the big dance numbers, the choral harmonies, the over-the-top theatricality. They are the ultimate escape from reality. A world where people speak in song, "jazz hands" are normal, and everyone gets their moment in the spotlight. I think I know the words to more musicals than to pop songs. I know I've seen more musicals than concerts. I even reference lines from musicals more than from films. They have had a big impact on my life and, in some way, I think they have saved my life, or at least steered it in a better direction.

I grew up in an alcoholic home. My early childhood was full of a lot of dysfunction and trauma, but it was also full of music and dance. That was one of the ways my sisters and I managed the stress, emotion, and confusion. Storytelling and performance allowed us to process our experiences and move that energy through us in a good way. It's no surprise that we all became performers. And we still remember all the words to those early musicals we sang together when we were children.

There was one song in particular that became my personal anthem. When I was twelve years old, I was part of a children's choir that toured with Raffi to the United Nations in New York for Earth Day. I was invited to my first Broadway show, *A Chorus Line*, and my world was changed forever. I watched a bunch of people sing about their love for performance, their desperate need to be seen, and their struggle with rejection. Almost halfway through, a Puerto Rican actress sings a song called "Nothing," with lyrics by Edward Kleban and music by Marvin Hamlisch.

Before the song begins, a spotlight comes up and I see a young Latino woman (the character's name is Diana Morales) who kind of looks like me. With my Anishinaabe/Ashkenazi mixed heritage and dark features, I was already used to people looking at me and asking, "Um, what are you?" I was also used to not seeing people that looked like me on stage or screen. So in that theatre, when this woman who looks like me introduces herself as an aspiring actress, I completely lose myself in her story. With humour and so much heart, she describes an acting class with ridiculous theatre exercises that make her feel nothing inside, and an acting teacher who makes her feel like she is nothing. On so many levels, I could relate.

At this point in my life, I had already put in four years at performing arts school, and had yet to make it into any choirs, dance troupes, plays, or musicals. It was as if I was the only one who knew I was *really* talented. And that's what I heard when Diana Morales sang "Nothing." She knew she was special, even though no one else around her saw it or believed it. Even worse, the people around her denied her talent and crushed her dreams.

There's a point in the song when her acting teacher says she'll never be an actress—never! It is a critical moment, a moment I have faced hundreds of times throughout my twenty-five-year career as a performer: rejection, dismissal, humiliation. Instead

> **I learned a lesson in that song that has stuck with me to this day. No one's word means more than my own. No one's opinion of me means more than my own.**

of crumbling into despair, Diana finds her power. She realizes: this man is nothing, and if she wants something, she just has to find a better class. Then she'll become an actress.

I learned a lesson in that song that has stuck with me to this day. No one's word means more than my own. No one's opinion of me means more than my own. It is all perspective. And in an industry that offers me a success rate of 9:1 (nine auditions for every one job booked), I had to find a way to know my worth and value and truth, *regardless* of what anyone else said.

It's not that what other people think of me means nothing. It's just that what I think of myself means everything. And so, almost thirty years later, I sing this song regularly to honour that teaching, to thank Mr. Kleban for his words, and to remind myself of my own power.

Tamara Podemski is an actress, singer, dancer, and screenwriter. She won the Special Jury Prize for Acting for the 2007 film *Four Sheets to the Wind*, and starred on Broadway in the musical *Rent*. She has recorded three albums, two in the Ojibwe language. With her actress sisters, Jennifer and Sarah, she produces, writes, and facilitates multimedia workshops for Indigenous youth.

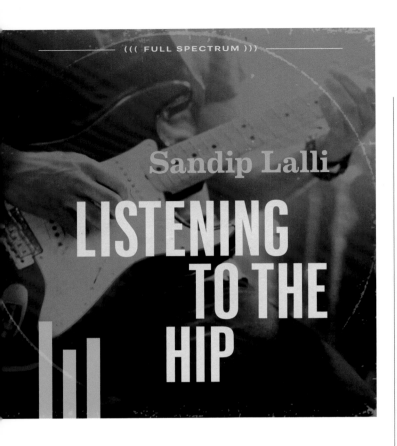

Sandip Lalli

LISTENING TO THE HIP

I **always tell** people, if you want to know who I am, just listen to the Hip. Listen to the lyrics; I've always been a lyrics person. There are three lines from three Hip songs that have guided me in who I am for many years—that have compelled me to be a better person.

The first one is from "Courage": "Courage, it couldn't come at a worst time." When I was growing up in Edmonton, then going through college and far more in my professional career, I've often come back to that line. It's all about your obligation to do better, do the right thing, act on your principles, move forward in a way that adds to the community you're in.

Sometimes it's got me in trouble—they say you should shut your mouth, and then I don't. The line can weigh on you, but it can also make you do incredible things. And it does always come at the worst time! Though the worst times are less and less frequent these days, now that this thinking is part of my DNA.

The second line is from "Wheat Kings": "No one's interested in something you didn't do." That sort of picks up where "Courage" leaves off. To me, it means that good intentions are fine, but if you don't follow through, they don't mean a thing. Every day I think of that and make sure I don't leave things unsaid or undone, make sure I say what really needs to be said in every conversation. My sense of urgency and pace often intimidates people.

The third song is "Hundredth Meridian," which always makes me long to come back home to Alberta. I have had the privilege of working all over the world—the US, Europe, Singapore, Latin America, Southeast Asia, China, Australia—and when I was away, I kept listening to that song and longing to be back at the hundredth meridian. I was working for an American firm at the time, so the opening line—"Me, debunk an American myth?"—struck a chord. And I love the line right at the end, about being buried "unceremoniously/Away from the swollen city breeze."

The band didn't talk too much about their songs, so you need to make up your own stories about them. We know little bits, but not much. I like that. It allows me to make the songs mean what I need them to mean. For me the connection was deepest when I was struggling with some epic life stuff, the kind that makes or breaks you. The lyrics gave me a sense of belonging, of mental strength, and a no bull-shit attitude to move forward. Plus, I finally had the permission I needed to not take myself so seriously.

That's the power of music—sometimes it gives me the strength to kick ass, and other times it gives me the lyrics to wallow in my own pity. It lets us be human. It's fantastic.

Sandip Lalli is president and CEO of the Calgary Chamber of Commerce. She grew up in Edmonton and spent many years outside of Canada leading teams for Cargill International.

My mom graduated in the 1950s with a music degree from Toronto's Royal Conservatory of Music and in the blink of an eye had four children under the age of six to keep her more than occupied. As well as looking after all things domestic and raising four kids, she shared her love of music by teaching piano in our home in the evenings.

Once my dad was home from work and a boisterous dinner consumed, my mom retreated to the den, where she shared her art with her students. Sitting at the kitchen table doing our homework, we could hear the ever-present tick, tick, tick of the metronome accompanied by the trials and tribulations of pianists, beginner and advanced alike. All four of my parents' children were encouraged to find my mom's musical genes within but only my youngest brother succeeded. The rest of us, to her chagrin, were, and still are, tone deaf.

Being the eldest, I got to stay up later than my siblings and sometimes, when the last of the students left, I was taken in by my mother's magic. Time stood still as she took to the keys for herself and only herself. In those few minutes alone she often played one particular piece that never failed to move my world, and still overwhelms me in such a great way.

"In a Persian Market" by Albert W. Ketèlbey took this ten-year-old on the greatest adventure she had ever experienced, both in the notes it knit together and the way playing it transformed my mother into her most passionate self. It is both delicate and chaotic, foreign and familiar, and takes you by surprise in its final notes, exactly how an exotic market would come to life and conclude until another day. Watching my mother's body sway and live the music, watching her close her eyes and transport herself to another world was mesmerizing. That piece of music fuelled my imagination and became mine. It was uplifting and adventurous and showed me a part of my mom that was independent and intensely creative.

In a Persian Market

DEB KRIZMANICH

Many years later I had the great opportunity to take my mom on a trip through the Middle East, where she could experience the culture that accompanied the music for the first time. I will never forget that time with her. She is now eighty-three years old and still loves playing the piano, though she sometimes finds it difficult to recall the notes. Her audience are her neighbours in my parents' retirement village at Saturday night happy hour. They enjoy my mom's love of music as much as we do. And on very special days, she plays "In a Persian Market" for me and I am once again ten years old and transported to a most wondrous place . . . with my mom.

Deb Krizmanich is CEO of Powernoodle and since her early days at IBM has been passionate about technologies that unleash the innate potential of individuals and groups. She believes that amazing things happen when diverse backgrounds and perspectives are encouraged to shine through.

RAISE A LITTLE HELL

Rick Mercer

QUADROPHONIC

I **was maybe** twelve years old when my sister brought the Trooper album *Thick as Thieves* into the house. I remember listening at her closed bedroom door as she played it with a friend. Being a little brother, admission to her bedroom was strictly prohibited at all times. One track captured my attention. The song was telling me to throw caution to the wind, to be bold, to take drastic measures if need be. It was telling me to seize the day.

The next morning I did just that. I had a stomach ache, I had a headache, and I didn't feel well. There was no end to my symptoms and no end of excuses. My early acting skills were on bust and I somehow convinced my parents I wasn't up to the rigours of school and should stay on the couch for the day.

Once my father was out of the driveway, I leapt into the unknown. I was in my sister's bedroom like a shot. This was a high-risk operation; the consequences of entering her room were dire, and touching her record collection and record player was a crime that was probably punishable by death. It didn't matter. The music demanded it.

For the next few hours it was all Trooper, all the time. I played "Raise a Little Hell" over and over again. I played air guitar, I sang along, I danced, I became the front man in a rock and roll band. I remember thinking, *This is my favourite song! I have a favourite song!* I decided that "Raise a Little Hell" would be my favourite song forever.

Turns out I was right. As I grew up, I went through a Top 40 phase, a Motown phase, an extended punk rock phase, a singer-songwriter phase. My tastes are eclectic and vast but "Raise a Little Hell" still holds the title of favourite song.

Professionally I have used the song more than any other piece of music.

When I was on *This Hour Has 22 Minutes*, I shot a music video on Parliament Hill that involved all three major parties, the prime minister, and the opposition leaders, all urging young people to vote. The music I chose was "Raise a Little Hell." The lyrics were perfect. The leaders, the caucuses, and the young people sang along to the words with gusto:

If you don't like what you got why don't you change it.
If your world is all screwed up, rearrange it.
Raise a little hell.

In the very first pitch meeting for the *Rick Mercer Report*, I said that the only thing I knew about the show was that the theme song would be "Raise a Little Hell."

That never came to be—we needed a song that sounded like a current affairs program, not a rock anthem. But the song showed up in the show consistently over the next fifteen years. It was always there, in the background or foreground.

And when I finally wrapped up the show, when I said goodnight for the very last time, "Raise a Little Hell" played under the credits as I walked out of my studio. That was a big moment for me. I was glad that song was the soundtrack.

"Raise a Little Hell" has been with me my entire life. To me, it is the ultimate Canadian rant set to music.

To this day when I perform live, when I walk on stage and off stage, that's the song that plays.

I once got pulled over for speeding. When the officer asked why I was going so fast I told him—"Honestly? Trooper just came on the radio, 'Raise a Little Hell.' I got carried away."

"Raise a Little Hell" has always been my personal anthem. It not only speaks to me but also gives everyone great advice.

He said, "Best excuse I've heard in a long time," and let me go.

It is and has always been my personal anthem. It is a radio-friendly rock and roll hit from the past that not only speaks to me but also gives everyone great advice. Words to live by in the face of adversity, or during difficult times.

In the end it comes down to your thinking
And there's really nobody to blame.
When it feels like your ship is sinking.
And you're too tired to play the game.
Nobody's going to help you.
You've just got to stand up alone.
And dig in your heels and see how it feels to raise a
*   little hell of your own.*

When they throw my ashes into the wind, feel free to play this song and play it very loud.

For the lyrics by Brian Smith and Ramon McGuire, and the production by a young Randy Bachman: thank you, Trooper.

Rick Mercer is a comedian, television personality, satirist, and author from St. John's, Newfoundland. He is best known for his work on *This Hour Has 22 Minutes* and the *Rick Mercer Report*, both on CBC TV.

A MENU OF EMOTIONS

CLAIRE DUBOC

For me it was a show: *A Chorus Line*. It's one of longest-running shows on Broadway, and was made into a film. The plot is simple: the cast is auditioning for a part in a show and each member is asked to share their personal story through song and dance. There are stories of awkwardness, unrequited love, lack of confidence, over-confidence. The things every kid goes through.

Music has been at my core forever. As a child I drove my family crazy because I sang all the time. I'd been in love with musical theatre since I was ten and played Buttercup in my first show, Gilbert and Sullivan's *H.M.S. Pinafore*. My parents came and thought, *Wow, she can really sing!* After that I was in a show every year.

I was lucky to go to a high school in London, Ontario, that was quite famous for its drama and music programs. They did shows every year, and being in the cast was as cool as being an athlete. It was co-ed and a safe place for everybody, a bit like summer camp. It was a great equalizer, which is so unusual at high school—everybody was so thrilled to be part of the production. These shows became my safe place, the catharsis for my adolescence. And *A Chorus Line* was my touchstone. I knew every song in it and picked the one that went with each particular moment.

Music involves so many senses, that's why it's such wonderful therapy. You hear it, and with a musical you watch it (I've seen *A Chorus Line* so many times). And I loved the physical act of singing those songs, the vibration in my chest, being able to sing loud when I wanted to express loudly, or quietly when I was feeling introspective. I used that show as my menu of music; I could literally connect into anything; pick the song that would get me through, make me feel like it was my friend.

Now I work in mental health. I talk to a lot of organizations about wellness, and see how they have embraced healthy eating, sleeping hygiene, and wellness. Everyone says: go do something you love. But we don't as easily go to music. We should.

I still sing—in the house, the car, the shower, just because it makes me feel better. It's my version of going for a run.

Emilia Nippard

CATCH YOUR BREATH

Early in the winter of 2016, I found myself in a dark place: caught between friend groups, struggling with schoolwork, feeling isolated and misunderstood. I was fifteen years old. Looking back, I was likely just one among many of my peers feeling a first serious bout of anxiety and hopelessness. At the time, however, I felt sure I was the only one.

I recall walking home from school one day in February, taking my time, dragging my heels. I put my earphones in and blasted some music in an effort to block out the daily malaise. I chose *Oh Fortune*, a Dan Mangan album my brother had been telling me about. I was halfway through and in the final stretch of my journey when the opening drums of "Starts with Them, Ends with Us" rolled into my ears.

Instinctively, my breath began to sync with the beat as I listened closely to the hypnotic guitar. About two minutes in, the drums drop out for a moment before building back up again slowly. I'm not sure I can explain why, but the song had me completely captivated. Before long, the lyrics stop and the music dives into a horn break. In a moment of serendipity, I exhaled at the exact second the trumpets made their first ascent. I was sure that my feet had lifted off the ground, that I was soaring away from everything around me.

For the next minute or so, I stood on the sidewalk, bubbling over with ecstasy. But, as with all songs, it eventually ended. I quickly pulled out my earphones, afraid that anything I heard next would pull me away from the joy I was feeling. I felt like I had taken a full breath for the first time in months, and that things were now okay.

That afternoon, I sent a message to Dan Mangan on Facebook. I told him how his song had made an impact on me and thanked him for writing it. A few days later, he replied, saying, "It's such a gift to be in people's lives even if I don't know them." He told me of his own intent with the music. He described the horn section as the sounds of a revolution—of people breaking free, parading through broken streets and waking up. This was different from my interpretation, but the sense of musical release is the same.

I won't lie and say that this four-minute song cured all my mental health struggles or radically changed my life. I will, however, say that it instilled in me a steadfast understanding of the power of music as a coping tool. In the three years since that day I have hit many lows, but I can say that each of them was, at least in some way, mitigated by a good song.

Emilia Nippard is a student at the University of Toronto. She is a passionate musician and a strong believer in the power of music as a tool for coping with challenges and trauma.

follow the sun

JODI KOVITZ

AMPSONIC 054

I **started learning** the violin at six, then moved on to the piano. I really appreciated the discipline involved in mastering the art; it developed my grit. To play well you need to be able to focus and stick to things, from the highest to the most minute level.

I remember learning a really hard piece, "Bloody Well Right" by Supertramp. I was totally daunted by the complexity of the music, but my teacher just said, "You can do it—you just have to learn it one note at a time." That's how I approach my life and how I am building my business today: one note at a time.

Some work days are so hard. Right now, for instance, we're planning dozens of events in various countries, including one in Toronto for 2,500 people; supporting an employee with a personal challenge at home; writing the minutes for yesterday's meeting; deciding who is coming to meet Ellen DeGeneres this weekend; working on a report on women and retention; all in the same day. My approach is: one note at a time. That's how I get things done.

Music is also key to my well-being. When I was young I was influenced by Bruce Springsteen, especially "Thunder Road." A counsellor taught me every word of that song on a canoe trip in Algonquin Park one summer. I went back to it for years, and still always associate the beauty of nature with that song. I've had different songs for different times in my life, and love to listen to the same song on repeat day after day. When I was getting divorced it was Katy Perry's "Roar."

One really beautiful song I feel blessed to have found is "Follow the Sun" by Xavier Rudd. I discovered it a time of serious transition in my life, about a year before I started #movethedial. I was moving from one way of existing in the world to another, very different one, confronting some really big issues inside myself to become what I wanted to be. I had done a lot of inner healing, and knew I had to look for the light and follow it. There was something very powerful in that moment that allowed me to pursue my dream, which is what I am doing now. "Follow the Sun" helped me do that.

Like all great songs, "Follow the Sun" combines a beautiful melody with powerful lyrics. It gave me permission to go the way the wind blows, to set my intentions, and breathe with care. And it reminded me that tomorrow is a brand-new day, with a brand-new sun. We're all so small in this huge world, but every day we have a chance to try again.

I knew my self-talk wasn't positive, but learning to tell yourself a new narrative is hard. Having self-compassion is hard, too—I had to work consciously at being kind and compassionate to myself. Whenever I disappointed myself, that song would remind me that tomorrow is a new chance.

Jodi Kovitz is founder and CEO of #movethedial, a global movement she launched in 2017 dedicated to advancing the participation and advancement of all women in tech. She has a background in family law, business, and tech.

I have a really annoying tendency to, as my parents put it, "play music to death." I set my sights on a band or singer, or even just one song, and play it on repeat for days on end. I do this so often that there is a list of songs I'm no longer allowed to play aloud because everyone around me is so horribly sick of them. Usually the artist or song ends up on the "do not play" list—and finally gets buried in my iTunes library in favour of my newest obsession.

But my family, who have blacklisted so much of my favourite music, all know there is one singer I will never let go of. His likeness is on the calendar above my bed, the prints on my wall, and the vinyl records on my shelf. Only my closest friends (and now all of you, I suppose) know that I even wear my favourite lyric of his on a ring.

I was introduced to David Bowie when I was fourteen. That was two years before I discovered the Knowledge Society and started exploring tech, so I didn't have much of a sense of identity yet. I had floated through high school, never getting quite close enough to anyone to develop a sincere friendship. I never found "my people" at school.

But Bowie is the patron saint of misfits. And his music, particularly the song "Starman," with its promise of a higher purpose, was my battle cry.

As songs and artists have come and gone in my house, Bowie has remained an unshakeable constant. He embodied the intrinsic confidence that I wanted so desperately, a deep-set assurance of his own worth.

As I've grown up and come to realize that the world is not contained by the four walls of my high school, Bowie's role in my life has evolved alongside me. No longer is he the boy in the makeup I once used as an exaggerated role model for self-esteem, or the singer of the song I'd play for days on a loop.

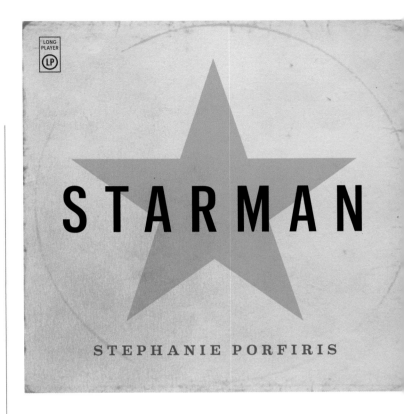

LONG PLAYER LP

STARMAN

STEPHANIE PORFIRIS

Today, he doesn't represent shock value or high school drama; Bowie represents freedom of spirit.

Instead of being the artist I'd listen to distraught after struggling to find a seat in the cafeteria, Bowie is now the person whose songs I play when I need to be reassured that everything I'm doing and sacrificing is worthwhile.

I take one look at him and the lightning bolt across his face and remind myself that experimenting and exploring *is the point*. How much would I be limiting myself if I just stayed comfortable?

And then I remember what he says in "Starman"— "it's all *worthwhile*."

Stephanie Porfiris is a member of the Knowledge Society, the world's leading innovation program. She is currently exploring the Internet of Things and building an Arduino David Bowie Bot (and, yes, it plays "Starman").

four chart-topping tracks from research on music

1

Listening to Music Reduces Stress

- It improves immune system function by increasing production of immunoglobulin A.
- It reduces levels of the stress hormone cortisol.
- It is more effective than prescription medications at reducing anxiety before surgery.

source: According to a review of more than 400 research papers into the neurochemistry of music, published in the March 2013 edition of *Trends in Cognitive Sciences*.

2

Music Reduces Agitation in Dementia Patients

- Music therapy reduces stress and anxiety, enhances emotional well-being, and even increases social interactions.
- Dementia patients had lowered anxiety and stress levels after two thirty-minute therapy sessions per week.

source: From a study published in the August 2001 edition of *Nursing Times*, led by Nottingham University Hospitals nurse Jacqueline Craig; the study reviewed a number of scientific articles on the subject of music therapy and dementia care.

Premature Babies Benefit from Live Music— and So Do Their Parents

- Live music improves both physiologic and developmental outcomes in premature babies in neonatal intensive care units.
- The infants experienced lower heart rates, better oxygen saturation, higher caloric intake, and increased sucking behaviour.
- Live music or rhythms also soothed the parents.

source: From a 2018 study at Queen's University Belfast, led by Sam Porter of the School of Nursing, in which rhythms or lullabies were played or sung to 272 premature infants suffering from clinical sepsis, respiratory distress, and/or small for gestational age symptoms.

Music Therapy Eases Depression in Kids and Teens

- Children who receive music therapy have significantly improved self-esteem.
- They also show significantly reduced depression, and improved communicative and interactive skills.
- These benefits are being shown to be sustainable in the long term.

source: From a study by the School of Nursing and Midwifery at Queen's University Belfast in Northern Ireland in 2014. The study was the largest of its kind, involving 251 children and young people who were being treated for emotional, developmental, or behavioural problems.

HOW MUSIC MAKES YOU (WANT TO) MOVE

MUSIC & THE BRAIN

GABE NESPOLI

> **All styles of music are associated with some form of movement—be it dancing with friends, marching in a band, or rocking a baby to sleep.**

Have you ever thought you were sitting still, only to find that you are tapping your foot along to music? This kind of reaction is spontaneous, effortless, and often unconscious. Practically all styles of music are associated with some form of movement—be it dancing with friends, marching in a band, or rocking a baby to sleep—and historically you would be hard pressed to find music without movement. So why does music pair so readily with movement? And how does it create a desire to move our bodies to the beat?

Music provides a rich and robust temporal structure that makes it straightforward to synchronize with. Repetitive rhythmic figures and a consistent underlying beat are very predictable, and thus well suited to being followed. *Groove*—the desire to move along with music—depends on this kind of regularity, and yet some of the grooviest music is not the most predictable. For example, Stevie Wonder's "Superstition" or Weather Report's "Birdland" have syncopated rhythms that deviate from a strict sense of meter, and yet listeners have no trouble finding and moving to the beat. More than that—these kinds of rhythms *compel* people to move along, inviting them to spell out the simple underlying structure of a complex rhythm. Your hips don't lie.

Many different regions of your brain are engaged when you listen to music. Most notably, regions that plan and control movement, like your premotor cortex, are active even if your body isn't moving. Neurons in your brain will also spontaneously synchronize their firing with the beat of music, so the rhythmic patterns you are hearing resonate inside you. In this way, your brain can create a model that predicts how the music will unfold over time. By drawing on the rhythmic expertise of the motor system, your brain might be able to do a better job of predicting the patterns you are hearing. Engaging the motor system and actually moving along to music might be your brain's attempt to validate this internal model. In creating a desire to move, then, your brain is simply attempting to better understand and predict its surroundings.

Understanding the world is what your brain strives to do. If involving the body in the process means it can do a better job, then it's no wonder you find pleasure in moving to music. So the next time you find yourself grooving along to a song, let your head nod along, and know that your brain is just trying to understand the rhythm.

Gabe Nespoli is a data scientist at Sonova in Kitchener, Ontario. He received a PhD in psychological science from Ryerson University for studying how the brain tracks the beat in music, and how this can create an irresistible urge to move along.

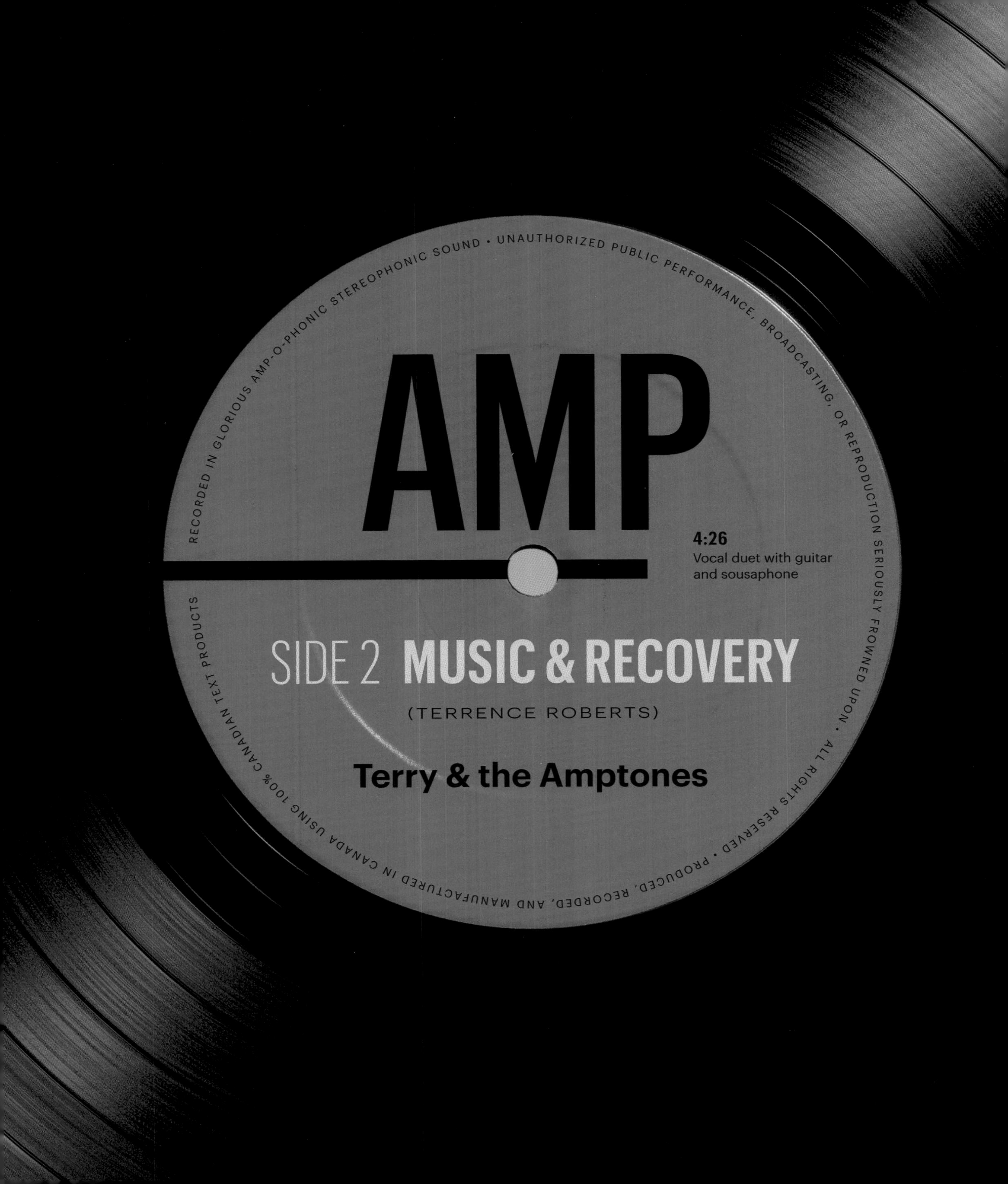

RECORDED IN GLORIOUS AMP-O-PHONIC STEREOPHONIC SOUND • UNAUTHORIZED PUBLIC PERFORMANCE, BROADCASTING, OR REPRODUCTION SERIOUSLY FROWNED UPON • ALL RIGHTS RESERVED • PRODUCED, RECORDED, AND MANUFACTURED IN CANADA USING 100% CANADIAN TEXT PRODUCTS
AMP
4:26
Vocal duet with guitar and sousaphone
SIDE 2 MUSIC & RECOVERY
(TERRENCE ROBERTS)
Terry & the Amptones

STEREO

WOLVES DON'T LIVE BY THE RULES

ELISAPIE ISAAC

I didn't know why, but three years ago, after my son was born, I suddenly felt lost. Ever since I moved to the south, almost twenty years ago, I've been trying to adapt to survive. I adapted too well, forgot about a real way of thinking.

I was still a kid when I arrived in Montreal: twenty-one years old. I loved it here, loved the freedom of being on my own. But the price you pay when you leave a small community is feeling isolated. My adoptive parents were a long way away and didn't even say goodbye at the airport; my mother was sick, she acted like I was ruining her life. The artist in me paid the price of being alone.

I come from Salluit, an Inuit community in the very north of Quebec. In the 1950s, the federal government decided they didn't want the Inuit to be nomadic any more. Over the next few decades, lots of kids from Salluit were sent to residential school, in places like Churchill, Manitoba. Sad and confused, they listened to Bob Dylan and Neil Young,

> I had a dark side, a sadness, but I kept it hidden, except when I made music. Now I feel like I'm content with that. I have kids now, I have to find a way to go to that lightness, that brightness, that we all need.

and learned to play the guitar. I listened to the songs they sang when I was growing up, years later: music inspired by American and British sounds, but often sung in Inuktitut.

I didn't want to take pills when I was feeling down, so I started listening to that old stuff again, songs I remembered from when I was a kid. I got stuck, I couldn't listen to anything else. That music was my shit! I didn't know if I was depressed, having an identity crisis, maybe it was about my adoption— it all surfaced. Wow. I kept asking myself: could I make music like that?

I found the original CBC recordings, the old vinyl. They have an amazing, very raw sound. A lot of the songs are about the land, and missing home. Both the tunes and the lyrics are super simple, they are naïve and beautiful. We can't write like that anymore, because we didn't grow up hunting on the land and weren't sent to residential school. Knowing it's my uncle (with his band, Sugluk) who wrote some of those songs is amazing. I ended up recording one of them, Willie Thrasher's "Wolves Don't Live by the Rules," for my next album, *The Ballad of the Runaway Girl*.

I was brought up by parents who didn't over-stimulate me. That's how Inuit are: really quiet. I was taught to never speak in front of an elder person, just to listen. We could answer a question, but that's all. It's another way of life, and it doesn't go well with all the sadness and identity crises we are having. We need to learn to talk more, to counter things like the panic attacks my sister is suffering from.

On the beautiful side, it's healing sometimes not to overthink, not to talk, to be in the presence of elder people with all their knowledge. It's a non-verbal culture that can be very soothing. It's still very important for Inuit to be among nature, among elders, to stay in contact with our spirituality, even if people don't live with shamans or rituals any more. Make eye contact instead of talking, slow down and observe.

When I perform I get super high. The stage is like a drug, you share this thing with the audience and discover another side of yourself. But the rest of the time I've always been melancholic. Listening to those songs, I realized I had always put on a front, since I was a kid. I had a dark side, a sadness, but I kept it hidden, except when I made music. Now I feel like I'm content with that. I'm neutral, in the middle, and that's fine. I have kids now, I have to find a way to go to that lightness, that brightness, that we all need.

I wouldn't have got there without Willie Thrasher, an Inuit boy who was taken away from his summer camp at the age of five to go to residential school. And sang about it.

Elisapie Isaac, or just Elisapie, is a Juno award–winning singer, broadcaster, filmmaker, and activist. She began performing with her uncle's band, Sugluk, at age twelve. Her song "Far Away," from the film *The Legend of Sarila*, was nominated for Best Original Song at the Canadian Screen Awards in 2014, and her album *The Ballad of the Runaway Girl* was longlisted for the Polaris Prize in 2019.

WHAT HEALING SOUNDS LIKE

Karyn L. Freedman

As I write this, I'm listening to one of my all-time favourite albums, Herbie Hancock's *River: The Joni Letters*, his tribute album of Joni Mitchell covers. Music has always provided a soundtrack to my life. Sometimes it's a treasured album on repeat. Other times, it's a song that punctuates an experience. And then there are those rare occasions when music opens up the world in ways that we never knew possible. I had one of those profound experiences when I was halfway around the world, in Botswana, in the fall of 2008.

Two decades before that, in the summer of 1990, I had been raped at knifepoint at the age of twenty-two, while backpacking through Europe. Although for many years I tried to pretend otherwise, burying the truth of what had happened to me, the experience had marked me for life. The trauma had taken root in me like an occupying force, and before long I began to go through the anxiety, panic attacks, and sleepless nights that are part of the aftermath of traumatic experiences. As time passed things got worse, not better, and so, close to a decade in, I decided it was time to get help. With the support of a therapist, I began the slow work of recovery.

It wasn't easy. Trauma is a chronic condition and healing is not a linear process. But, eventually, I began to feel lighter, freer, and when I reached a point where I started to feel safe in the world again, I decided it was time to come out as a rape survivor. Keeping that a secret had taken a terrible toll on me. It had intensified the humiliation and shame that is part of the cost of living in a distorted, victim-blaming culture. Talking openly about being raped had lifted an enormous weight off my shoulders. It was my way of saying that this was not my fault, that I had nothing to be ashamed of. I began to see the value in talking publicly about surviving sexual violence.

It was with that in mind that I applied to do a short-term volunteer placement at a rape crisis center in Maun, Botswana, called Women Against Rape (WAR), to work alongside support workers and counsellors and share personal and professional knowledge about the impact of sexual violence on individuals and communities.

Maun is a small town of about fifty thousand people on the southern tip of the Okavango Delta, in a stunning part of northwestern Botswana. I spent my first day there getting groceries and settling into my rental apartment, which was in a one-storey complex, the only one of its kind in an area of town dominated by traditional thatched huts. After a fitful sleep I woke early, propelled out of bed by a combination of jet lag and nervous anticipation of the day ahead. I was excited to start work.

I arrived at WAR just before 8 a.m., the spectacular Botswana sun already warming the day. The staff, whom I had met briefly the day before, welcomed me into their daily morning meeting. Everyone gathered in the front office for announcements and a

These songs, with their irrepressibly joyous melodies, are what healing sounds like.

discussion of agenda items. The informal tone of the proceedings belied the seriousness of the work ahead, which would bring us face to face with survivors of sexual violence, women and girls of all ages. I was observing this all with great interest, and then, just as the meeting was wrapping up, the most surprising thing happened: the entire staff broke into song, an awe-inspiring and soulful African hymn. The song was in the traditional language of Setswana, but it resonated with me nonetheless. It stirred something deep within, moving me in ways I could not have expected. When it ended, someone said a quiet prayer, and the workday began.

I spent the next few weeks intoxicated by the power of these songs. The staff at WAR are devoted to helping others heal from the trauma of sexual violence, and, like frontline workers all around the world, they face very harsh realities every day. But despite the darkness, they begin each day with these uplifting songs. It's a remarkable display of generosity of spirit. These songs, with their irrepressibly joyous melodies, are what healing sounds like.

Karyn L. Freedman is an associate professor of philosophy at the University of Guelph. Her book, *One Hour in Paris: A True Story of Rape and Recovery*, won the 2015 BC National Award for Canadian Non-Fiction. She was born in Winnipeg and now lives in Toronto.

AMPLAPHONE

mono

matt
clarke

I WANT TO HOLD YOUR HAND

Everyone joined in between sobs, and the '60s pop hit took on the air of a southern hymnal.

It never ceases to amaze me how a song's meaning can change from one moment to the next. Cohen's "Hallelujah," for example, is a completely different song to me now than when I first heard it as a teenager. Or in Springsteen's "The River," when he asks if a dream is a lie (or something worse) if it doesn't come true—that's a cool-sounding line when you're angsty and trying to impress a girl, but after you've actually had a couple of dreams crushed, it's like a punch in the gut.

It's the same for my own music as well. I'm never really sure where a song comes from. A chord change just seems to appear out of the rubble of a mistake, or a chorus sneaks up on me like a sneeze. From there I find myself scrambling to suss out what the hell it's about—like reading tea leaves or something. That journey of discovery, to understand what a piece of music is about, is what I still find most exciting and rewarding about songwriting.

Spanning my twenties and early thirties, my grandfather made his descent through Alzheimer's to his inevitable end. After he died, my dad asked me to play a song at the funeral that I had written years earlier, called "Familiar." In it I had imagined what it might be like to watch your life slowly disappear. I had written the song as a way to come to terms with a tragedy of the human experience, to attempt to find some kind of insight into it. My dad had always liked the song—I think it helped him see the whole experience from a different perspective as well.

So I agreed to play "Familiar," and someone else requested we play a cover of the Beatles' "I Want to Hold Your Hand." As grandpa lost his ability to hold anything resembling a conversation, and eventually his ability to speak much at all, he never lost his habit of reaching for the hand of anyone who sat near him. It was a habit that got him punched in the face a few times by other random patients at the nursing home. But like a child's impulse, it was a way to find connection and also a sense of comfort and safety.

So the funeral comes along and my wife, Leila, and I sing "Familiar." It's a bit of a sad bastard song, but what better place for a sad bastard song than a funeral? But as we were singing it, the song, which in the past had felt cathartic, this time offered me little comfort. His death had changed my relationship to that song. It didn't hold the same meaning.

Then we launch into the Beatles' classic—a joyfully simple tune. And to my surprise, before the first chorus hits, everyone in the place, including Leila and me, are in tears. There wasn't a person in that room who hadn't held old Bud's hand on countless occasions. Everyone joined in between sobs, and the '60s pop hit took on the air of a southern hymnal.

I cannot imagine when Lennon and McCartney were writing that song that they considered for even a fraction of a second that it could be about an elderly Alzheimer's patient grasping for his last straws of human connection. But on that spring afternoon in a Calgary funeral home, that's exactly what it was about.

Matt Clarke is a singer-songwriter, actor, producer, and writer. Since *Convos with My 2-Year-Old* went viral on YouTube, he's been busy writing, acting, and producing comedy for TV and any other medium that will have him.

angith mohan

Music Is for Everyone

When I was twenty, I was diagnosed with obsessive-compulsive disorder (OCD). I was in my first year at York University and I knew something was going on. I had been struggling for years, but now just getting to class was difficult.

To help manage my anxiety and my day to day, I was put on medication, Prozac, and on the wait-list for cognitive-behavioral therapy at CAMH (the Canadian Centre for Addiction and Mental Health), where I was lucky to be accepted after a year.

My parents had moved to Canada from a third-world country. So when they found the pills in the bedroom of their eldest son, they were confused and upset. They saw me as a role model, and didn't understand why I was on medication. I eventually dropped out of university for a year, to address my condition and commit to being happy.

Luckily there was another way to tackle my OCD: music. I had been playing music from an early age. My parents saw how much I loved it and encouraged my interest. I got a five-piece drum set in grade 5 and played that well into my twenties. In grade 7, I started dancing; by grade 8, I was acting and singing. I did a lot, all for the love music.

When I decided to take a pause on my education, I remained as a student and committed myself to my happiness by joining the university dance team and competing in interuniversity dance competitions. It kept me afloat. Dancing and playing music complemented the CAMH program and helped me deal with my compulsions.

With this second chance, I knew I had a new meaning to my life: I wanted to use performing arts as a platform to help others to identify with, experience, and express their greatness. For the next six years, I helped with creating a dance community and dance team based on the philosophy of "We Not I." The result was a family of talented individuals continuously pushing artistic boundaries and excellence. A spectacular moment in my life that has now forever defined me.

I still deal with the OCD, it's always there. But tackling it through music and dance has allowed me to see the other side of what it could be. Music has this intrinsic benefit. It brings me joy and a sense of peace and takes me to a place of balance with myself and the world around me.

Music is not just for artists or musicians, it's for everyone. There is no logic and there are no prerequisites to appreciate it. You just experience it as a human. We all feel, and music and dance can help us do so clearly and calmly. Performing brought me that awareness, that connection, and has allowed me to help other people achieve them, too.

Angith Mohan is an artist and an advocate for positivity. He grew up in Scarborough, Ontario, and has a masters of design from OCAD University.

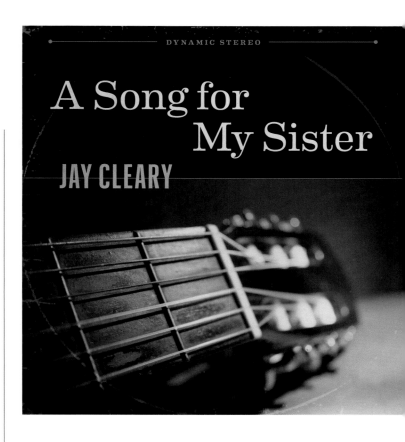

A Song for My Sister

JAY CLEARY

I've produced more than a thousand music shows in my day, but the most profound one revolved around my sister Jenny's fight with cancer. When I came home to Toronto one Christmas from Nova Scotia, where I was attending university, my mom sat me down and told me Jenny had been diagnosed with leukemia. I was tested to be her bone marrow donor, but was not a match, though luckily our youngest brother was.

The waiting was unbearable. There were all sorts of complications that kept pushing back the operation. A year later, when I had moved back to Toronto, I was struggling to find a way to help her, outside of visiting often. Talking about her health every day with the family was very difficult. My mom, who was with her the most, would tear up all the time and it was hard to know what to do except hope for the best.

While playing guitar at home, I stumbled across a guitar riff that was very enlightening and a song wrote itself. I named it "Jenny's Song" because the melody and emotion felt like a perfect fit of hope and positivity. The next time I went to the hospital, I brought my guitar and played her the song. She really liked it, but was very weak.

The chemotherapy had been really intense and now she had a huge blood clot sitting right outside her heart; if it were to enter her heart, it would kill her. She had been very strong throughout her ordeal but this was a pivotal moment—she was losing energy and the will to live. She became delirious, unsure where she was and rambling about odd things, living in a dream world, partially because of the pain meds. While she slept I would continue to soothe her with my song, and, with the help of blood thinners and luck, the blood clot dissipated and she resumed her chemotherapy treatments.

The day of her bone marrow operation, we were very nervous and exhausted. I tried to soothe my family with "Jenny's Song." Talking about her situation was difficult, but the song helped to inspire a positive outlook. The operation was a success and Jenny slowly recovered, much to everyone's delight. She has now been cancer-free for ten years and has built a wonderful life.

"Jenny's Song" has taken on a life of its own. I've been asked to play it during sad family events like funerals and memorials. I've played it live with my many bands and I keep intending to record it, but somehow the timing never seems to work out. I'm gonna get on it ASAP.

Jay Cleary has toured Canada and the US as a musician. He has produced events in Toronto and New York City through his company NuFunk Concerts, and as an agent for 360 Degrees Artists, Cleary has booked shows at major venues across North America.

ALWAYS THERE

NICOLA CAVANAGH

When I was fifteen, I was diagnosed with depression. I was given Prozac (it was 1993, so that particular drug was all the rage) and things were better for a while. Turns out, this was Step 1 in my (so far) twenty-five-year mental health adventure. A couple of months later I picked up a bass guitar and started a band with some guys (it was 1993, so having a girl bass player in your alternative rock band was all the rage); it was less obvious at the time, but this was Step 2.

The path I took as I attempted to be mentally healthy was kind of like the one Alice takes in Wonderland (the 1951 Disney animated version). I wandered around on instinct, trying to unravel well-intentioned information wrapped up in riddles. Then every so often some weird dog with a broom for a face (a.k.a. my malfunctioning brain, or an unexpected event) would come along and dust the path away, leaving me frustrated, occasionally hopeless, and unsure of what to do next. It's been a long and sordid tale, full of crises, questionable decisions, some good times and good decisions, and clichés such as "emotional roller coaster." But bit by bit, my path has become clearer.

Though all this, music has been a constant. It has often been the force that has allowed me to get things done. It's been a reset button when I felt overwhelmed, a release when I felt anxious, and a source of pride when I felt unworthy. It isn't just the playing of music, either, but also the community of friends I have built through our shared love of rock and roll. A community I love dearly and who have never hesitated to support me, even when I didn't have the energy to ask.

To share just one story: in 2015 my marriage ended. It needed to. Still, it was a difficult thing. It was a change in identity, an unclear path (that broom-faced dog again), an attempt to reconcile what I thought would happen with what I was being presented with. We have a daughter, who was turning six at the time, so her feelings had to be handled with the utmost care. There was a home, and stuff, and bank accounts . . . Fortunately we also still had respect for each other, and I was confident that we could do this right.

I returned to therapy with fervour. I also threw myself into music in a way I hadn't done for years. I had always played, and was co-boss of Girls Rock Camp Calgary, but I had often been overwhelmed by the feeling that *I shouldn't be doing this*. Playing music seemed selfish, and I hadn't been able to admit what it really meant to me. So I changed that. Quickly. I started playing bass in a band I had always dug (Night Committee) and writing songs for my ongoing project, Sequicons. I travelled to music festivals and played at a couple, too. When I felt anxious, frustrated, depressed, sad, worthless, I went to a show with my friends and they wrapped me up in affection.

> # Music has been a reset button when I felt overwhelmed, a release when I felt anxious, and a source of pride when I felt unworthy.

One day, at the 2015 Girls Rock Camp, a well-known TV news reporter came by to do a story about me; it turned out I had been nominated as an "Inspiring Albertan." When the story aired, a former camper talked about how my influence had allowed her to pursue music. I think about her when I feel unimportant.

In 2017, Night Committee played two great shows at the Sled Island Music & Arts Festival. The response was awesome, and I shared the stage with a longtime hero, Mike Watt. I think about that when I want to feel proud.

That Canada Day, Sequicons recruited a young violin phenom, and I wrote an arrangement for a song by a local band. It went incredibly well. I watch the video of that performance when I want to feel joy.

My daughter has seen me play a number of times, and while she always feigns disinterest I sometimes hear her singing our songs, and she started playing guitar this year. I think about that when I worry that music is making me an absent mom.

I have achieved a lot over the past fifteen years. I have struggled, but I have also had periods of stability and joy. My life is like that, and likely always will be. Music has always been there, and I am eternally grateful for it.

Nicola Cavanagh is a Calgary-based musician who founded that city's chapter of Girls Rock Camp.

WHEN I SEE THE POWER OF MUSIC, I WANT TO DO THINGS TO INSPIRE PEOPLE AS MUCH AS EMINEM INSPIRED ME.

I've been rapping since I was twelve years old. Because I have cerebral palsy, I was bullied when I was a kid: called a cripple, whipped with skipping ropes. I'd come home from school and cry to my mum, ask her, "Why do I have this disability, why does it have to be this way?" Luckily I have a tight-knit family who treated me just like every other Filipino Canadian.

Everything changed the first time I listened to Eminem. My cousin slipped me a copy of *The Marshall Mathers LP*, pulled it out of his coat like it was a drug deal. I went to my room and played it over and over.

I really connected with those songs. Eminem was taking everything he'd struggled with, growing up poor in a trailer park, and putting it into his music. It was mind-blowing. I remember thinking, *Why can't I do that with my struggles, with what I have to face at school?*

I asked my mum to buy me a journal and began writing everything I was my feeling in it. Sometimes it was just random words. Then I'd take them and try and make them into a song. At twelve years old I had enough material to write my first rap. I had an old-school boom box and recorded myself, and thought, *Man, I can do this*. I made my first mixtape and sold it to my mum and dad for a dollar. I thought I was a rap star.

The first time I performed one of my raps for my mum, I was so nervous. At the end she was crying, and I was thinking, *Wow, am I that bad?* She hugged me and said, "That was really good, Calvin." It was the first time she'd seen me comfortable.

When I got to high school, everything was better. Rapping gave me confidence. They asked me to rap at every school event: lunchtime shows, the yearly pep rally. Everyone gathered in the cafeteria and I would perform. I got so much support, this little guy on crutches who looked like he was super shy. I'd take the mic and be really loud and people would be amazed.

Meanwhile I was teaching myself how to record. I set up a mini-studio in my bedroom and put out album after album.

In grade 12 it was 2010 and the Olympics were in Vancouver. I had a family friend who was an event coordinator. She called me up one day: "Calvin, how would you like to perform at a Yaletown event in front of twelve thousand people?" I jumped at it.

I performed a remix of Jay-Z's "Empire State of Mind," about Vancouver instead of New York, plus two originals, on an outdoor stage. When I started singing people started to chant my name, "Kalvonix, Kalvonix." It was cold and I was so nervous, but it was an incredible feeling.

The next day, my friend called me again to tell me that Chin Injeti, a music producer, was in the crowd and would like to meet me. Turned out he was working on Eminem's latest album in a studio in Gastown. So my friends and I went down.

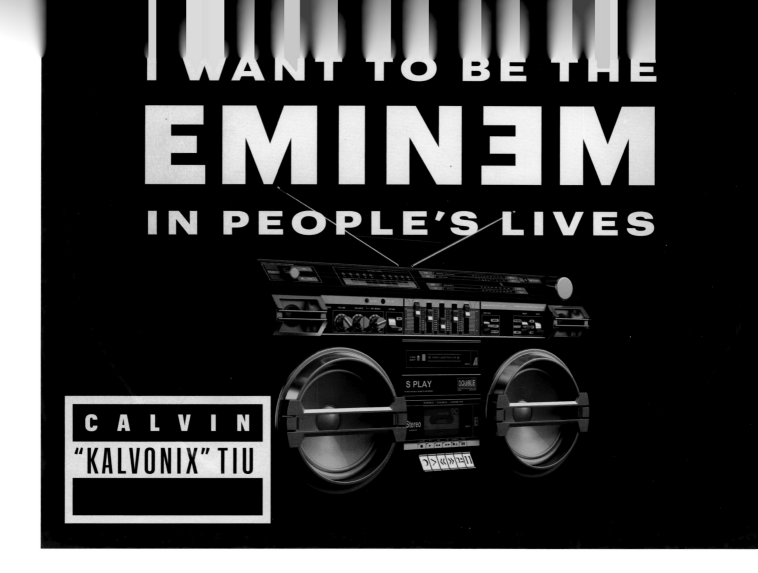

I WANT TO BE THE EMINƎM IN PEOPLE'S LIVES

CALVIN "KALVONIX" TIU

Chin was sitting at a computer with his back turned to us, and he stood up to shake my hand. But first he grabbed a crutch, and I realized, *Wow, he has the same waddle as me. Oh my goodness, this guy has a waddle too, and he's working with my heroes.* I later found out he had polio as a kid.

He asked me to rap for him, so I got one of my cousins to throw on a beat and rapped. After a minute he said, "That's hip hop, Calvin, real hip hop." Then he asked us if we'd like to hear what he'd been working on with Eminem, and he played the beat to the song "Talkin' 2 Myself."

"Keep doing what you're doing," he told me. "You inspire people, you inspire me. Keep grinding."

The next year he won a Grammy for *Recovery*, the Eminem LP he'd previewed for us.

When I see the power of music, I want to do things to inspire people as much as Eminem inspired me. I want to be the Eminem in people's lives. If one person thinks, because of me, I want to attend university, I want to pursue my passion in painting or whatever, I'll be happy.

Calvin "Kalvonix" Tiu leads a music curriculum in schools and is a trained and certified Jack Talks speaker for Jack.org. Listen to his latest album, *I Don't Know Yet*, on your streaming service.

MAKING MUSIC
MATTER
Darcy Ataman

◀ STEREO ▶

First come the drums. Then a searing guitar riff. Then the voices, a chorus of girls and women, singing in Swahili, calling out all the negligent men, the rapists, and the ones who stood by while the soldiers abused them.

The song is called "The Criminal Father," and the girls and women singing it are all survivors of sexual violence in the Democratic Republic of the Congo (DRC). They have lived through horrendous suffering and are now laid low with post-traumatic stress disorder (PTSD), anxiety, and depression. If you survive a rape, you might need two years of surgery to repair yourself physically, but what about the emotional and psychological side? How do you heal that? That's where Make Music Matter and our program Healing in Harmony comes in.

All of the music for songs like "The Criminal Father" is written by the survivors, who we call artists. We build studios in the hospitals where they are recovering. All of the operational staff are local, because they have to understand the cultural nuances. Rural Mulamba is one thing; Beni has a very different musical style. We find producers who know the local rhythms and traditions.

The artists write the lyrics and melodies, then producers build the tracks with computers. Sometimes we add live drums. The artists do it all: composing, singing, writing lyrics, creating melodies. Then they get a completed album, which is sent out worldwide. The songs go on local radio and they do concerts. It's all about rebuilding confidence. When you're raped in a war, you have no power, everything has been taken away from you. Making music gives you back some control.

In October 2018 our main partner, Dr. Denis Mukwege, founder and medical director of Panzi Hospital in Bukavu, DRC, won the Nobel Peace Prize. I've known him for a long time. It's a huge validation. Dr. Mukwege is set to become one of those global figures who everyone knows. It will help the work, and help protect him a bit, too. He has treated thousands of survivors of sexual violence, performing up to ten operations a day. He practically lives in the hospital, under UN protection.

"The Criminal Father" is a gutsy, angry track calling out all the men who allowed these rapes to happen, standing by while the military assaulted people. You can imagine how cathartic it is for the women to sing it. And the incredible thing is, whenever the local radio stations play it, the military calls in to complain. They insist that *they're* not the ones committing the rapes, they're not the bad guys—which is a total lie.

That members of armed militias are scared enough to call in repeatedly really says something. It's fascinating that the people with the guns are afraid of the people with the songs. They're the ones with power, but they can't control the music, and that terrifies them. That tells you what music can do.

Darcy Ataman is a music producer and the founder and CEO of Make Music Matter, an NGO that brings music therapy to survivors of conflict and trauma. Born in Winnipeg, he is a frequent guest speaker and a contributor to the *Huffington Post* and various other publications.

On **April 14**, my thirteenth birthday, I was in the operating room at SickKids Hospital in Toronto for what was supposed to be a not-quite-routine-but-still-manageable spinal cord decompression. It was not routine. What was expected to be a four-hour surgery turned out to be a ten-hour surgery, as they realized when they got in that they needed to remove more than planned. After I came out, we thought everything was fine.

I have spent a lot of my life in hospitals. At the age of two I was diagnosed with a metabolic disorder called MPS VI. My dad, Andrew McFadyen, created the Isaac Foundation to raise money and awareness around rare diseases like mine. So far, they have raised more than a million dollars, with a lot of help from musicians like Danny Michel and John Mayer. All the money goes to research.

After three or four days in recovery, we realized something was wrong. I was not improving as fast as I had after previous surgeries, and had barely any appetite. Then, in the middle of the night, I woke up feeling unwell. My voice was all screwed up, I vomited, and, over the next few hours, I developed intermittent paralysis. We were still at SickKids, so the doctors did an emergency MRI and decided that the paralysis was caused by high intercranial pressure, and they needed to put in a drain to relieve it. As they were prepping for the surgery, I had another paralysis episode and stopped breathing. Luckily, my anesthesiologist was visiting at the time, so he put in a breathing tube. I was then rushed to the operating room, where they put in a drain.

I spent the next five days in the intensive care unit, with a breathing tube and a ventilator in for most of them. I was delirious, because I needed to be suctioned and have neuro checks done every fifteen minutes, so the most I ever got was fifteen minutes of sleep at a time. As a result, I was hallucinating and in deep distress.

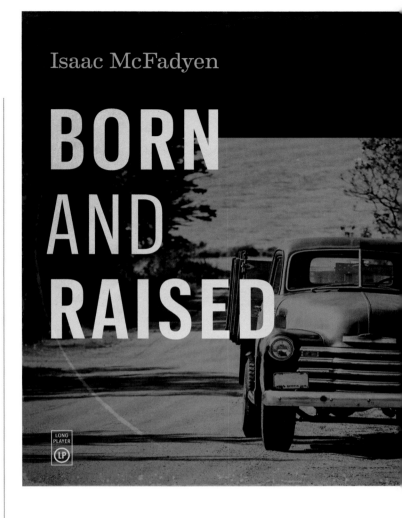

Isaac McFadyen

BORN AND RAISED

I was in a really bad mental state; Dad tried everything to calm me down, but failed. Then he thought of music. He knows how much I love John Mayer, so he put a phone beside my head and put on the album *Born and Raised*. I know John quite well (he's supported our foundation for years) and listen to his music often. That album is so familiar, and is naturally mellow and calming. It was the one thing that succeeded in relaxing me and letting me sleep.

Isaac McFadyen is fourteen years old. He likes reading, playing video games, and cooking; his favourite foods are pasta and pizza (especially Neapolitan).

CHRIS HADFIELD

What a Friend to Have

I've always been a musician. I think we all are, it's just that only some of us learn to play instruments. I grew up with music; it's how I meditated, how I learned about life.

With the jobs I've been in—military pilot, engineer, astronaut—I've lost many friends and colleagues. But the first, and the toughest, was Captain Tristan de Koninck. We were both CF-18 pilots, defending Canada during the Cold War, scrambling out to intercept Soviet bombers practicing dry-run attacks on North America. We were in our late twenties, we'd both been through military college and got married;

he had two girls and Helene and I had two boys. We flew together, we were going to be lifelong friends. He was a very good guy, physically fit, and a great pilot; a better pilot than I.

Then in May 1986, after an air show on Prince Edward Island, Tristan crashed his CF-18. He had taken off, pulled up hard into low-lying clouds, then flown straight down into Malpeque Bay at 700 miles an hour. Nobody knew why. Maybe he got disoriented as he pulled up, or maybe it was a technical malfunction. Either way, it was a horrible, horribly short end to a vibrant life.

> **Music gave me a way to deal with the most harrowing thing I had yet faced in my life, a way to say the kind of things I would have said if I'd known how.**

I was flying down in Bermuda when I got the news. His wife, Sue, asked if I would come back and speak at his memorial. Of course I said yes, and in no time I was in my CF-18 on the 1,000-mile flight back to CFB Bagotville. It was a very sombre flight home, trying to digest what all this meant. He had a lot of plans. We had a lot of plans.

As soon as I landed I went to see Sue, who gave me Tristan's twelve-string guitar and said, "I'd really love it if you could play a song with this." I had a six-string, and she'd put up with so many evenings of us jamming together in their living room over the years.

Again I said yes, but this time I didn't know if I was up to it. I was angry, at the vehicle for killing him and the sheer injustice of the accident. And sad. But I took the twelve-string back to my place and started going through our songbook. And the song that made sense was "This Old Guitar" by John Denver. We'd had played it together, harmonizing our voices, so many times. I had always loved the lyrics, but now they packed an extra punch: Denver sang that his guitar taught him to sing love songs, how to laugh and to cry; it brightened his days and was his friend on cold, lonely nights.

The problem was, once I sat down to practice the song, I didn't make it through once. I probably tried two hundred times, but it was just too raw; it brought the memory of him too cruelly alive. I couldn't reconcile that with the fact I'd never see him again.

Then the moment of the memorial came. There was a big picture of Tristan, and his wife and all our friends were there. I went up and played the song.

I made it through, mostly by imagining Tristan was playing beside me. Music gave me a way to deal with the most harrowing thing I had yet faced in my life, a way to say the kind of things I would have said if I'd known how, instead of keeping them bottled up inside.

That was thirty-three years ago. When I play or hear "This Old Guitar" today I'm exactly there, in Tristan's living room, or at the memorial. That song is both a moment in time and a treasured thing that keeps my friend alive in my mind. It allows me to invite Tristan over to play.

People often ask me, "Do you miss walking in space?" It seems like an odd question; that's just one thing of so many I've done, and I usually say, no, I don't miss it. What I do miss are people, and one of the people I miss the most is Tristan. I wish he was here, beside me in our late fifties, to enjoy life with me.

That's a big part of music. It can help remind you of a person or a time or a place that meant a lot to you. "This Old Guitar" is not one of John Denver's biggest songs, but when I play it, I'm much more liable to smile than to cry.

Chris Hadfield is a retired engineer, military pilot, and astronaut. During three space flights he was the first Canadian to walk in space and the first to command a spaceship. Hadfield is an author and professor, and his cover of the David Bowie song "Space Oddity," the first music video ever recorded in space, has had more than forty million views on YouTube.

AT THAT MOMENT I SAID TO MYSELF: I AM GOING TO FIGURE OUT A WAY TO PLAY ONE-HANDED ACOUSTIC GUITAR.

At age forty-seven my life changed forever when I was suddenly felled by a stroke. I woke up one morning feeling dizzy and nauseated and decided to take the day off work. I eventually called 911, from bed, and found that I couldn't talk properly. I totally blubbered it out: "AMBULANCE." Half my tongue, my mouth, my whole body wasn't working; it had shut down.

It's been an incredible journey since then. The sensation slowly came back over weeks. At first I couldn't eat solid food, or even drink water, for fear of choking. Having a stroke is not a gradual decline; you go straight off a cliff. One moment you're fully capable, the next your life has changed entirely. That was November 2011.

I had been playing guitar since my early teens. I had toured in a band, played in church, even recorded a few times. I grew up with music at home; my mom was a guitarist and a fiddle player who'd performed her whole life: square dances, church, family events. It's in you when you're young and you don't even realize it, it's part of life. Being a musician is just who I am.

I had always played guitar, with my left hand on the frets and my right hand strumming the strings. Now I found myself with no control over the whole right side of my body.

When I first got out of hospital my occupational therapist asked me to set goals. My goal was to get back to playing the guitar. Then one day she asked me if I had ever considered some kind of one-handed technique. I had naïvely believed that it would all come back one day. But it wasn't about the old way of playing guitar, it was about *making music with my guitar*. That was an "aha" moment. I said to myself: that's something I can work on *right now*.

About six months after getting out of the hospital, I went out one night to Hugh's Room, a music venue in Toronto, and saw an artist performing that brought it all together for me: Jon Gomm. He's an unbelievable guitar player who creates rhythms, melody, bass, and percussion, all on the guitar body. I'd never seen someone play like that before. I was watching what he was doing with his two hands, totally independently, and thought, if I could just do the left-hand part, that would be musical enough for me.

At that moment I said to myself: I am going to figure out a way to play one-handed acoustic guitar. I came up with my own approach; I had to find a way to make my one hand do all the things I wanted, and work out how to tune the guitar. Then I started writing songs for one-handed playing.

On my website you can see me playing a song called "Best Foot Forward," with just my left hand. It's from a CD called *On the Other Hand*. That's an expression that has extra meaning for me now. As does "It cost an arm and a leg."

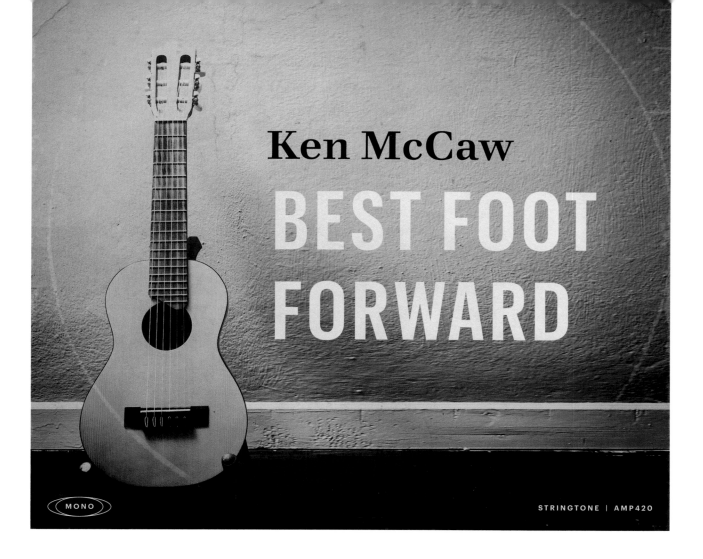

Ken McCaw

BEST FOOT FORWARD

MONO

STRINGTONE | AMP420

I now have an electrical device I wear around my leg that allows me to walk without dragging my right foot; it raises it in a controlled way while I step. I have full sensation on my right side, I just have no motor control. Another part of my brain would need to step in and take over, which is hard to fathom.

That's not a priority for me now. I can live life entirely with one hand. I'd rather put the time and energy I have into making music and helping other people. I speak and perform regularly at conferences. My goal is for people to leave the room like I left at that Jon Gomm concert—believing, "There is another way, because I just saw this guy do it!" It's more than just one-handed guitar, it's how we approach our perceived limitations and roadblocks.

Your life's not over. It's easy to feel that way, and I wouldn't fault someone for succumbing to it. But I believe, as Jon Gomm says in his song "Passion-flower," that we are what we grow into, not what we were. That is what I am living now. Maybe just sharing that one thing—how I learned to play the guitar one-handed—can help one person approach things a little bit differently.

Ken McCaw is an IT consultant who lives and works in Toronto. He speaks at conferences and inspires others to take some crappy thing that happened and find real value in it. Listen to him play guitar at kenmccaw.ca.

RAIN

CAMERON ESPINA

SONG

When I was in hospital, in grade eleven, my mum brought my guitar in to help soothe me. I hadn't put enough time into playing before that, not enough to progress, but it gave me something to do and helped with the healing. Now I play every day; music has been a real gift that has helped me to manage my mental health issues.

I've suffered from anxiety and depression for a number of years. I've been on several different medications, but the combinations weren't good. That's how I ended up in hospital two years ago, after a really deep bout of depression that led me to take overdoses of pills. Now I'm off all the medication and focusing on music.

I grew up listening to tons of older music. My mum used to play a lot of Marvin Gaye, Stevie Wonder, Eric Clapton, stuff like that. And dance around the house. Older rock and soul music always made more sense to me than the new stuff.

This year, a few friends and I formed a band called Wescali. We started jamming for fun, me on lead guitar, and entered a battle of the bands contest to help raise money for our local skate park and ended up winning. We've performed at a lot of concerts and festivals since, recently as headliners.

A huge inspiration is Led Zeppelin's live album *The Song Remains the Same*, one of my favourite albums ever. It's the epitome of their style: a tight but loose, high-energy live show. And I could listen forever to that recording of "The Rain Song," a great breathing rock ballad that always makes me feel more powerful, like everything is going to be okay.

The guitar rhythm in itself tells a story throughout the song. You can feel it going through the seasons. Then the full band breaks in and all the emotion from the first half of the song cuts right through you. It's hard to explain, it just hits me in a way that makes me reflect on everything, appreciate everything, life itself.

I had been feeling down for a long time, and that song just broke through the shell I was trapped inside. I had been under a rain cloud for so long. The song says a lot of powerful things: about the lasting coldness of the winter inside us, and, in the powerful last verse, about how the seasons of our emotions rise and fall like the wind; how a little rain must fall on all of us.

I am the co-contributor for the lyrics and melodies for Wescali's songs. I'm too shy to be a front man, I say what I need to say with the guitar, though I do enjoy doing back-up vocals and taking the odd lead. I have a hard time putting together words and speaking sometimes, I feel like I can say a lot more with sound and melody. It's definitely the best way I have to express my emotions, to convey happiness, sadness, confusion. If I'm feeling down or worked up, the only thing that can take my mind off everything is playing. I just feed that energy through the music. It feeds right through and out of your soul. My dream is to pass my energy through my music directly into someone else's soul.

When I'm writing, most of time I come up with the guitar parts and the lyrics come later. Sometimes we'll jam for an hour or more without stopping, trying to find something cool we can build on. It's a weird process, it's different every time. Songs just come out of nowhere; you can't really bust them out from nothing. Often the first idea is the purest, the best—a melody, a lyric, that just makes sense.

Music comes from nowhere but your soul. It's completely real. Good music is true and will take you away from your bad thoughts or help you to understand them. They give you medication to take the edge off, but medication won't fix your problems, you have to learn to look at it the right way, to grit your teeth and learn how to get by. Music's the best medicine of all.

Cameron Espina graduated from Haliburton Highland Secondary School in 2018 and now plays lead guitar for Wescali, a classic and psychedelic rock band. Follow them on Facebook!

MUSIC FOR DOROTHY

Jennifer Budd

As babies, the first rhythm we hear is our mother's heartbeat. Those early sounds soothe and calm us. And so the journey with music begins. Hearing a piece of music can transport you to a time and place. Music can wake up a memory, tell a story, and be the vehicle of communication when speech is unavailable.

My mother-in-law, Dorothy Budd, was loved by all who knew her. She was a registered nurse, farm wife, mother of three, faithful church and choir member, gardener, and a most gentle soul. She loved music and made sure all of her children—Stuart, Brad, and Shelley—received piano lessons.

Many of you reading this will be familiar with the ravages of Alzheimer's disease, a cruel and devastating illness. Dorothy lived in a long-term care facility for six years as Alzheimer's slowly took her from her family.

After she had lost the ability to speak, conversing with Dorothy was challenging. It was so sad; Dorothy had loved a good chat about everything and anything. Now her adult children found it difficult to sit with their mom. It can be tiring when you are the one doing all the talking.

Then her eldest son, Stuart, got a violin for Christmas in 2011. He persevered with lessons, learning a few Scottish reels. During his next visit to Dorothy, he took out his violin and started to play. Her response was immediate. Her eyes lit up and she smiled. It was clear that the music was sparking something in her. She could not tell us what it was, but she appeared to be enjoying what she was hearing. Residents started to gather in the hallway beyond her room to hear the music.

Stuart's brother, Brad, plays the bassoon and his sister, Shelley, plays the piano. Somehow they found music for bassoon, piano, and violin and formed a trio to play for their mom. They soon found themselves playing for the entire unit. What had started as a means of finding a meaningful way to engage with their mom became a music session for many.

A dementia unit can be a sad and sorrowful place. When Dorothy's adult children played, the joy in the room was palpable. When the spoken word becomes lost and confused, music can connect us.

On September 27, 2015, as the moon was eclipsed by the earth's shadow, Dorothy slipped away, quietly and gently after much music-making at her bedside.

Music can help us navigate some of the most difficult days of our lives.

Jennifer Budd is a retired occupational therapist who believes in the transformative power of music. She now works as a fibre artist out of her home-based studio in Paris, Ontario.

Four words changed my life forever: "Your daughter has cancer." With that pronouncement our whole family entered another dimension. Telling my sixteen-year-old the news was the hardest thing I have ever done.

From dancing to playing instruments to singing, music has always been important to our family. Megan was a very musical child and teenager who had won an award for most promising young vocalist. That's why we invited the music therapist, Erin, into our lives as soon as Megan found herself at British Columbia Children's Hospital. That changed everything. For the next four and a half years, music was part of Megan's routine.

Seeing how much the therapy was helping Megan cope with her illness, Erin suggested she write a song about it. That's how "A Will to Survive" was born. Megan's initial intent was to share it with other teens going through treatment, but the song soon took on a life of its own. She was asked to sing it and speak at many events. Then she recorded it professionally, with the help of Vancouver producer Garth Richardson and indie singer-songwriter Ryan McMahon and his band.

Megan battled cancer four times. Her song and her appearances turned her into a spokesperson for teens fighting cancer, to emphasize how young people deal with treatments differently; for example, they are more susceptible to anxiety and depression than children or adults are. Megan sang with celebrities like Michael Bublé, and performed "A Will to Survive" with Chantal Kreviazuk and Ryan McMahon. This was just a few days before another round of chemo, and she insisted on performing even though she had a fever of 103.9 degrees.

Although Megan lost her battle with cancer in January 2011, her legacy lives on. People around the world are still inspired by her song. Her story shows

A WILL TO SURVIVE

Suzanne McNeil

teens how they can control their own destinies by facing severe life challenges through music. She went through so much but continued to use her music to give herself an expressive outlet.

My husband and I have continued to listen to her song, and are still working to spread the support. Whenever we face rough times, Megan's song inspires us. I can still hear her voice in the back of my mind, reminding me to find that will to survive.

Suzanne McNeil was privileged to be the mother of Megan McNeil. A registered holistic nutritionist, she has worked with Canadian Mental Health Association (BC division), where she learned firsthand the impact of mental illness on families—and many methods to deal with it, especially music. She has lived on both the east and west coasts of Canada and now lives in Delta, BC.

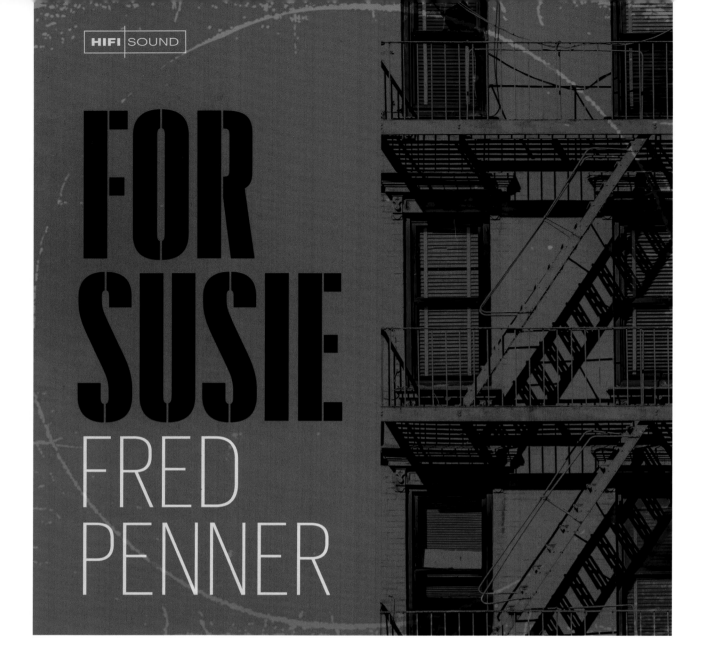

FOR SUSIE

FRED PENNER

My younger sister Susie was born with Down's syndrome. As is often the case, she also had a heart murmur, and back then (1954) the operation to fix it was experimental and risky. After much discussion, my parents opted against it, knowing that she would probably not live beyond puberty. Sure enough, despite a regimen of blood-thinning drugs, the symptoms got worse and worse, and she passed away at age twelve.

My strongest memories of Susie are her love for music, especially the soundtrack for *West Side Story*. She had an openness to receiving musical patterns to the depths of her being, and those amazing Leonard Bernstein arrangements got right inside there. They would bring tears to her eyes. All of her reactions were non-verbal—grunts and facial expressions— but they just seemed so intuitive. This was a lesson I would never forget.

Every time I perform I have been approached afterward by people with tears, with a story, with thanks. Every time it fortifies my appreciation of the power of music.

I was twenty when she died. I had just graduated from the University of Winnipeg with an economics degree. It was a huge turning point in my life, because my father died the year after that, from cancer. Those two mortality checks within a year of each other rocked my foundation and gave me the impetus to try to discover what my bliss was, where my life would go.

I had studied economics to satisfy my dad, who had never been to university. I realized I was never going to be an economist. I had been playing the guitar for years and been involved in dozens of musical productions, but nobody had ever told me I could make a career in music. Now I knew that this was what I wanted to do with my life. That decision led me down all sorts of paths, from dance and theatre projects to an offer to make my first record: *The Cat Came Back*. The delight in my journey was to realize how deeply others were affected by the music, as Susie had been.

After one of my first concerts after releasing *The Cat Came Back*, I saw a lady at the back of the theatre, waiting for me to finish signing autographs. She approached me and told me how important the record was for her and her three children, one of whom was in a nearby hospital with a brain tumour. She wanted me to hear how she'd bring the record in with a record player and they'd bond listening to it, her and her four-year-old son. He ultimately passed away.

Every time I've performed since then I have been approached afterward by people with tears, with a story, with thanks. Every time it fortifies my appreciation of the power of music. My mantra now is: never underestimate your ability to make a difference in the life of a child. That message is just so crystal clear to me now. And it all goes back to Susie and seeing how deeply she was affected by *West Side Story*. That touched everything I've done in life.

As time went by, I became more involved in the Down's syndrome world. This inspired me to writing a song called "Celebrate Being," the title of a Down's syndrome conference I attended. The chorus is simple:

Celebrate being a dreamer
Celebrate being real
Celebrate being good, good friends
Telling each other how you feel.

Fred Penner has been performing and recording songs for children since *The Cat Came Back* was a worldwide hit in 1979. He has won four Juno awards for Best Children's Album, most recently for the 2017 album *Hear the Music* (distributed by Linus Music), which includes the song "Celebrate Being."

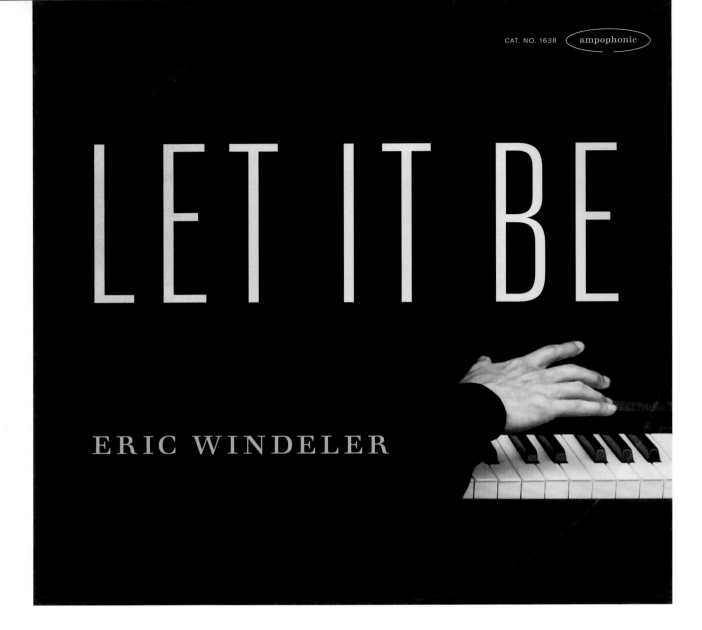

LET IT BE

ERIC WINDELER

One **Saturday** morning in March 2010, I received a call from a police officer. He rushed to our house and had the unenviable task of telling us that we had lost our first-born son, Jack, to suicide. Jack was just eighteen years old and in his first year at Queen's University. The death of our child, a parent's worst nightmare, came as a complete shock. We always thought we had three happy, healthy kids. We had no idea Jack was struggling.

As a family, we knew very little about mental health or suicide. But somehow, there were three things that we knew immediately after losing Jack. One—if this could happen to us, it could happen to anyone. Two—we were going to be open and honest about what had happened to our precious son. And three—we would do our best to help others whose stories are similar to Jack's, so that far fewer families would have to go through the horror we had experienced.

The days leading up to Jack's funeral were long and difficult, a blur of compassionate words and sorrowful embraces. Family and friends were at our side around the clock. These people and their support saved us. They came and they stayed with us, with love and without judgment. They were there to express their condolences and commiserate in the grief-stricken finality of the loss of our beloved Jack.

During the funeral service, a young family friend performed a haunting rendition of the Beatles' song "Let It Be." I knew right away why he had chosen that song. It resonates so strongly with all who find themselves in times of trouble. Its message is one of loss and consolation, of comfort and moving forward. Paul McCartney wrote the song during a painful moment in his life, after his mother, who had passed away when he was fourteen, came to him in a dream. She told him that everything would be all right if he could just "let it be."

The song's "Let it be" chorus is a mantra we can repeat over and over again in moments of difficulty. It encourages us to release our sorrows and surrender to circumstance.

The song was perfectly appropriate at Jack's funeral and remains dear to me, despite the years that have passed since we heard it that day.

But the thing was that I, along with my wife Sandra Hanington, and Jack's siblings Ben and Julia, could not just let it be. Not this. Not possible. The loss of Jack, and the many other young people lost to suicide every year, was not something we could let be. Things needed to change, and we wanted to make sure they did. We didn't know precisely *what* needed to change just yet, but the song that was intended to provide us with some small semblance of solace during the most difficult time of our lives also lit a fire beneath us all. We were not able to just lose our son and move on. For Jack, we had to let it be. But for others, *we could not and would not* let it be.

My initial inclination was to find out exactly what had happened, how it had got to the point that it did, and how neither we, nor anyone around Jack at

I knew right away why he had chosen that song. It resonates so strongly with all who find themselves in times of trouble.

school, had seen the warning signs. I started asking questions. I spoke with every mental health professional I could find. I spoke with faculty at Jack's high school and university. But most importantly, I spoke with Jack's peers. I wanted to learn everything I could about the mental health landscape surrounding youth in Canada, and most importantly, what young people felt should be done to improve it.

Armed with this knowledge, we started what has become Jack.org, a national charity focused on training and empowering young people to revolutionize mental health for their generation.

The work that we do through Jack.org has helped me and my family get through our personal tragedy. But we know that Jack.org has helped countless others as well. We will continue to work tirelessly, motivated by our endless love for our dear son Jack. Our hope is that one day we will live in a world where no parent has the impossible task of choosing the funeral song for their child, and that all young people can get the help they need and deserve.

Eric Windeler is executive director and co-founder (with his wife Sandra Hanington) of Jack.org. He has received many awards for his work in mental health, including the Queen Elizabeth II Diamond Jubilee Medal, an honorary degree from Queen's University, and (with Hanington) a Meritorious Service Cross (Civil Division) from the office of the Governor General.

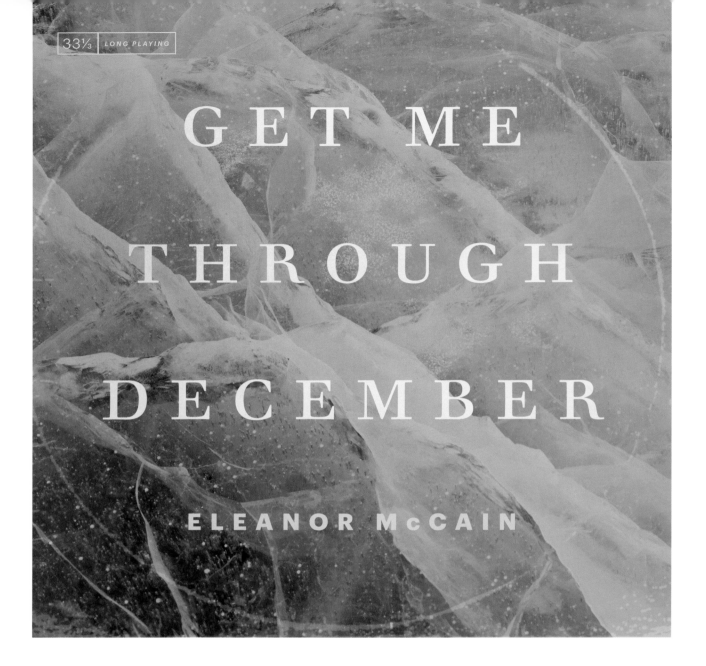

GET ME

THROUGH

DECEMBER

ELEANOR McCAIN

Music has always been part of my life. My mother tells me that I was singing before I could talk. I was drawn to it as a career because I have always found it therapeutic. I can be shy, so I've had to nurture that performance side of me. But music has the power to heighten emotions and connect us to something deeper. It takes me beyond my shyness and acts as a release. It's a form of expression and catharsis I don't get anywhere else.

In 2014, I spent the year thinking about our vast country for *True North: The Canadian Songbook*. I wanted to celebrate the 150th anniversary of Confederation in a recording of our most iconic Canadian pop and folk songs. I wanted these songs to be reimagined in new orchestral arrangements by Canadian arrangers, and then record them with ten orchestras from coast to coast. I also wanted to make a book of Canadian landscape photography

> Music takes me beyond my shyness and acts as a release. It's a form of expression and catharsis I don't get anywhere else.

that would accompany the CDs. The scope was epic and the logistics daunting, which is why I thought about it for a year.

Early in 2015, my short-lived marriage came to an abrupt end. I was in shock, devastated, not just because the relationship was over but also because there was a significant amount of misrepresentation and deceit involved in the aftermath. It was extremely difficult to comprehend. I was traumatized. I had to decide: *Can I move forward with this project or not? Should I crawl under a rock in a little ball or hold my head up and move forward?* What became clear almost immediately was that I knew I would heal through music. As hard as it was to put one foot in front of the other, I had to do this project because I knew the music would heal my heart.

I really connected with the songs I chose for the album. They are so full of deep, raw emotion. The more I immersed myself in the lyrics and the music, the more I kept finding my own story in them. Every time I showed up for a session, I would relate new aspects of the songs to things that were happening in my life. The whole journey was profoundly cathartic.

I planned to record thirty-two songs. In February 2016, we were all set to begin laying down the band tracks when I had a deeply cathartic moment. I had been dealing with a huge wave of personal crises, debilitating events that were unfolding simultaneously: not just the divorce but other difficult events in addition to being a single mother to a teenage daughter while leading a major recording project. I was on emotional overload.

I finally had time to myself on my drive to a rehearsal with the Kitchener–Waterloo Symphony.

I started listening to one of my favourite songs, "Get Me through December" by Gordie Sampson and Fred Lavery, as recorded by Alison Krauss and Natalie MacMaster. As the words unfolded, the lyrics hit me so hard that I could not stop crying. I ended up spending the entire hour and a half of my drive weeping. The lyrics depicted how my heart had grown cold and my love was stored away, in a way I could relate to. These experiences had just made me turn inward. My capacity to love hadn't disappeared, but it was sheltered away for safe keeping while I healed.

Then came the next verse, which brought me to my knees. Hearing the line about a girl taking on more pain than she should endure was a huge release.

I texted my producer and said, "You're going to kill me." He knew what I meant. Ten days before we started recording, adding one more song was not a small request. But how do you leave out a song that expresses your deepest emotions during the most difficult time of your life?

This is the power of music: it expresses our innermost feelings and releases them so we can heal.

Eleanor McCain is a triple ECMA-nominated vocalist who has recorded six albums and accompanied symphonies across Canada. In 2017 she released *True North: The Canadian Songbook,* an award-winning album and book showcasing thirty-two of Canada's most iconic songs and photography of the majestic Canadian landscape. From Florenceville, New Brunswick, and now based in Toronto, McCain is also an active philanthropist.

KELLYLEE EVANS

A SHOCKING LESSON

Music has been a part of who I am for as long as I can remember. I had my first solo in kindergarten, and knew instinctively that this was what I wanted to do for a living, though it took me almost twenty-five years to finally make music my sole focus. Then, in 2013, my new career was threatened when I was hit by lightning. I didn't stop touring, but I did take a long time to acknowledge how much my body and brain had been affected by the trauma of that strike. In the process I learned a powerful lesson—music heals.

People ask me what it's like to be struck by lightning. I always say "shocking," not just to be funny, but because it's true. The accident itself was freakish. I was standing by the kitchen window in my Ottawa home washing the dishes during a lightning storm—

something, it turns out, you are never supposed to do—when I saw a flash of light. I felt a surge go through me and everything seemed to stop.

At first, the effects were hard to place. When I finally got checked out by doctors, my bodily movements and functions were deteriorating fast. I didn't know what to do, so I just kept moving forward. I had a big tour planned the following week and didn't want to cancel, so I just kept on travelling.

It turns out I had suffered a brain injury from the jostling caused by the electrical charge. I found myself in a wheelchair, the left side of my body so weakened that I couldn't coordinate my arms to roll the wheels. I couldn't cut my own food, sign autographs, or write, and couldn't even hold my microphone for long. And at the end of every day, after many hours pushing myself to talk to people, remember my lyrics, and perform, I would start slurring and forget the names of everyday objects or the people around me. The symptoms were like those of a stroke or a concussion. Without the help of my bandmates and my family and friends, I wouldn't have made it through a very challenging time, when I had no idea if my body would ever function normally again.

That experience changed my life in so many ways. I went from being super active and full of energy to having to learn how to slow down and listen to my body's needs. At first, I took a lot of pride in saying that I kept working through my injury. But the truth was that I didn't know how to stop, take a break, and take care of myself. I've spent the past five years learning how to listen to my body.

I was on vacation in the French countryside, at my guitarist's summer home, when I began to notice the power that playing an instrument can have for

I was on vacation in the French country-side, at my guitarist's summer home, when I began to notice the power that playing an instrument can have for healing the brain.

healing the brain. I picked up a ukulele lying near the couch and asked my guitarist to teach me the lick in one of our songs ("Désolé," off my 2013 album *I Remember When*). At first, it was so hard to even move the fingers on my left side, much less work out how to coordinate them to learn the chords. But he was a patient teacher and I was excited to be learning something new.

I spent days just mastering the simple pattern, and a funny thing happened along the way: my brain seemed to be working better. I was slurring less, and my memory was sharper. My mental and motor skills improved steadily over months of this therapy. I got into a rhythm of playing every day, soon moving onto a new love: the electric bass.

Today, my health has greatly improved and my bass sits mostly untouched in the corner beside my bed. But that doesn't change my firm belief that music heals. I don't know what I would do without it in my life.

Kellylee Evans is a jazz and soul singer from Scarborough, Ontario. She has been nominated for three Juno awards, winning one, and won a Gemini award in 2007.

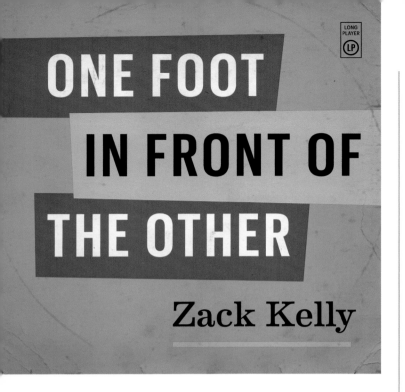

ONE FOOT IN FRONT OF THE OTHER

Zack Kelly

I was nineteen years old and sitting on the back of a car, slowly following a sea of students in the University of Toronto Frosh Parade. All around us young adults were smiling, cheering, and dancing, so excited for what first year had in store. Unfortunately, I wasn't sharing their energy. I had two crutches and a leg brace, and gone were my hopes of a career as a varsity athlete.

Two weeks before the parade I was training for pre-season football camp when I blew out three ligaments in my left knee. The doctors put it this way, "If you were a professional athlete, this would be the end of your career." Things only got worse from there.

Over the next few months, I slowly distanced myself from friends and social outings, stopped going to class, and eventually dropped out of first year. All my peers were having the time of their lives, but I was camping in my parents' basement.

In January I had surgery and, despite some nasty reactions to pain medication, it went well. My mom was kind enough to drive me to the first string of physiotherapy appointments, but after that, I was on my own. The temperatures were sub-zero, I was on crutches and it was a fifty-five-minute walk, subway, then bus ride to my physio. I slowly adopted a nocturnal lifestyle, so, needless to say, when my alarm went off every morning, I felt like gravity had exponentially increased.

Then, late one night, I was staring at the ceiling in my basement when I noticed my cousin had left a copy of the Eminem movie *8 Mile* at our house. I threw it on, and at some point the beat for "Lose Yourself" started. I got tingles down the back of my neck. It wasn't the first time I had heard the song, but it was the first time I had felt anything good in weeks. Eminem was mad, he had fire, and he wasn't giving up. Before the movie was over I had re-downloaded the *8 Mile* album and listened to it a few more times.

One line spoke to me the most, where he realizes this is his only shot, and asks his feet to fail him not. This felt like a wake-up call—my opportunity to recover. I had to trust that if I continued to put one foot in front of the other, things would get better.

The next day I woke up excited to listen to the album again. I was coming off about four hours sleep, but still felt energized. I knew I had found something that could help snap me back to reality. I promised myself from that day forward that if I wanted to go back to sleep after my alarm I could, but only after I had listened to "Lose Yourself."

Before I knew it, my sleep cycles were returning to normal and I had a wake-up playlist with forty-five tracks, from "Gimme Shelter" by the Rolling Stones to Meat Loaf's "I'd Do Anything for Love." It was vast and eclectic and more than a little corny, but it made all the difference in how I started my day.

These days my songs have changed, but the lesson they teach me remains the same: music has the power to facilitate healing. I still use this motivational strategy to generate healthy behavioural changes in myself and my clients.

Zack Kelly is a personal trainer and health coach at Toronto's Medcan clinic. He has degrees in kinesiology and psychology and is currently pursuing a master's degree in neuroscience and health and fitness behaviours.

Need to Feel
SAL TALON

DEEP STEREO | AMPOPHONIC 054

A lot of my friends don't know that there was a long stretch of time when I wasn't doing anything musical at all. Starting from a deep depression at age seventeen, I decided that my passion for music was irresponsible. I remember passing the Cameron House on Queen Street West in Toronto every week and seeing names of artists up in the light box. Then I started to see familiar names. Old friends, people I went to school with, people like me. Whatever I felt, I pushed it down.

By the end of this dry spell I was in rough shape. Neglected feelings became fatigue became migraines. By the end of it, when I was too tired to even cry, I saw that denying my feelings was denying me the energy of life. I was like a car without gasoline.

I remember sitting in my room under the soft glow of my computer with almost no life force left, and softly singing the words, "I fear I need to feel, to be a part of this."

That line went into the vault, until one day when a musician friend, Jordo Arnott, started playing a riff on the guitar. Everything about the music we're now making together taps into some aspect of that bleak time in my life. And so, without thinking, the words flowed again:

Gave up music when you left
Never played guitar again
Broke the strings and cut my hand
Been denying where I been
I fear I need to feel, to be a part of this

One Saturday a few months later, Jordo and I walked on stage and played that song, "Need to Feel," as well as a handful of other originals. At the Cameron House, of all places.

Our band is called Cleanse It with Fire, and that's exactly what we're doing.

Sal Talon is an artist specializing in dramatic, bluesy rock. Born in Alabama and raised in various states across the US, she has lived in Toronto since the age of thirteen. You can see her at the Paddock, where she lurks on Tuesdays.

STEREO

BELTING IT OUT

AMANDA LANG

Music—and singing—was something my older sister Maria shared with me. With all of us, actually—even though, as the eldest of seven, she had a serious amount of responsibility on her small shoulders. But she was always singing, and often dancing, too. The songs were from the albums my older brothers let us play: Styx, Wings, Billy Joel, the Eagles. I lay on my stomach on the floor of the den, changing the records and singing along. Not the Beatles; they were too precious, though my eldest brother, Timothy, would play them for us on the turntable in his room.

Maria took me to my first concert, the Eagles, and although our seats were so high we could hardly make out the stage, it didn't matter a bit because we knew every word to every song. Maria taught me that the best way to enjoy a song is to inhabit it, by singing along. I'm that person that makes other drivers giggle when they catch me singing alone in my car. But if I love a song, I have to sing it. None of which should imply that I can sing; Maria couldn't either, for that matter. But as one of the things you can do badly and still enjoy (like dancing and skiing), singing became central.

Boys in high school made me mixed tapes—remember those? Songs carefully chosen with you in mind, with everything from the order they played to the lyrics they contained considered with the utmost detail. The songs were always anthems or ballads, and because the words moved me so, I fell a little bit in love with the musician—if not the boy offering it. Bryan Adams was an early love, the lyrics to his album *Cuts like a Knife* so perfectly matching everything my sixteen-year-old self felt. At some point my musical taste diverged from Maria's, whose interests ranged from rock and roll to musicals while mine strayed heavily into soft rock. But when I think of her, I think of her singing.

Maria died when I was twenty-one years old. She was killed in a freak car accident that would claim no other victims. The hours after I learned of her death remain a blessed blank to me. The next thing I remember is finding ordinary tasks like showering or standing too much to bear. How could we be in the world, breathing, walking around, seeing sunlight, and Maria be dead?

But true to form, she left us a gift. Not many twenty-seven-year-olds write wills, but Maria did. Perhaps because she was a lawyer, or perhaps because she had an old soul. It was a holographic will, meaning she had written down her intentions but not had them notarized legally. Still, it was a

I'm that person that makes other drivers giggle when they catch me singing alone in my car. But if I love a song, I have to sing it.

message from her to us about what should happen next. And—this is so like her that I still smile through a tear—she left instructions about her funeral.

In those instructions was a request for a song. Not a Beatles or a Billy Joel song, because in the Catholic funeral service only hymns can be played, but a beautiful hymn called "Lord of the Dance." This was 1991, so playing it meant finding a record or tape, and it so happened that my best friend's parents had it in their album collection. We sat on the floor in her dining room, looking through the vinyl, playing the Beatles' *Sgt. Pepper's* while we searched for it. The gift she gave us was something to do. A sense of purpose when all purpose had fled. And, more importantly, a feeling that I was doing something for her.

And so we played the song at her funeral, and as we did, what else could I do? I belted it out.

Amanda Lang is a business journalist who has worked for the *Globe and Mail*, CNN, CBC TV, and BNN Bloomberg. She has written two books: *The Power of Why* (2012) and *The Beauty of Discomfort* (2017). Born in Winnipeg, Lang lives in Toronto.

MULTI-DIRECTIONAL STEREO

SURROUND

Grant Lawrence

THE TEARS POURED OUT

> The song's haunting melody, strained organ notes, and fragile vocal delivery spoke directly to me at that exact moment. The tears poured out.

When I worked at CBC Radio during the mid-2000s, I co-hosted one season of Radio 3 on air with a guy named Alexis Mazurin. We were supposed to do a second season, but never got the chance.

Alexis made a huge impression on anyone he met: he was a highly physical, barrel-chested man, the son of South American immigrants. He loved hip hop, capoeira, Wreck Beach, and making radio. He was, as the saying goes, larger than life.

I still remember the first time I heard Alexis's booming baritone: I was at my desk at the CBC, and my job at the time involved recruiting new voices. Across the office and around the corner, I heard this rich, loud voice cutting through the open-office chatter.

I rose from my desk to see who this young Barry White was. Alexis Mazurin had already been freelancing for the CBC, but I hired him pretty much on the spot for Radio 3, and he stuck.

The summer of 2005 was a bizarre time. CBC employees were locked out in a labour dispute and forced onto the picket lines outside of CBC buildings across the country. Alexis and I spent a lot of time "walking the block" in Vancouver. When Labour Day loomed and it appeared that we wouldn't be going back to work, Alexis announced that he would take advantage of the time off by attending the Burning Man festival in the Nevada desert.

I remember saying goodbye to Alexis at the corner of Georgia and Hamilton streets in front of CBC Vancouver. My last words to him were, "Don't do anything I wouldn't do." It would be the last time I would ever see Alexis conscious.

At Burning Man, Alexis suffered a massive heart attack in his sleep and fell into a coma. He was airlifted to Vancouver, where he remained in his coma for several months. His robust physique faded away as he lay there, being fed and hydrated through tubes, his breathing heavily laboured. Finally, determining that his brain was too damaged to ever recover, the family made the impossible decision to let Alexis go.

The morning Alexis died was heartbreaking. The CBC was filled with tears. My executive producer informed me that they'd like to broadcast an on-air tribute to Alexis that Saturday night in place of our regular show. Would I be up for hosting it? The show must go on.

When I sat down at my desk to program the memorial, I noticed a new package that had arrived in the mail. Inside was *Porcella*, the latest CD by Toronto band the Deadly Snakes.

On that record is a beautiful song called "Gore Veil" (named after a street in Toronto). Its haunting melody, strained organ notes, and fragile vocal delivery spoke directly to me at that exact moment. The tears poured out. It became the lead-off song for the Alexis Mazurin memorial special, and is the song that always reminds me and many others of my larger-than-life co-host who left us far too soon.

Grant Lawrence is a broadcaster, musician, and writer based in Vancouver. A mainstay of CBC Radio 3 for twenty years, Lawrence is also the vocalist for the indie rock group the Smugglers and the author of three successful memoirs; the latest, *Dirty Windshields* (2017), about life in the band.

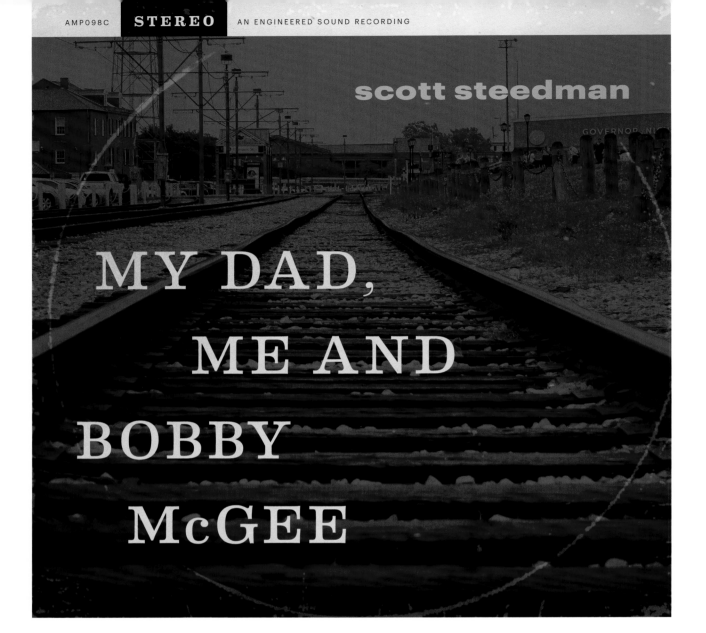

scott steedman

MY DAD, ME AND BOBBY McGEE

One of the last times I saw my father alive was on a sunny day in June 2014. In the elevator up to the third floor of the nursing home I was seized with panic. He had been slowly declining from Alzheimer's disease for years, and my mother had finally accepted the inevitable and moved him into this clean but drab facility a year earlier. It was in Ross Bay, a charming old neighbourhood of Victoria between downtown and the Strait of Juan de Fuca, but visiting was always gut-wrenching.

Dad's room was in a secure area, so I had to enter a code to get the elevator to stop on the third floor. Stepping through the door, I entered a sea of confused old men and women, some slumped in chairs, others striding about aimlessly in their confusion. Where was that familiar face? Ah, there he was, standing by the window in the lunch room, looking out at the blue sky. Thank God the rain had stopped long enough to take him for a walk. The Pacific Ocean was only three blocks away, but with his unsteady gait, the trip to the boardwalk on Dallas Road and back would take close to an hour. But what a relief it was to get out into the fresh air. And sing a song or two to Dad.

We had all tried to pretend otherwise for as long as we could, but my father didn't recognize any of us by this time, not even his wife of fifty-two years. He was still his gentle, attentive self, but he had no idea who I was; he probably imagined I was some random do-gooder who liked holding his hand and blabbering on while I steered him through the streets. But one thing remained in the honeycomb of his memory: songs. Scottish folk songs (which his parents, immigrants from Ayrshire, had sung to him when he was a kid); Newfie fishing songs (they'd lived on the Rock all through the Second World War); and hits from my childhood, too.

My parents were children of the '60s, and my sisters and my brother and I grew up singing along to the Beatles, Bob Dylan, Gordon Lightfoot, and Simon and Garfunkel. But my siblings were musical; I couldn't carry a tune for the life of me and had always been mocked for even trying. All my life I had done it anyway, though, and for once I had an appreciative audience.

So as we ambled through the back streets of Victoria I serenaded my rapt father with every tune I could remember, often humming the verses when I wasn't sure of the words. To passersby it must have been a strange scene, but I didn't give a fig—Dad nodded along, and sometimes even smiled with recognition. He didn't know me, but he sure knew "Wild Mountain Thyme."

Like I said, I really can't sing, but some songs were easier than others to evoke. "Blowin' in the Wind," probably the tune my mum loves the most, is pretty basic; just drone through your nose like Dylan as you ask about the number of roads a man must walk

On that sunny June day in Victoria, it felt like we'd flagged a diesel down outside that Louisiana town, and rode it all the way to New Orleans. Music can do that.

down. I worked out years ago that that was a rhetorical question, but here father and son were putting it to the test.

Tougher was my father's all-time favourite: Janis Joplin's version of the Kris Kristofferson song "Me and Bobby McGee." Janis really belts it out and hits some high notes I wasn't ever going to touch. Luckily, it has a great "na-na-na-na-na-na" chorus, and some hokey lyrics you can ham up about being broke in Baton Rouge and feeling faded as your jeans.

My father died a few months later, just before Christmas. I'd never been to Baton Rouge, and neither had he, but on that sunny June day in Victoria, it felt like we'd flagged a diesel down outside that Louisiana town, and rode it all the way to New Orleans. Music can do that.

Scott Steedman is an award-winning writer, editor, and publishing consultant who has worked in book publishing for more than thirty years, in the UK, France, and Canada. A professor in the Publishing department at Simon Fraser University, he is also co-founder and publisher of Locarno Press. He lives in Vancouver.

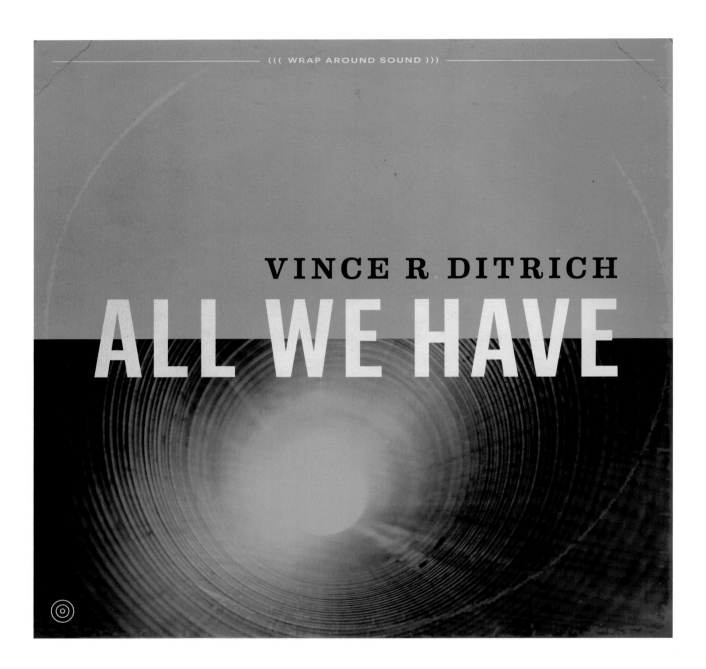

VINCE R. DITRICH

ALL WE HAVE

I **get tired** of hearing music called the "universal language"; the term has become cliché, gutted of meaning. But after a lifetime of performance, musicians realize that we have an in with every human on earth because of our relationship with music. The only thing I've experienced that's as profound is the act of holding a baby.

My friend and bandmate Johnny Mann, singer of Spirit of the West, loves kids. And he loves music—in fact, he has lived through it, as his fans have lived vicariously through him, all his adult life. But John suffers from early-onset Alzheimer's disease, which has cruelly robbed him of the capacity to communicate or perceive much of the world around him.

> Music is the last stand. It is the last tunnel out of the bunker, the last fingertip touch before the grip is finally broken. It is all we have.

He has gone from a performer so electric that even subtle eyebrow moves made audience members twitch, to a man who cannot speak at all.

But chuck a pair of headphones on him, put on one of his favourite songs, and watch the transformation. The low embers in his eyes begin to glow again, the intensity ratchets up and his lips stiffen into a rictus of intensity; frustration as he tries vainly to spit out the melody, the lyric, the emotion of the song. The tunes draw him out and make him want to come forth to be with us once again, and share what he feels.

And he certainly still feels it. John hears the music, reacts strongly to it. If you want to have a good visit with him these days you almost certainly need to introduce music to the conversation. It is the only way Johnny can reconnect and rejoin all of us.

So not only can music bridge cultural gulfs, it can also reach deep into our brains, our psyches, and help us remember who we are, who we were, and who we ideally would like to be.

I don't think many people visit Johnny anymore without a guitar or iPod in hand. As soon as he hears the strumming or the song, he is up and probably trying to sing, certainly dancing, fingers snapping, reminding everyone present that he is still Johnny. He is in there, he is in there, buried under increasing layers of darkness that frankly scare the hell out of me.

I know what music has done for my perception of the world. Without it I'd probably never have succeeded in life, unfulfilled and spiritually depleted, able only to look on like a jealous voyeur at the colour of life.

The physiological mechanism of musical perception within the human brain is mostly unknown to me. But I experience its effects daily. Kooky things take hold, such as being able to see music, feel its textures and flavours, through some form of synesthesia. I am in no way unique in this—I am just fortunate in having been allowed to experience and analyze it endlessly, and hone my mind's-eye vision. Johnny has done the same; I know that he still "hears" music in the abstract sense because I can see it in his face, in his manner. I can tell you about someone's personality after doing nothing more than hear them play their instrument; Johnny can feel the emotion and is still moved by it, his inner world richly savouring the moment, even when he cannot use his words to describe his experience.

Music is the last stand for him. It is the last tunnel out of the bunker, before the attacker shuts communications down completely. It is a radio antenna attached to a balloon, a single telephone wire along the trench, the last fingertip touch before the grip is finally broken. It is all we have.

Vince R. Ditrich is a musician, composer, and producer who has played with many artists, including Long John Baldry, Paul Hyde, Doug and the Slugs, Great Big Sea, and, since 1989, Spirit of the West, as drummer. He also acts as the group's manager and refreshment coordinator.

WHY I BECAME A MUSIC THERAPIST

JENNIFER BUCHANAN

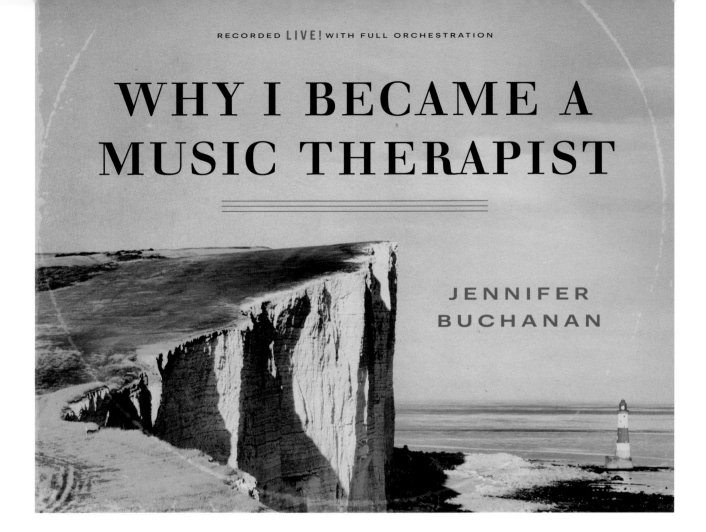

My granny was perfect. Truly. Everything about her said, "I know what I'm doing and you are in the best care." She was wonderfully generous with her love, and it showed in all she did.

Grandad, her husband, was the complete opposite. He tucked himself away in the basement, where he spent endless hours in his workshop far from the visiting grandchildren. When I did see him, he always seemed grumpy. It would be many years before I learned that his stern look was sparked by his resolve to be a successful provider, and to give my dad and his brother what his parents hadn't been able to give to him.

I don't remember Granny and Grandad laughing or talking together much but I do remember them hosting many family gatherings: BBQs, Christmas parties, Sunday dinners. I loved it when all of my cousins would get together to play. At dinnertime we would all head to the buffet line for roast beef, ham, and heaping bowls of potatoes doused in gravy. Through it all the stereo would play an endless array of classics until someone started to play the piano. On leaving Granny's house you could count on three things: you were full, you had had a great time, and you felt loved.

I was twelve when Mom received a phone call informing us that Grandad had been rushed to the hospital. At the age of sixty-two, he had suffered a stroke that left him partially paralyzed and unable to speak. In no time he was in the local extended-care hospital.

We continued to visit Granny and Grandad every Friday evening. As we walked into Grandad's room, I would mumble a greeting and then immediately zero in on the only thing that interested me: the little black-and-white television set on the corner table. My sister and I rarely interacted with the adults as we were too busy adjusting the rabbit ears of the television set. Granny looked over at us from the corner of her eye. She wanted us to tune in to something else: Grandad.

One Friday, Granny walked over to me, gave me a hug, and handed me a piece of music, saying, "Jenny, I brought this sheet music from home. It is your Grandad's favourite song. Would you please learn it and sing it to him next week?"

Her request took me off guard. It seemed odd, but with some reluctance I said, "Sure." I arrived the following Friday with my guitar. Granny pulled up a chair beside the bed where Grandad was resting, leaned down into his ear and said, "I've asked Jenny to sing a song I think you'll like."

Grandad looked puzzled as I sat down beside him. I felt nervous and looked down at the words on my lap. It took me a moment and then I began to sing a song written many years before I was born—"The White Cliffs of Dover," the Second World War song made popular by Vera Lynn.

After I finished the final lyric, a hope for peace "tomorrow, when the world is free," the first thing I noticed was a change in the sounds around me. The typical commotion and loud conversations in the hallways stopped. Although my back was to the door, I could tell that people were beginning to look in. One of the wandering patients came right into Grandad's room, and Granny gave him a chair. It surprised me when he started to sing. Even the woman who regularly yelled in the hallways stood behind me and joined in. I had no idea so many

I finished the song and looked up into Grandad's eyes. He was crying. He reached out for my hand and squeezed it.

people knew this song. Granny smiled and nodded for me to keep going, so I sang on about the shepherd tending his sheep, the valley blooming again, Jimmy in his bed, and the bluebirds flying over those famous white cliffs.

I finished the song and looked up into Grandad's eyes. He was crying. He reached out for my hand and squeezed it. I looked around the room and knew something big was happening. Granny rested her hand on my shoulder and announced proudly, "Jenny will be here to sing every Friday night." I couldn't help but smile.

Fortunately for me, many more musical moments like this would be in my future—with all sorts of people, from many different backgrounds and all stages of life. Those hospital visits would eventually lead me toward a career as a music therapist where, after many years of school, I would learn how to use music to calm, connect, even change the behaviours of people, including many more broody teenagers and grumpy old men.

Jennifer Buchanan is a health entrepreneur and music therapist, and the author of the books *Tune In* and *Wellness Incorporated*. A past president of the Canadian Association of Music Therapists, she has appeared on NBC, CBS, CBC Radio, CBC Television, CTV, and Global TV, and has been featured in the *Huffington Post*, *Chatelaine*, and *Canadian Living*.

I have known Roger Hodgson, the lead singer and songwriter of Supertramp, since June 23, 2013. On that night, my life changed forever during a concert in Kitchener, Ontario, thanks to the kindness and caring of Roger and his manager, Linda Tyler.

I am a retired police officer who worked for thirty years with the police service in Belleville, Ontario. I was involved in numerous life-and-death situations during the course of my duty. I was critically injured, and then lost two sisters within a year of each other. I didn't know at the time, but I had been suffering from severe post-traumatic stress disorder (PTSD) for almost twenty-five years, since I saw my first fatal shooting, and my life was falling apart. Four days before I met Roger and Linda, I walked off the job and quit policing. I was done with everything. I couldn't cope any longer with the violence, all the things I'd had to do and had witnessed and lost. It literally broke me.

I still live with PTSD to this day, and probably will for the rest of my life. Luckily, I have help, including a service dog, who I named Babiji, in honour of the Supertramp song. The lyrics to "Babiji" are about Roger looking for God in life, but they had another meaning for me, because I needed Babiji the dog so that I could continue in life. We are inseparable.

I grew up listening to Supertramp. Roger sent me a lifeline with his song "Hide in Your Shell," which was always my favourite. Little did I know as a teenage boy that later that song would change my life. There is a line that says the cure for pain is love. Those words have always been so meaningful to me. I had a cabin cruiser named *Cure for Pain*. I used to travel alone for months at a time in that boat, trying to get away from all the emotions and thoughts of work; I enjoyed my solitude, but I had to keep "running away" from my issues. This was my "shell," where I could be alone and try to deal with my troubles. As a police officer I had to be tough and not let people see I was human with emotions. It's a terrible burden.

That night in Kitchener I happened to say hello to Linda before the concert. I told her my life story in a few minutes and she listened to every word. I asked her if she could have Roger sign my ticket and write "Cure for Pain" on it; I was going to frame it and hang it in the cabin of my boat. Linda said she would see what she could do, and that I should meet her at the stage door before the concert started.

I met Linda at the door and she apologized that Roger hadn't signed my ticket. Then she looked at me and said, "Roger is going to do something special for you during the concert." She then placed a backstage pass in my hand and said, "Roger really wants to meet you after the concert." I was overwhelmed with emotion and excitement.

Three songs into the concert, Roger introduced "Hide in Your Shell," then spoke for a couple of minutes about me and how this song had helped me deal with trauma. I cried during the entire song.

After the show Linda took me in to meet Roger. It was such an honour to be able to thank him in person. He took me aside and we talked privately for a long time. At that moment I knew my life was going to change for the better. Having a few minutes of Roger's time saved my life.

Roger encouraged me to put my feelings down in writing, as he did. I started writing poetry and continue to write every day. I have published five books so far; the first one was titled *Cure for Pain*.

Doug Norman is a retired police officer who lives in Belleville, Ontario.

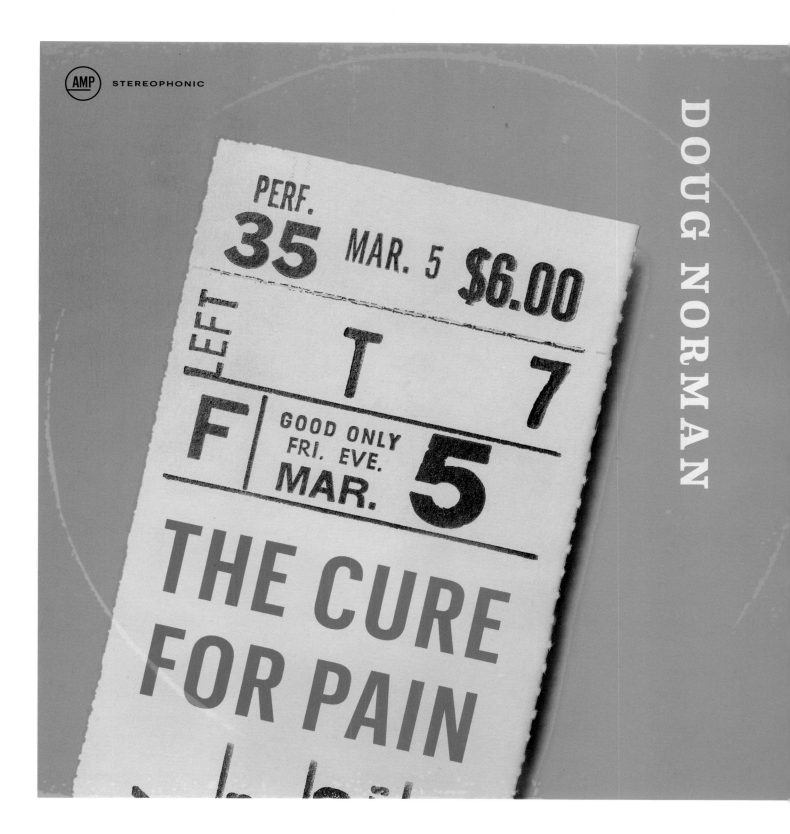

Cathy Tait
STAND BY ME

◀— STEREO —▶

One of my favourite songs is "Stand by Me," the John Lennon version. Talk about songs that bring smiles. My daughter and my son both got married in the last two years, and it was played at both of their weddings.

My daughter had started suffering after she moved to Brisbane, Australia. She'd just got a masters in museum studies at University College London in the UK, and had worked around the world in the field, but there her experience and qualifications weren't recognized. She went into a deep depression. Her partner, a geologist and a fantastic guy, told me music seemed to help, so I started sending her songs, including "Stand by Me."

Then they moved to Melbourne, a much better place, and she started to come out of it, thanks to a combination of therapy and medication. He proposed to her, and they got married at our place on the beach back in Canada, on Georgian Bay. After dinner I played a video of photos of the two of them over the six years they'd been together, and the music that played in the background was "Stand by Me," sung by John Lennon. Our daughter's husband says he plays the video every once in a while because it makes him smile. Even now it brings tears to my eyes. She had tremendous breakthroughs with her depression, and they are now expecting their first child in August.

A year later I found myself at another wedding, at North Arm Farm in Pemberton, BC. It's an absolutely majestic spot, surrounded on 360 degrees by mountains. Unbeknownst to me, the processional song for my son's bride and her father was "Stand by Me." I asked them how they came to choose that song, and they replied, "Because you loved it so much, Mom."

That song brings back a lot of memories. Some are happy; others are of people breaking through illness and suffering. It's a very hopeful song. The joke is that Lennon was in his heroin days then, and they say he was higher than a kite when he sang it. He made several recordings of the song, and there is a rumour that he did one in Toronto.

The lyrics are simple and very, very powerful. I have played it at conferences and workshops. One time I had a huge hall down by the convention centre filled with internationally educated professionals, highly trained folks, and I put on "Stand by Me" and they got up and danced. It was quite remarkable. It's just a very hopeful song that appreciates the people who support you.

There's something about Lennon's voice, a grit to it. Think about it—the guy was a full-on drug addict at the time, and he recorded this anthem to standing by the one you love. You have to wonder how that juxtaposition worked.

Cathy Tait is a management consultant from Toronto. She spent two decades at Xerox, was a principal at Western Management Consultants, and is now an independent consultant with Connecting the Dots in Sydney, Australia.

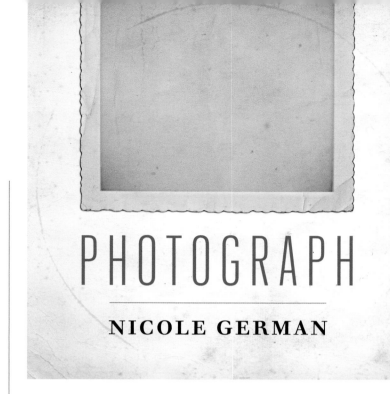

PHOTOGRAPH

NICOLE GERMAN

The loss of a child is indescribable. The loss of a child to suicide is surreal and unimaginable. On April 11, 2015, we lost our beautiful, athletic, funny, smart, giving daughter Madeline (Maddie) to depression. She was fourteen.

When she was born, my life changed forever, fulfilled with a lifelong purpose. When she died, our world was rocked beyond imagination. Yet today and every day, her presence feels even more vivid than when she was alive.

The smallest everyday actions bring her absence to life. In the morning when I brush my teeth, I look for her toothbrush among the others. When setting the table for a meal, I contemplate the empty spot. As I travel through the day, I see little signs of her: purple flowers, bunnies in the garden, music on the radio.

Music brings great reflection. Sometimes sadness, but often comfort. It also carries memories. Certain songs remind us of a special event or our first concert. And many songs remind me of my childhood—mostly very happy times.

Maddie adored music. She played it all the time and loved to sing along. She would sing at the top of her lungs in the shower. I can still hear her belting out Adele songs so loud we could hear her all the way downstairs in the kitchen. Lucky for us, her voice was beautiful.

As a family with three very active kids, we spent many hours driving to and from sports and activities. Maddie always rode shotgun and subjected her two younger brothers to the back seat. This meant she could control the music selection in the car. So we often listened to Top 40 hits or the latest rage in music—*loud*—with Maddie's singing voice added on top. And we would all join in when the chorus kicked in.

One favourite was Ed Sheeran's song "Photograph," in which he talks about keeping love in a photo, where time is forever frozen still. The irony of those words. The day Maddie died, time froze still. I carry her in my heart and literally in my pocket. She is always with us.

When you lose someone there is nothing more precious than a photograph that brings to life a memory or their presence. Maddie's friends come across a photo of her once in a while and share it with me. It's like winning the lottery.

Listening to "Photograph" and some of the other songs Maddie played on her iPhone or in the car or sang in the shower brings those days of happiness and fun right back to us. Life with the vividness we had when she was with us. And while it's hard sometimes to listen, more often than not the songs bring back memories of happy moments. And those memories can't help but make me smile.

Nicole German is a global-tech marketer and business strategy executive, and the leading force behind the Maddie Project, which supports youth struggling with depression and other mental health-related concerns.

Rhiannon Rosalind

A BETTER FREQUENCY

I have always tried to use music to get through dark moments in my life. It even helped me overcome debilitating panic attacks.

I grew up in Toronto, an only child with a single mum who was a survivor of domestic violence. We lived with my uncle and my grandmother, and the whole family struggled. There was a lot of hardship and alcoholism. Like any kid, I learned how to navigate a very unpredictable environment, how to

chameleon myself. I knew when I could be fun and when I should blend in with the linoleum.

From a young age, music became a way for me to express my emotions, to connect with narratives that weren't part of my world. By the age of nine I was writing my own songs. Singing was my main escape. I would write the melodies and the lyrics and sing them into a little tape recorder. Later, in bands, working with trained musicians, I took those melodies and turned them into real songs. It was fascinating to see them come to life. They were such a huge vehicle for me to deal with my pain.

Come age thirteen, I started to repeat the cycle myself, began experimenting with drugs and alcohol and connecting with people who were broken, too. By age fifteen I had dropped out of school and was really heavily into drugs and alcohol, in a relationship with a person who was a decade older than me—I was in a really bad place. Again, music inspired me.

I had always banked on becoming a singer, using music and songwriting as my vehicle to improve my circumstances. Then I got a wake-up call. One day I suddenly realized—if I'm not going to be a rock star, I better get into school. I remember sitting in a field across from my house with paper and a pen, making a list of goals for myself: *If I don't become a rock star, what do I need to do to make something of myself?*

My first goal was to become the first person in my family to graduate from high school. Then, go to university. And stop using drugs, be somebody. Use my pain and experience to help others, if not through music, then another way. I achieved all those things: in my final year of school I was on the honour roll.

Then I hit another roadblock. At sixteen, the panic attacks started. I didn't understand what they were. I was finally doing everything right, so why was this happening to me? In those days, nobody spoke of these things: depression, anxiety. The panic was so debilitating that I was afraid to leave the house, my heart was beating out of my chest, I got really claustrophobic and scared of public transit.

So I turned to music again. I started to sing to myself as a way to not have panic attacks, while I sat on the bus or the subway. It was literally the only way I could get through. I would pace my breathing, prescribing music to calm myself. I never used medication, I used music.

From a young age, music became a way for me to express my emotions, to connect with narratives that weren't part of my world.

Now I get up in front of thousands of people and talk, as part of my job. Music literally allowed me to get past one of the most traumatic and tumultuous periods of my life. It was my saving grace.

When I was growing up, it was Bob Dylan, Led Zeppelin. I'm actually named after a Fleetwood Mac song! But Alanis Morrissette, *Jagged Little Pill*, that was my anthem. I knew every breath she took on every song. That was a huge album that has meant so much to me. And Lauryn Hill and the Fugees. And Jewel—I couldn't believe it when I heard her singing about things like sexual abuse, racism, and heartbreak in such a raw way.

Now, I'm president of a major organization. I still sing, though I don't do it on a stage much anymore. The last time I got up in front of an audience was two years ago, when I did a couple of songs at a charity concert. I sing in the shower, and to my kids—it's still such a part of my life.

And I try to incorporate music into my work. We recently had Michelle Obama here—she did her first talk in Canada at the Economic Club, and we invited an incredible musician to perform for her. That's a great way to open people up; it opens our hearts and gets us onto a better frequency.

—————————

Rhiannon Rosalind is president and CEO of the Economic Club of Canada.

TYLER MacLEOD

Sweating It Out

Two years ago, my sister and my best friend both died, within a month. She took her own life, after struggling with mental health problems. He was into ocean conservation and had a diving accident; we had made several films together.

I hit a pretty dark place in the months that followed. I was working in New York and I knew I had to change the patterns in my life. So I made a list of what we would call self-love now, all the things that really mattered to me: yoga, hanging out with animals,

nature, horses, and riding. I have a friend who owns BIG Heart Ranch in Malibu—it's a farm attached to an addiction centre, where they do equine therapy. I moved to the west coast to be around the animals. I started going to animal shelters on weekends and doing yoga every day. I still do; it's been the biggest pillar of healing for me.

I found a studio where they played my favourite kind of music: slow house music, with beautiful vocals. One day, in the middle of class, I started

I realized why this music was speaking to me. Our ancestors sat around a fire, beat a drum, and danced. Ever since we've been on the planet, music has been a part of who we are.

crying. I had been struggling to open up to the pain of losing my sister and my best friend, and somehow that music let the emotion come out. Every time I did that class, I shed tears. Not jagged wailing, just good, cathartic crying. The music was the trigger; it took me into a space where I felt really connected. In the heat of that room, I felt like I was shedding my skin, sweating out all the toxins. It's the most powerful experience I've ever had. It transformed me.

Not long afterward a friend and I went to Standing Rock to take part in the pipeline protests. I met some Native American kids there—they were the ones you saw on TV riding horses. They were camping next to us, and whoever could ride a horse could just jump on one. They were a little suspicious of a couple of white guys with video cameras, but we gradually earned their respect.

One day they started leaving, to go on the Dakota 38, they said. Turns out this is an annual two-week ride through South and North Dakota, to commemorate their 38 Sioux ancestors who were hanged following the Dakota Uprising of 1862. It was the largest mass execution in US history, at a place called Mankato, Minnesota. Anyone could come, so we tagged along. It was amazing to be part of it.

At the start of the ride there were only five to ten people. All along the way, people came out to clap and cheer us on. It was a hard, cold ride; our companions said they could feel the pain of their ancestors. More and more people joined every day, until the caravan was several hundred strong. We would stay every night at a pre-determined place: a hockey arena, a church. Total guerilla style.

Every night we would hold a ceremony. We sat through a lot of drumming and sweat lodge ceremonies. The sounds were simple, just humming and drumbeats and some basic vocals, maybe a couple of singers, a girl and a guy. It reminded me of the type of house music I like; it had similar traits.

By the end of the ride, as the caravan arrived in Mankato, I realized why this music was speaking to me. Our ancestors sat around a fire, beat a drum, and danced. Ever since we've been on the planet, music has been a part of who we are. It was very powerful, being allowed to be part of that ritual. I think back on it a lot. It makes me respect where we come from and the basic goodness of music.

Tyler MacLeod is an entrepreneur who is passionate about mental health and art. He has produced several films, including *Revolution* (2012) and *Sharkwater* (2006). His latest project is Habitas Tulum.

In June 1990, I was as successful as I'd ever been. I was on the radio and in magazines, and had been a speaker for six years, criss-crossing Australia, Canada, and the northern US. I was having a great old time.

I came back exhausted from a tour and took a few days off in Whistler, BC. On June 20, a buddy and I hiked to Brandywine Falls, this 200-foot glacial waterfall. We stood at the base, looking up, and it was absolutely stunning. I challenged him to go behind the falls, which was pretty incredible. We felt like supermen when we came out, so I said, let's not hike back, let's climb the face. But free-climbing when you're soaking wet is moderately insane. I reached for a rock, which dislodged another rock, and sent me hurtling 120 feet onto the rocks below.

I won't tell you all the gruesome details, but suffice to say, I died several times, first on the rocks and then later in the hospital. Twelve reconstructive surgeries later, I was in a dark, dark space. I was born in a ghetto, around extreme poverty, addiction, violence. It made me tough; I was a boxer and a leader. That's how I'd always dealt with adversity. So when people asked me how I was doing, I'd say, "I'm great." With my jaw wired shut.

Needless to say, I wasn't great. It was all ego and machismo. I fell into very dark depths. For nine months I never left them. Occasionally I'd have a night out, but when I came home I'd think, *I'll never laugh again*. Then one night I did laugh, and when I walked through the door I was telling myself, there is hope. I saw light in the kitchen, and went in to find the room festooned with garbage: empty meat trays and cans. The smell was horrendous, and I went from joy to rage.

I knew who the culprit was and I went looking for him. I found him on the couch, curled up, totally comfortable. I lost my shit and all that anger and depression spilled forth. By nature I'm not a violent person but a switch was flipped. I lifted my hand to strike him, but halfway down something in me put the brakes on. I touched my cat, only to find that he was cold. Dead. I fell to my knees and wept, over a cat I didn't even like. I held the frigid body in my arms and broke down completely.

I realized instantly that I wasn't crying for the cat, but for me. I finally had to admit that I had lost the life I used to have. There were only three paths. The first one was going back—but there is no going back. The second path was to stay the same, become the victim. That was seductive. The third option was to find my true purpose, why I am actually here on the planet. To become fulfilled, make the difference I really want to make. That was the path I chose.

In the first phase of that process, I allowed myself into my own darkness. No more avoiding; the time had come to actually feel the depths of my own sadness. As Joseph Campbell said, "The treasure you're looking for is in the cave you fear to enter." I did enter it, fully. I allowed myself to move into the darkest depths. I got to know parts of myself that had been disenfranchised for decades.

And I used music to let me go there. I played a lot of music that opened up those deep, dark parts of me. One album that helped a lot was *Listen without Prejudice* by George Michael. I loved that title, and

I got to know parts of myself that had been disenfranchised for decades. And I used music to let me go there.

every time I put it on, I gave myself permission to listen to myself without prejudice.

In the next phase, the album that really moved me was U2's *The Joshua Tree*, especially "I Still Haven't Found What I'm Looking For." My whole life I had kept on finding what I was looking for, but I was just finding success. That song made me commit to staying the path. Not just stating "this is okay," but really going into the depths of what the truth is for me, what I really want, deep inside of myself.

It's a song by an Irish band inspired by an American desert. There's nothing there—that was how my world felt. Where was I going to find that oasis, that truth?

Dov Baron is a leading authority on leadership and corporate loyalty. He is twice cited as one of *Inc.* magazine's Top 100 Leadership Speakers to hire. Baron's bestselling books include *Fiercely Loyal* and *One Red Thread;* his *Leadership and Loyalty Tips for Executives* is the number one podcast for Fortune 500 executives.

A SONG

RENAE MORRISEAU

GIVEN...

As Indigenous people of Turtle Island, we all have our ways, processes, and protocols in how we honour the moments that need to be acknowledged. And we usually do so with a song. Some of these songs are really old, passed down with their story, their dance, and a ceremony; our songs call out to the land and water, to home and family.

One day, back in 2006, I was driving to my ceremonial brother Frank's place to request a family song. I was hoping I could put it on a CD I was helping to create and produce with other Indigenous women.

I was a little worried. I was traversing an unknown area: recording a spiritual family song. I had to speak to Frank and get his guidance. It was also going to be

a ceremony, because I would be activating the responsibilities of a song carrier.

Growing up, I heard songs that could only be sung in ceremony. Other songs are social songs that are shared publicly. Now you can go online and learn a peyote song or a sundance song. I once heard a woman sing a beautiful traditional song, and when I asked her where it was from, she told me she'd learned it from the internet.

Back then, Frank lived in Stó:lō territory (the Fraser Valley, near Vancouver). A Cree/Anishinaabe ceremonial man, he had told me stories of his grandfather's trap-line. This was before Frank was taken away to residential school, where he spent more

> As Indigenous people of Turtle Island, we all have our ways, processes, and protocols in how we honour the moments that need to be acknowledged. And we usually do so with a song.

than ten years. Frank spent time in jail, too, when he was young. When he got out, he began to go back to the ceremonies, and then worked in prisons as an Elder, conducting sweats and pipe ceremonies for the inmates.

Ceremony. Spiritual connection to Ancestors and to the Creator. To be a spiritual conduit, where you get out of the way and connect to creation. I had received all of this from Frank. But as I pulled up to his place, I suddenly remembered why I had stopped sweating with him. We had had a bit of a disagreement. Okay, I had an issue, not him.

After years of doing sweats with Frank, I began to question some of the Christian concepts he used in his ceremonies. I would ask him why he spoke of such things in the sweat. He would say that many of the inmates needed to believe that their time in residential school wasn't a waste. They needed to hear that the word of God was beyond those who purported to be their saviours. These "saviours" had abused many of these men when they were children. Yep, most of the men Frank did ceremonies for in the institutions were residential school survivors.

Over the years, I have seen many First Nations live in the commonality of being both ceremonial to their Indigenous cultural ways and also speaking of the teachings of the bible.

I sat across from Frank and brought out my gifts: a bag of tobacco and some home-canned salmon. Then we began our ceremony. We smoked the pipe, burned the sacred medicines, and sent our prayers of gratefulness to the Creator. Then he sang "The Honour Song." This was a ceremonial song, and he said to me, "It's okay to record it."

Frank gave me various songs over the years, and the one I recorded back in 2006 was "The Honour Song." It's about honouring all life: the winged ones, the four-legged ones, the ones in the water, those sixteen-legged little bugs, as well as the two-legged ones, the humans.

As I sat and listened to him speak of honouring life, I realized that the gift given to me in that moment was the gift of family and community. Honour life every day, with a simple thought, a smile and a handshake, a hug. All life is spiritual. That was one of the last ceremonies I did with Frank before he died.

Recording a spiritual song used in the sweat deepened my understanding that my family are prayerful people. My ceremonial brother, Frank Settee, honoured me by sharing this song, so I can now sing it for you. The Honour Song.

Frank Ewart Settee/Manitou Mahkwa, December 18, 1941–August 7, 2012. Thank you, Frank. You are with me. You are always with me.

Renae Morriseau is from Manitoba and of Saulteaux and Cree descent and has lived on Vancouver's Coast Salish shores for thirty years. A producer, writer, and director, she starred in CBC TV's *North of 60* and performs with the Indigenous women's hand-drumming group M'Girl. Morriseau received the 2015 City of Vancouver Mayor's Arts Award.

When I think of Samya, I think of her dancing to Caravan Palace. I'd never heard this French band before, and I'd only just met Samya, but she loved their wonderful fusion of gypsy jazz and electronic dance beats. Her love for the music, and for dancing to it, was infectious.

Samya came into my world like a whirlwind, radiating life and gliding effortlessly through crowds with her enchanting energy. She was such a delight and so utterly herself that she left those around her spellbound. She was the girl that was taller than most guys around, yet wore high heels anyways, because why shouldn't she? As she danced through life, her comfort with exactly who she was was contagious. She made you feel like you should just be you.

When life ends, it's always devastating. When it is one too young, too full of life, it's tragic.

As an avid and frequent traveller, I have always hung on to the statistics that it's safer to fly than it is to drive to the airport to take that flight. Whenever there is turbulence, or a nervous flyer is sitting nearby, I remind myself, and anyone looking to be comforted, of those statistics. So when I heard two days ago that Ethiopian Airlines Flight 302 had crashed, I wasn't worried.

It wasn't until a few hours later that I noticed Samya's boyfriend had sent a message asking if I had her friends' phone numbers. I didn't think too much of it. Samya is a free spirit who goes where the wind blows, and he was probably trying to locate her. Then the phone rang and I learned some devastating news. Samya had been on the Ethiopian Airlines flight. She was gone.

How could this be? How did it possibly make sense? We had just been in touch! She's too young, still in her twenties, too full of life, too brilliant to be gone! I cried. Right in the middle of a conference floor. It was no use trying to stop it, and why should I? Her smiling face flashed in front of me, together with the word "gone."

With death comes shock, loss, and sadness. But you also face the existential crisis of "It could all be gone so suddenly, so what does it all mean?" And those reminders seem to be coming all too frequently these days, from those around me losing friends, siblings, and parents, to my own loss of my aunt, uncle, grandma, father, and grandfather, all in the span of several years. Time heals all, life goes on, but when none of it makes sense, music can connect with us on a visceral level and reach a place words cannot access.

So here I am, away from home at a conference, living this moment in a house full of colleagues, many of them teenagers. What is allowing me to reflect and write this is listening to Caravan Palace.

I picture Samya dancing in the living room of her house, filled with instruments and her musician friends, alive with her spirit and brilliance. Dancing and being more present in the moment than anyone I have ever met.

Dancing and smiling. Present and musical. Musical and magical. Rest in peace, Samya. Or better yet, keep on dancing to Caravan Palace, wherever you are.

Jennifer Brown leads partnerships for the Knowledge Society in Toronto and was previously leading global business development for a biotech company based in Vancouver. She has lived in or travelled to more than sixty countries. She met Samya while living in Barcelona.

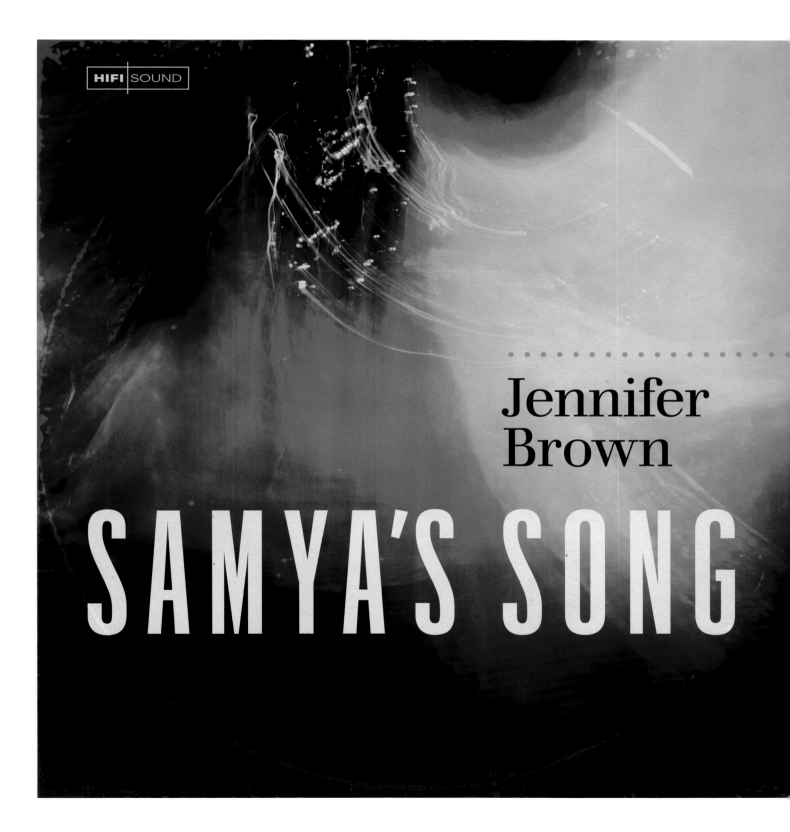

Jennifer Brown

SAMYA'S SONG

SUAD BUSHNAQ

GRIEVING THROUGH MUSIC

Music is the only constant in my life. Nothing else is as reliable, as true, and as rewarding as music. Listening to or creating music is my refuge and my true home, where I feel fully alive.

I grew up in Jordan in a home filled with music. My father, a pharmacist, dreamed of becoming a violinist. He had a huge collection of vinyl records and cassette tapes of music of the masters: Bach, Vivaldi, Beethoven, Mendelssohn, Chopin, Rachmaninoff. My mother, also a pharmacist, loved '80s pop and Middle Eastern music.

I remember sitting in the back seat of my dad's silver Toyota as he picked me up from preschool. I can still see his hand grabbing a blue and white cassette tape with "Vivaldi: The Four Seasons" written on it in faded pencil. For the first time I became aware of a beautiful world in which sounds combined to create something magical.

I started taking piano lessons at the age of five. My parents bought me a secondhand Wurlitzer piano, which became my favourite "toy." I hated piano lessons but loved improvising. I composed my first piece at age nine, and fell in love with Bach, my favourite composer, at sixteen. I loved math, and admired the way he combined math with art. I studied music in Damascus and then earned a scholarship to study music composition at McGill in Montreal.

Being of a mixed heritage (my mum is Syrian, my dad Bosnian/Palestinian/Arab), I grew up in Jordan and Syria feeling that I did not fully belong.

When I immigrated to Canada, I was still a visible minority, and still have a slight accent. I have never felt 100 percent part of any place—except music, the one place I can be fully me.

As a Canadian, I've learned to honour my mishmash of identities through cooking and travelling, but I pour everything into the music I compose. It is a place of comfort and release, where I can explore who I truly am as an Arab-European-Canadian. It is the only home that has managed to stay with me despite my constant moving around, and that has enough space for all aspects of my ethnic makeup.

In 2007, only three years after coming to Canada, my mom got an aggressive form of breast cancer that took her away from us within months. Part of my grieving process involved recording a piano album of nine pieces, most of which I had composed in Damascus. In honour of my mother, I decided to sell the album for no profit. I raised more than two thousand dollars for the Canadian Breast Cancer Foundation.

Four years later, Syria went up in flames. My mother's beloved hometown of Damascus, which we both adored, was now at war. I continued to compose music but was engulfed by all the ugliness and bloodshed on TV. Then, in 2015, a former colleague told me about the Syrian Expat Philharmonic Orchestra, formed in Bremen, Germany, of Syrian refugees from across Europe. It was apolitical and had one mandate: to spread the beautiful culture of Syria to the world, to counteract the images of bloodshed.

They asked me to compose an orchestral piece for their inaugural concert, which would be in a week. I locked myself away and spent the next seven days composing "Tomorrow." It was later performed at the Berliner Philharmonie and the Konzerthaus Berlin,

and toured Europe and the US. Once again, music was my way of grieving, this time for Syria. I am now composer-in-residence for this orchestra, which has premiered four of my orchestral works.

In 2016 my father, a healthy, stylish, trilingual man, was diagnosed with Alzheimer's disease. I watched helplessly as he began to lose focus, memory, and weight. I eventually had to move him into a long-term facility. I quit my math teaching position in North Carolina and came to Toronto to be near him.

During this time, I was composing a score for a documentary, *The Borrowed Dress*. My anguish was so intense that the score soon took a personal turn. The end credits I composed became a homage to my dad. Seeing a proud, educated man become a shadow of himself is something I'm still dealing with. I ended up turning the credits into a full-fledged piece for orchestra and accordion dedicated to my dad that was performed in Berlin in 2017. That piece truly allowed me to wear my agony and my love on my sleeve.

Suad Bushnaq is a film and concert music composer.

1

Writing
songs

2

Analyzing
lyrics

3

Improvising

4

Listening to
music

5

Playing
instruments

music therapy's greatest hits

FIVE GO-TO TECHNIQUES

source: Psych Central

Medical Areas That Have Used Music Therapy

- Acquired brain injury
- AIDS
- Autism and other pervasive development disabilities
- Critical care
- Developmental disabilities
- Emotional traumas
- Geriatric care
- Hearing impairments
- Mental health issues
- Neonatal care
- Obstetrics

THE MUSIC THERAPY SONGBOOK

- Oncology
- Pain control
- Palliative care
- Personal growth
- Physical disabilities
- Speech and language impairments
- Substance addiction
- Visual impairments

And more...

source: Canadian Association of Music Therapists

THE RHYTHMS OF LIFE AND CONNECTION

I have always been drawn to music. As a child it was my refuge. As a teenager it kept me sane and grounded. As a mother, I saw the benefits for my children. As a musician it fulfills me and gives me pleasure. And as a neuroscientist, and director of the McMaster Institute for Music and the Mind and the LIVELab at McMaster University, I try to answer questions about music. Why is it an important part of every human culture? How does it have the power to move us to tears? Why do parents around the world sing to their babies? Why do we turn to music when we are sad? Why do we feel compelled to move to the beat of certain songs? Why did our ancestors make music more than thirty thousand years ago? Why do we turn to music when we want to connect with others, at a party, a wedding, a funeral, a hockey game? Why do we attend live music concerts with other people when we could listen to music at home?

It could be argued that rhythm—the unfolding of sounds over time—is the most fundamental aspect of musical structure. Rhythms are ubiquitous in nature. We walk rhythmically, our heartbeats are rhythm, our speech is rhythmically organized, and, of course, rhythm and timing are at the heart of music. Rhythms are so powerful because their regularity enables us to predict when the next beat(s) will occur. Brain studies show that neural circuits fall into sync with musical rhythms, even in infants, and

Rhythms are ubiquitous in nature. We walk rhythmically, our heartbeats are rhythm, our speech is rhythmically organized, and, of course, rhythm and timing are at the heart of music.

that interactions between different brain oscillations focus our attention at the points in a piece of music that contain the most information. Deficits in our ability to process rhythm and time are even linked with major developmental disorders such as dyslexia, autism, attention deficits, and developmental coordination disorder. And research suggests that music can help alleviate all of these disorders.

Humans have been able to record music for just over a century. For the first three hundred millennia of our history, people had to make their own music, typically with others in social gatherings. Connections between auditory and motor areas in the brain for timing, honed through evolution, make us feel compelled to move in time to music. So when people experience music together, they tend to move in sync. And, after moving in sync, they feel more attached to each other—they report liking and trusting each other more, and cooperate more in games. Our studies show that even fourteen-month-old infants help a stranger more (for example, picking up objects the stranger "accidentally" drops) if that stranger had bounced in sync with them to music. Listening to and moving to music with other people has profound social consequences.

The LIVELab at McMaster University is a unique research-performance laboratory for studying the neuroscience of music at realistic venues. It is a fully functioning 106-seat concert hall in which we can measure EEG and other physiological responses (such as heart rate, galvanic skin responses, or muscle tension) simultaneously in multiple performers and audience members. We can also film and analyze the movements of musicians and audiences during performances. Our studies show that musicians continually predict the movements their fellow performers will make, and that this communication is critical for high-performance quality. Our studies also show that the brains of lead musicians influence the brains of the other musicians more than the other way around. And the brains of audience members are different when they experience live compared to recorded music, and when they experience the music in an audience rather than alone.

As we uncover the critical role music plays in people's development, well-being, and social interactions, it becomes imperative that we expand and research the incorporation of music into an increasing number of therapeutic contexts. Music has the capacity to transform all of our lives for the better.

Laurel Trainor is founding director of the McMaster Institute for Music and the Mind and the LIVELab at McMaster University in Hamilton, Ontario. She has done groundbreaking neuroscience research on musical development in children; her research spans perceptual, cognitive, and social aspects of pitch and rhythm.

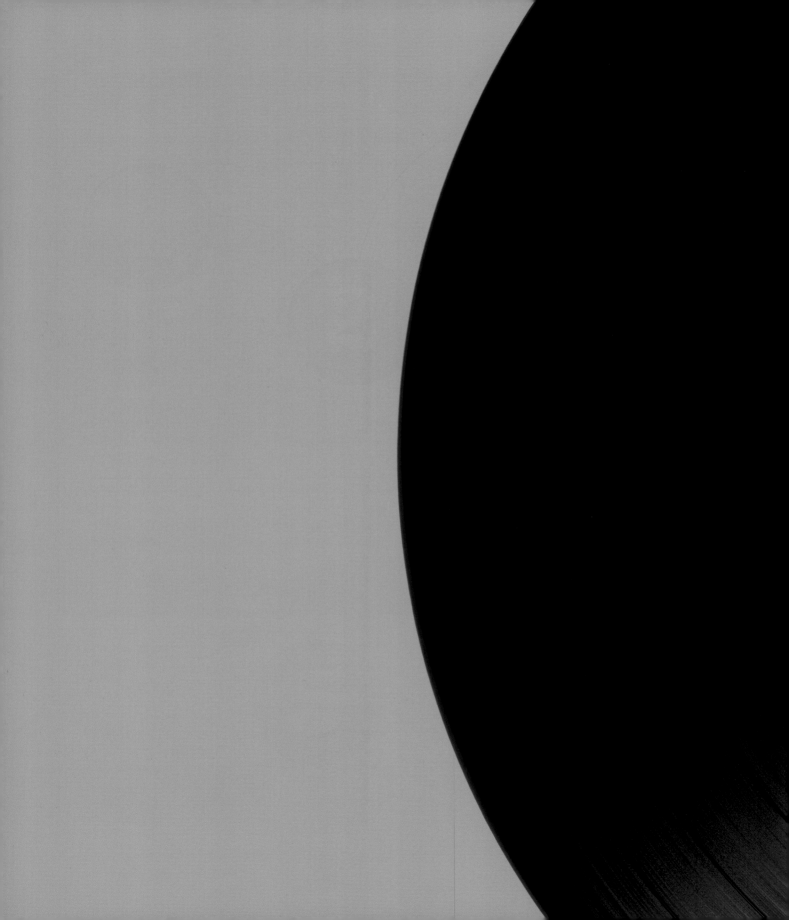

AMP

3:42
Instrumental with
featured soloist

SIDE 3 **MUSIC & EXPERIENCE**

(P. SCOTT–S. PETERS)

The Robert Terry Sextet

HERE COME THE DRUMS

Robert Wiersema

You know those mornings where you wake up and feel paralyzed, crushed by the weight of the world? I had one of those mornings the other day. I was falling further and further behind at work, and felt like a mess. And then there was the usual stuff: the grind of a merciless schedule, trying to balance family and work with too few hours in the day, all with too little money in the bank and too many bills outstanding.

A gnawing sadness and sense of desperation clung to me as I worked on the morning's writing, as I got ready for work, as I left the house.

It was raining. Not a hard rain, more of a heavy mist, with a strong enough wind that an umbrella would have been no use. Not that I could find mine.

There was something appropriate about standing at the bus shelter, cold and getting wetter by the minute. I was miserable, and everything was conspiring to keep me that way.

Well, almost everything . . . I've always got music playing.

Especially on my morning commute. So that morning, mired in funk (and not the good, James Brown/Parliament/George Clinton kind), I was plugged in. And over the course of the bus trip, things started to get a little better. An old Tori Amos song came up on the rotation, and I smiled. Then Lissie's cover of Kid Cudi's "Pursuit of Happiness" perked me up.

And then, as I'm getting off the bus . . . here come the drums.

Literally.

I had never heard of the Rogue Traders before watching *Doctor Who*'s third-season finale. I still don't know much about them, except that they're an Australian band.

But I broke into a huge grin. I did a little shuffle-bop across the sidewalk. The rain stopped, and the clouds parted, and the world was right again.

Why?

It was "Voodoo Child." The song itself is a catchy, hooky little number, percussive and danceable. But the boppiness of the song alone wasn't the main reason my day turned.

Most weekend mornings, my son, Xander, comes down to my office to hang with me while we give my wife, Cori, a few hours to sleep in. It's one of my favourite parts of the week. It's our time, his and mine. I'm supposed to be writing, but we end up hanging out, watching TV shows; most recently, *Doctor Who*.

Our second or third time through the latest series, Xander developed a fondness for the finale: Rogue Traders' "Voodoo Child," with its refrain of "Here come the drums, here come the drums." It comes at a big moment in the show, and he started to sing along, then asked if we could find it on YouTube. Which we did.

He fell in love with it.

Ten years old, my son was falling in love with music through a song from a semi-cheesy British sci-fi TV show.

Whenever I hear that song, I can't help but think of Xander, those weekend mornings hanging out with him, that look of sheer joy he had on his face when he listened to the song for the first time.

How can that not make me smile? How can that not bring me joy?

That's what music does for me.

Robert Wiersema is a novelist and bookstore owner who lives in Victoria, BC.

Alison (and Scott) Stratten

Magic in the Car

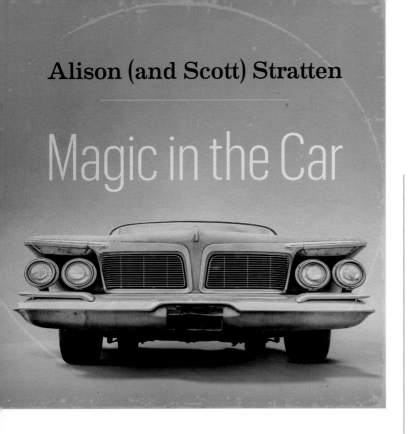

Music can be medicine, and in the car, magic. It's a sixteen-year-old, with Metallica too loud for home blaring, just out for a drive. Because they can. The window open. The world passing by.

It's singing Maria Carey's "Hero" at the top of your lungs, talent be damned.

It's Moby quieting a fussy baby.

It's Raffi bringing together three sweet little voices into a giggle-filled rendition of "Banana Phone."

It's "Hey, have you heard this one?" for a teenager, and a parent, both looking to connect.

Something about the way music brings the motion to life. The way the sounds make a car feel like a private place, where conversations can begin. The way music and motion make silence between people, comfortable.

In our car, the kids pick the music. One of them recently told us they were in a friend's car and had to listen to their parents' music. They wouldn't believe him when he told them how things work in our car. As a parent, when the right song comes on, all of a sudden you can be learning all about your child. You're talking about the hard stuff, and the good stuff. Or, like a fly on the wall, you hear them speaking to one another or their friends—the music providing a blanket over your presence, like magic.

Classical music is long drives with my mom, tapping her finger on the steering wheel.

Country is my sister, on a road trip unfortunately timed to correspond with the height of Billy Ray Cyrus's fame.

Barenaked Ladies is a first date, on the way to a movie.

It's a mixtape you spent hours crafting, only to have it get stuck in the tape deck.

It's camp songs on bus rides, and Ani DiFranco cross-country, late at night, across the plains.

Broadway is hours of *Hamilton* and *The Book of Mormon* on the way to school, until we know every line by heart.

Hip hop is the music they play for us, as we calmly explain that yes, we know who Kendrick Lamar is.

Coldplay is New York City, because it was playing in the taxi the first time I ever saw the skyline, and now that's how the city sounds: like "Yellow," and traffic speeding past and my heart beating with excitement.

The car is the sanctuary, the music a soundtrack for the escape. Freedom to go, physically and emotionally. To travel, to get away from whatever is, and move into whatever can be.

Alison and Scott Stratten are co-authors of five best-selling business books, co-owners of UnMarketing Inc., and co-hosts of not only the *UnPodcast* but also of five children, two dogs, and two cats. They have advised companies that include PepsiCo, Saks Fifth Avenue, IBM, Cirque du Soleil, and Microsoft.

I knew at a very young age that music spoke to me. By the time I was sixteen I was working at a radio station, and I went on to do just about every job in the music business: selling records, managing bands, doing radio shows, DJing in bars, hosting on MuchMusic. I was lucky, I knew what interested me and I lived it. There was just one hitch: I can't sing.

Luckily, I met a jingle-writing musician, Tim Thorney, and we became songwriting partners. For more than a decade, writing songs is what I did when I wasn't on air at MuchMusic; I took the raw material of my life and turned it into stories for other people to sing. It was cathartic and liberating.

Tim and I have very different personalities, but when we walked into a room to write, we felt safe together. We trusted each other, easily building on the other's ideas. A lot of artists don't know when a song is done, but we weren't precious about it. We trusted our guts and didn't overthink it. Together we composed hundreds of songs and won a slew of awards.

On the final day of recording one album, Tim turned to me and said, "Ehmie, it never gets better than this." We had just written and produced the record for an up-and-coming country vocalist, Cassandra Vasik. I had had a big falling out with friends and had gone into therapy, so the songs were my way of working out personal demons. Sitting there in the dark studio with Tim, listening to Cassandra sing the stories of my life, was extraordinary. Not many people have had that gift, to be able to tell personal stories and hear them sung by the voice of a (country) angel.

That moment was pure. Tim and I had told the stories we'd wanted to tell in the way we wanted to tell them, and Cassandra's emotional performance had breathed life into them. After you finish producing a record, it's sent out into the world to

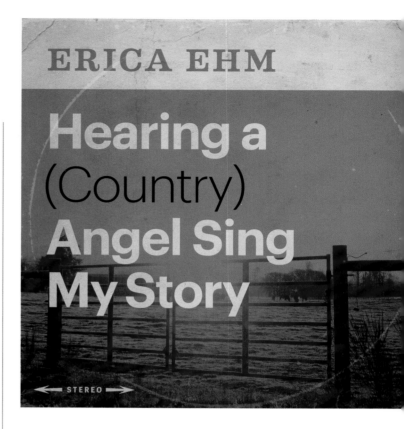

ERICA EHM

Hearing a (Country) Angel Sing My Story

← STEREO →

be judged. But what really matters is knowing you've done your best work. We were deeply proud of what we created together; and, what do you know, the album, *Feels like Home*, won the Juno award for best country female artist.

A few years later Tim asked me out to lunch. I had a feeling something was up, and I was right; he was breaking up with me. It was like a relationship splitting up; he told me he had met a new writing partner and after a decade of working with me, he wanted to explore things with her instead. It turned out to be Alanis Morissette.

Erica Ehm is a Canadian writer, songwriter, entrepreneur, and TV host. Her songs have been recorded by many artists, including Van Morrison. She founded Ehm & Co, a digital publisher and marketing agency for the mom market.

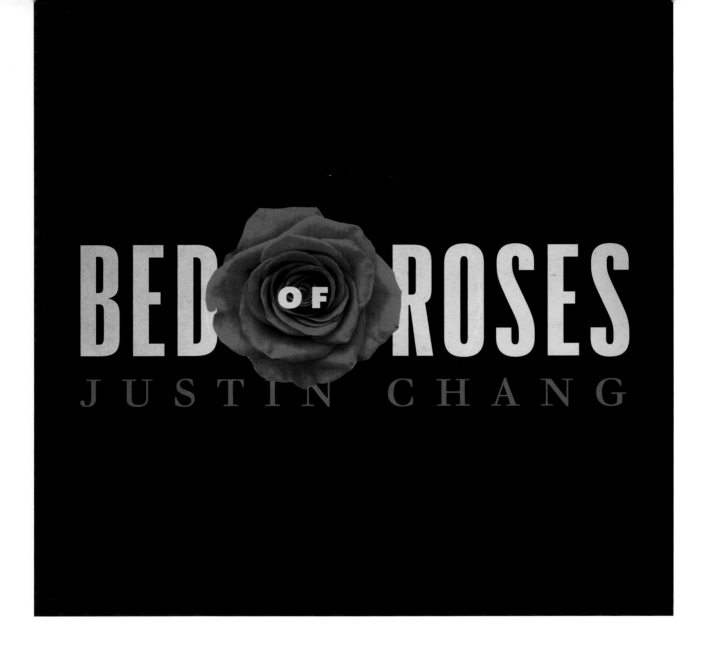

BED OF ROSES

JUSTIN CHANG

When I think about music and hard times, I remember bicycling down a country road in New Zealand, listening to Bon Jovi's "Bed of Roses" over and over again on my Walkman. I was fifteen and all alone. My parents had sent me there from South Korea, to attend Christchurch Boys' High School. They were supposed to follow, but we were waiting on the paperwork, so I'd gone on ahead.

When I heard the plan, I had thought it was awesome, an opportunity to see the bigger world and learn English. But looking back, I was so young and immature, a fifteen-year-old boy in a country I'd never heard of. It wasn't easy. My dad had come over to drop me off and find me a homestay. I'd started in a motel run by my legal guardian, who was also Korean. Dad worked for Samsung and couldn't get much time off, so after four days he had to go home.

There were kids studying English from all over the world there: Japan, Hong Kong, China. Then I passed the language tests and was put into regular classes, so I was separated from the international students, as well as from my parents, my country, my friends. I went through some tough times, including changing high schools. I bought a bike to get to the new school, and once a week I'd pedal forty-five minutes or so to my guardian's place, to say hello and get some Korean food. The bus system was erratic, so I decided to just bike everywhere. I didn't even know the rules of the road.

The only thing I enjoyed was music. Especially Bon Jovi, who were huge in Korea then. I'd been following them since their 1992 album *Keep the Faith*, and had bought the latest, *These Days,* just before I left Korea.

The song that really caught my attention was "Bed of Roses." The sound, the way the music starts, the cymbals, the tone, it just hit me. It's a rock ballad, with soaring guitar and piano. I didn't even have a CD player, just an old boom box and a Walkman. So I made a cassette with the same song repeated again and again on both sides, and listened to it while I was riding my bike. It had auto-reverse so I didn't even have to flip it.

I put my headphones on under my helmet and started pedalling, down an open country road, and let it wash over me. The first line is about being wasted and wounded—at the time I didn't understand most of the words, but I just loved the rhythm and the notes; it kept me pedalling over and over until I got to my guardian's motel. Then I'd get some Korean food, and a few hours later I'd head back home, listening to the same song.

Looking back, I must have been going through a depression. I didn't even know what that was. I started crying in my room, which is not good for a Korean boy aged fifteen; I was supposed to be macho, tough. I remember hearing the theme song from a Korean TV show and not being able to stop the tears, it brought back memories of watching with my family

When I was fifteen, I thought I knew everything. I thought I was ready, but I wasn't. I had to rely on something, and it turned out to be Bon Jovi.

in the living room at home. Now I was all alone and vulnerable. This was before cellphones or email; the only way to communicate was through letters, which took weeks to come.

In the end I was there all by myself for three more years. My parents' application didn't get accepted, but they got into Canada instead, so we all came here. I was the head of the family then, because I spoke English (I graduated with a first in economics): reading letters from the government, finding our first house, buying a store. The family ran that store for nine years.

When I was fifteen, I thought I knew everything, but I was still a kid. I thought I was ready, but I wasn't. I had to rely on something, and it turned out to be Bon Jovi.

Justin Chang grew up in South Korea and emigrated to Canada in 1999, after more than three years alone in New Zealand. He studied computer science and commerce at University of Toronto and has worked since 2004 at Deloitte Canada, where he is the Toronto greenhouse technology lead.

AMP132Z **STEREO** AN AMPOPHONIC SURROUND SOUND RECORDING

Lindsay McCabe

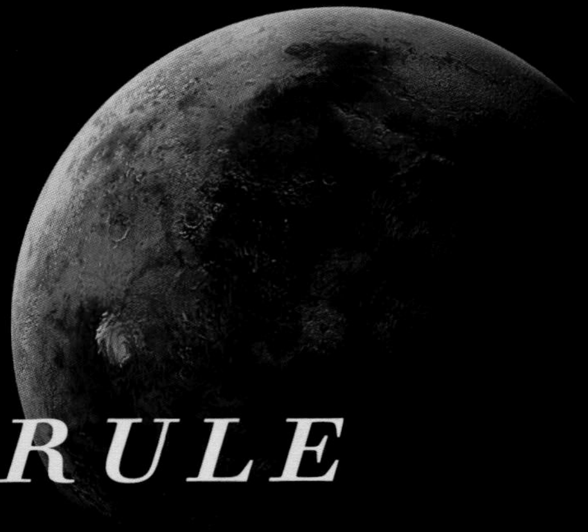

EVERYBODY WANTS TO RULE THE WORLD

My love of music started at a very young age, thanks to my dad. I was probably the only five-year-old who knew every Beatles lyric. Some of my first memories are of my sister and me dancing around the living room while Dad played piano. One song in particular was our favourite: "Everybody Wants to Rule the World" by Tears for Fears.

The other passion my dad and I shared was sports. He grew up an "average house league player" (his words) but loved hockey and coached me when I was little, then took me to games and practices when I played rep. It was great, as I got to see him a lot even after my parents had split up. When I switched to volleyball, a sport he knew nothing about, he stayed involved and celebrated my every accomplishment.

Dad always found a way to relate how I was feeling back to music. In between weekly phone calls he would send me songs over email, to cheer me up and motivate me.

Fast-forward a few years and I am playing D1 volleyball at Syracuse. The adjustment to playing at this level, both physically and emotionally, was really tough. I had struggled with anxiety off and on in my life, but had never felt anything close to the constant worry this brought on, a weight that sat on my chest for months without relief. Through it all, Dad was my biggest fan. He always found a way to relate how I was feeling back to music. In between weekly phone calls he would send me songs over email, to cheer me up and motivate me.

Things got better after first year and Dad and I kept sharing songs. Sometimes he even sent songs for me to play for the team in the locker room. After five great years I held a "Senior Weekend," where I invited fifteen friends and family members to celebrate the end of my collegiate volleyball career. I felt proud to have Dad there walking me out wearing his Syracuse Orange Converse runners. Everyone was telling me how great it was to see him after so many years, and I felt so happy and complete. My dad passed away suddenly from a stroke a week later.

In the aftermath I wasn't sure if I would play volleyball again. I had always dreamed of playing professionally, but the training and isolation were really hard following Dad's passing. I bit the bullet, and though I spent many days alone crying on my way home from practice, I made the national team

that summer and signed a contract to play professionally in France.

France was a whole other beast; it felt like first year at Syracuse all over again, except this time there was an ocean between me and my support network, and I was in a different culture in which I had to figure everything out on my own. Unsurprisingly, my anxiety worsened again. I spent a lot of time listening to music in my apartment trying to feel better.

At our first tournament, I was a nervous wreck. I'd never been anxious before games before, but could barely breathe on the drive to the venue. We stopped for a team meal before the game and I was convinced I was going to have a panic attack in front of all of these people I was just getting to know. I was trapped in a vortex in my own head until I heard my coach asking, "Who sings this again?" I came out of my fog to hear the song they were playing in the restaurant. "This is Tears for Fears," I replied. "Everybody Wants to Rule the World" was playing, and I could breathe again. I was going to be okay.

Lindsay McCabe has a BSc and an MSc from Syracuse and an MBA from Oregon State, and played professional volleyball in Béziers, France, in 2015–16. She is now a consultant in human capital at Deloitte in Toronto.

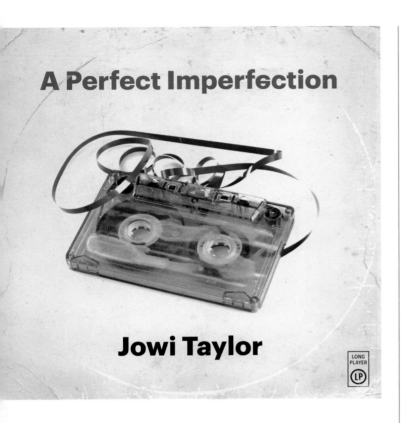

A Perfect Imperfection

Jowi Taylor

While it's tempting to write about the countless times I cranked up Talking Heads' "Once in a Lifetime" or New Order's "Your Silent Face" or Pete Seeger's banjo rendition of Beethoven's 9th to change regular old tears into tears of joy and release, there's another story that always makes me keenly aware of the extraordinary power of music.

While I was growing up, my dad did several extended contracts with the International Labour Organization in different parts of Africa. When I was fifteen he took a two-year job in Kabwe, Zambia. By that time my music obsession was well established and I fancied myself a master of the cassette mixtape, making them for friends and girls I was interested in. It was also my main way of communicating with my parents; I found it easier to play them a song that captured where I was at than go through the uncomfortable business of expressing complicated feelings in words. In fact, my parents were concerned that my obsession with music and DJing was getting in the way of making sensible decisions about what I wanted to do with my life. So, perhaps not surprisingly, I made my dad mixtapes instead of writing letters and sent them off by mail to Zambia, where he had a combination shortwave radio/cassette boom box that served as his home entertainment system.

My mother, sister, and I visited Dad in Kabwe in the summer of 1978 so I got to know that player pretty well. One tape I had sent to Dad earlier included a mix of Kraftwerk, Brian Eno, Peter Gabriel, and the Penguin Cafe Orchestra. Side B started with Gabriel's "Indigo." Before our arrival, the player had chewed the tape partway into the song. Dad had rescued it from the rotors and re-spooled the cassette but the song was marred by a distinctive garbly squelch about two seconds long. I still can't hear that song without hearing that squelch in my mind at the precise moment.

Two decades later, when I was thirty-six years old, my dad went into the hospital for cancer treatment and didn't return. One day I went to visit him and found him in bed with his Walkman on the little tray in front of him. He asked me to put the headphones on and pressed PLAY. I heard the sounds of Peter Gabriel's "Indigo," and soon, right on cue, the familiar squelch. He had saved the tape all these years.

When I took the headphones off he said, "You know, when I heard this tape I knew you were going to be okay. It was so smart, so well-chosen and sequenced, and it told such a story about who you were and what you cared about. I realized you were in better shape than we'd given you credit for."

It was an answer to a message I'd sent my father twenty years earlier, preserved in a damaged cassette and a perfect imperfection.

Jowi Taylor is the host, writer, and co-producer of the Peabody award–winning CBC Radio series *The Wire* and the creator of the Six String Nation project, focusing on an acoustic guitar made from pieces of history from every province and territory of Canada. He received Canada's Meritorious Service Medal (Civilian) for his work.

Aside from being a phenomenal mother, my mum was also a very good amateur pianist. She was one of nine kids, and two of her sisters, my aunts, were *professional* pianists. Music was absolutely the fabric of family gatherings; there was no such thing as a get-together that didn't involve piano playing and singing. There was a lot of classical music, and "When Irish Eyes Are Smiling," that sort of thing. If it was Christmas, there were carols. My father would be conscripted because he had a beautiful baritone. He couldn't sing "Danny Boy" because you needed a tenor, but he would sing Elvis songs, like "Love Me Tender."

My mum also appreciated jazz, and played her favourite classical records over and over and over again. At the time I didn't appreciate it, but I sure do now. A typical obnoxious male, I was like, *Why are these old folks doing this? Who cares about the piano?* It took a while for it to gradually sink in that I was being influenced anyway. I realize it now. After all, I did become a musician; and now I run a recording studio.

Because I was in a heavy metal band, people assume all I ever listen to is Led Zeppelin. Don't get me wrong, I love classic rock. When my wife and I are out on a Sunday afternoon, we'll listen to "Don't Stop Believin' " good and loud in the car, like everyone else. And Boston, Deep Purple, ZZ Top, all that good stuff. But I also listen to a lot of Mozart. And like a lot of my generation, I grew up on the blues. Prior to the British Invasion, it all came from Memphis, Muscle Shoals, Stax, Chess Records. I'm sure the members of the Stones and Led Zep would say the same thing.

As a kid I was pretty oblivious to the music my mum and my aunts loved, but it must have been permeating the back regions of my cranium. It comes back when you're much older and need it; that's when you gravitate back to the mothership.

I'M MY OWN MUSIC THERAPIST

Gil Moore

Now when I come home at the end of the working day, after ten, twelve hours of stress, I sit down at the Steinway grand piano my wife convinced me to install in the foyer of our new house. And what do I play? Some jazz, some Mozart. I self-prescribe; I'm my own music therapist. Just like my mother and my aunts.

Gil Moore was the drummer and singer for Triumph, a hard rock band whose fourteen albums received eighteen gold and nine platinum awards in Canada and the US. He is the owner of Metalworks Studios in Mississauga, Canada's biggest recording studio, which has hosted such acts as Drake, Guns N' Roses, Aerosmith, Katy Perry, the Black Eyed Peas, David Bowie, Prince, and many more.

PAOLO PIETROPAOLO

MUSIC IS A VERB

The most important thing I ever learned about music is that, just like dance or love, it's a verb as well as a noun.

It sure didn't feel like a verb growing up studying classical music. It was quite clear that, just like the dictionary says, music is a noun. A thing, even. It has two colours: black and white. It lives on manuscript paper. And it's to be treated with reverence and even a little bit of fear. A holy set of instructions, like scripture.

My first piano teacher sternly admonished me for my musical transgressions (thou shalt not slouch). By the time I started attending recitals, I had come to understand that music was a Very Serious Thing and that some sins were unforgivable—like showing any kind of emotion during a performance, or, God forbid, wanting to move to the music. Like everybody else, I learned to sit as still as death, too afraid to breathe for fear of offending someone.

Yes, music was a Thing: a limp and flabby thing that felt a little bit dead.

Still, I persevered. I wanted to be a composer. Maybe I liked rules. I learned very specific rules from a wonderful composition teacher in his seventh-floor apartment overlooking Bloor Street West in Toronto. His giant orange and white cat watched us as I strained to understand why the Gates of Music Hell might open if I put certain chords next to each other.

I met my next teacher on the first day of Composition 101 at university. He gazed impassively at us and said, "What are you all doing here? You have a one-in-a-billion chance of amounting to anything."

I loved classical music (still do), but it was hard not to feel as though it tries very hard to flog the love out of you. I felt lost that winter. I had already abandoned science after my first year of university. Had I made a mistake switching to music? I wandered up and down Bloor Street in quiet despair.

One fortuitous Thursday I picked up *NOW Magazine* and my eye landed on a review of a French film opening at the local repertory cinema. It was about the music of the Romani people. The reviewer raved that the film might change my life.

It did.

Latcho Drom runs for almost two hours. There's almost no dialogue, just performances by Romani musicians tracing the journey of the Romani diaspora from India through Egypt and Turkey all the way to Spain. I wasn't used to sitting through two hours of music without dialogue. Oh wait. I was. That's what going to the symphony was like.

But this was different. This was no Thing I was witnessing on the screen. No, it was very verb-like. Every performance was full of motion, from the expressions on the musicians' faces to the dancing, clapping, and swaying of their friends and families. It was completely unlike anything I was used to. It was alive.

There's one scene at a small train station in Hungary. A platinum-blond woman is sitting on a bench on the platform. She's bundled up in her fur-lined coat, an arm around her young son. She looks cold and miserable. A close-up reveals that she's crying.

On the other side of the tracks, some Roma gather to wait for the train, too. They start a little fire and huddle around it, holding their instruments. The boy, wanting to cheer up his mother, crosses the tracks and tugs on a coat. Out comes a fiddle, a jug drum, a set of spoons—and they start musicking. Whoever's not playing is singing, or dancing, or snapping their fingers. The boy starts dancing, too. And eventually, his sad mum smiles. It gets me every time.

I learned a few things from the Roma that day. Firstly, that music is everywhere—for the Roma, making music is a part of everyday life. It brings (and keeps) people together and lifts our spirits like nothing else can. Secondly, that we're all musicians. You don't have to spend your whole childhood worried about the opening of the Gates of Music Hell to earn some rite of passage into musicianship. It's inside all of us, in our hands, our fingers, our hips, our feet.

And thirdly, and most importantly, that just like dance or love, music is a verb.

Paolo Pietropaolo is a writer, producer, musician, and broadcaster. He is co-creator of the Peabody Award–winning CBC Radio documentary series *The Wire: The Impact of Electricity on Music,* and writer, host, and producer of *In Concert* and *The Signature Series* on CBC Music. He loves to dance.

STEREOPHONIC AMP

DAVID HEIN

Goin' Up

On the first day of school at York University, I met the incredible Irene Sankoff. We were friends for years, and then started dating. She brought me to musicals and I brought her to acoustic rock concerts—including countless Great Big Sea shows. We'd stay up all night listening to songs or driving on long car trips down to New York City, singing to each other.

Years later we got married and then, when we found we never saw each other between all of our day jobs and night jobs, we started writing musicals together so we could hang out. Our second musical, *Come from Away*, was set in Newfoundland, and was inspired by the incredible true story of the locals' kindness after 9/11—and by my love of Newfoundland music.

At first, Irene wasn't sure that *Come from Away* should even be a musical, but when we travelled out to Newfoundland on the tenth anniversary of 9/11, we went to a kitchen party benefit concert in the hockey rink. A local band, the Navigators, started playing and *everyone* started dancing: the locals, us "come from aways," the executives from Lufthansa in their three-piece suits. Even though we were there to commemorate a solemn day, the music and spirit of Newfoundland reminded us that we are all there *together*—and that you need to dance and sing to remember you're alive. We both realized that music is how Newfoundlanders come together, how they get through their ridiculously long winters. They bring over instruments and start to play; they sing and tell stories to stay warm and come together as a community. From that moment on, there was no way that *Come from Away* wasn't a musical.

Working on it, we dove deep into the songs of incredible Newfoundland bands like Shanneyganock, the Once, the Dardanelles, Figgy Duff, the Navigators, the Irish Descendants, Rawlins Cross, and many more. But I always came back to one of the first albums I fell in love with: Great Big Sea's second album, *Up*, which came out just as we started university, right before we started dating. It's the soundtrack for our friendship and falling in love.

Though there is a lot of loneliness, sea sickness, and heartache on the album, the second track, "Goin' Up," perfectly captures the kitchen party spirit of Newfoundland. Alan Doyle sings about jigs and reels, heel and toe, about music all around, and how there's no place like this place "if we get it on the go." It's the kind of song that makes you want to dance. That makes you want, as the chorus says, to "lock the world outside." It's the kind of the song that inspired our relationship and our show. It brought a lot of things together for me and I never get tired of it.

David Hein is a playwright, songwriter, and actor. He was born in Regina, trained in Toronto, and is now resident in New York, and he has written two musicals: *My Mother's Lesbian Jewish Wiccan Wedding* and the Broadway smash hit *Come from Away*, with his writing partner and wife, Irene Sankoff.

NOTORIOUS IN THUNDER BAY

VITALY PECHERSKIY

It was a fall day in 2005. I had immigrated from Saint Petersburg, Russia, population five million, to Thunder Bay, Ontario, population 110,000, two months earlier. I just had my first day of the frosh week at Lakehead University and, unfortunately, aside from the people, there was nothing nice I could say about Thunder Bay. I was one of the only foreigners and attracted a lot of unwanted attention, despite the fact that I spoke very little English. And I had missed my best chance to bond with my classmates, because I was seventeen and everyone had decamped to the bar.

Walking home down one of many quiet streets, kicking occasional yellow leaves, I sipped on my new obsession: Tim Horton's hot chocolate. I was frustrated at how incapacitated I felt. I had always taken great pride in my mastery of the rich Russian language; now all of a sudden I was mute. I had been the popular kid in high school; now I was an invisible, scrawny teenager with shaggy hair. My cool skater kicks that I wore when I rode my BMX bike felt out of place on the shores of Lake Superior. Not having a driver's licence, let alone a car, I felt imprisoned at home. I was beaten down.

"Notorious Thugs" by the Notorious B.I.G. became the soundtrack to that difficult year. I didn't understand the freeform lyrics at all, but the driving beat gave me the energy to get up every day, put a brave face on, and fight for my future.

Before writing this, I listened to the song again for the first time in more than a decade. Even though it's full of minor notes—the sure song of a sad song—it evokes many positive memories of challenges overcome. "Notorious Thugs" makes me feel good, even though I still barely understand what Biggie is rapping about!

Vitaly Pecherskiy is co-founder of StackAdapt, a venture-backed advertising technology firm that is one of Canada's fastest-growing companies. He was named a 30 under 30 by *Marketing* magazine.

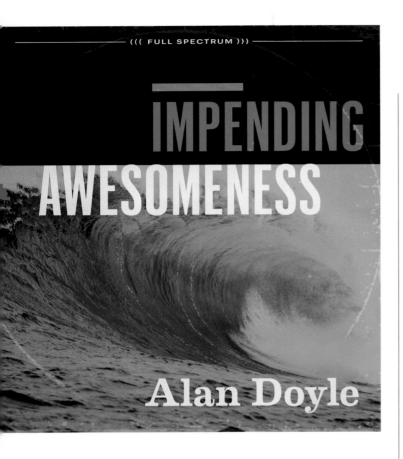

IMPENDING AWESOMENESS

Alan Doyle

At one of Great Big Sea's first big festivals, we opened for the Rankin Family. Back then, in the early '90s, they were the biggest thing in Atlantic Canadian music. I'd grown up on them and was a huge fan. I'll never forget standing in the pit at the Exploits Valley Salmon Festival as they launched into "The Mull River Shuffle," my favourite song of theirs. It began with Jimmy Rankin's Recitation, where he invites all the ladies and gentlemen to picture a dance in a small town years ago.

Having grown up in a small fishing town, Petty Harbour in Newfoundland, I knew what that was like. The whole town would be buzzing before a dance. There was such anticipation, everyone hoping that something foolish would happen.

You'd hope you'd catch one of your older cousins kissing outside the church hall, or a couple of older fishermen getting into a fight. Or someone sneaking

an extra cold plate—we had these at garden parties and dances, called turkey teas: you'd get a cold turkey plate with potato and beet or mustard salad and a cup of tea. Everyone would dance for a couple of hours, then it was time for the turkey tea break. Time for small-town drama.

After Jimmy's Recitation, the second piece of business was the instrumental lead-up, during which the girls danced onto the stage. That was really incredible. In Newfoundland we don't have a tradition of step dancing like in Cape Breton. Whenever I hear the song now, I see those three beautiful ladies legging it on stage, before the first verse kicks in, and Jimmy starts singing about going home, full of the devil and full of the rum. That says it all.

People wanted mischief, that was their release, their night out, a chance to act out of character. Or to act predictably in character! It's the summer dance, and Reggie's going to get into a fight. Reggie always gets into a fight.

That song has a perfect six-eight lift. Many of the best Celtic tunes are in six-eight time, not four-four like the blues. They actually wrote the rhythm right into the song—this really cool, bouncy bouncy rhythm to dance and sing to. And it perfectly demonstrates Cape Breton fiddle and piano playing, unique to that part of the world.

Whenever I'm back home, having dinner or getting ready to go out, knowing we're going to go down for a dance, that's the song I put on. Before we go, to get us all ready, it's "The Mull River Shuffle."

As a songwriter and performer, it's one of my biggest influences. I've always wanted to create what that song creates—that sense of impending excitement and awesomeness.

Alan Doyle is a musician and actor from Newfoundland. He has released nine albums with Great Big Sea, as well as three solo albums.

Music has always been a big part of my life. I started taking music lessons at age four and was soon turning every book I read into a suite of songs. When I needed cheering up, my parents would take me for a drive and I'd belt out songs from *The Lion King*.

I started teaching music eleven years ago, and I see firsthand the impact music has on my students every day. Making music truly is therapy. I've seen pupils come into lessons crying, because they are having a hard time at school or are struggling with friends. Music helps them work through those emotions by giving a voice to everything they're feeling. I've found that to be especially true when they just don't have the words to express their emotions, be they good or bad. The songs that play during the good times and the bad times stick with you. Like the song that was playing when my niece was born.

The birth was a magical, inspiring experience. My sister-in-law, who is also one of my best friends, put me in charge of the playlist. Three playlists, in fact. There was one for during the contractions that was really calming, like yoga music, and a second one for the pushing period, before the birth, that was more pumped up. During the delivery I played softer, more sentimental songs.

It was a water birth, at a birth centre in Calgary. It all happened really quickly, or so it felt; we barely had time to walk mom around the block as the contractions grew more intense. When it was time to push, we got her into the tub and, not much more than five minutes later, her daughter was born, during "Castle on the Hill" by Ed Sheeran.

That song welcomed my niece into the world, and has now become a family favourite. We always turn it on and say, "This is your song," and dance around the room. I can't listen to it without a smile on my face.

Now, my niece's birth and "Castle on the Hill" are all one memory. It's a song about looking back on your past along with family and friends, about feeling like you can't wait to go back to where you're from. There are some darker moments, but the rhythm and vocals are so inspiring. The overall theme is really positive.

Sometimes I wonder what my niece will think of that song when she grows up. Will she love knowing the song she came into the world to, or will she eventually say, "Okay guys, stop!"

Lauren Rodych-Eberle is trained in the Royal Conservatory of Music and has a BA in music from the University of Calgary. She is the owner of Miss Lauren's Music Studio, based out of Calgary, and is available on Skype, where she teaches voice and piano. She was born in Winnipeg, Manitoba, and now spends her time between Calgary, Alberta, and Garden City, New York.

Suddenly I recognize a familiar refrain—a song of the yearning within, both torment and delight . . . I say out loud: "I've played this for that listener from Burnaby!"

It does not matter that it is pouring rain. It does not matter that I am standing in the dark at a bus stop without a shelter, clutching an umbrella that could upturn any minute now. It does not matter that the bus into UBC is already five minutes late. What matters is this: soon I will be on campus, dashing up the stairs of the Student Union Building, all the cued cassette tapes will come out of my backpack, and promptly, on the hour, the delicate strums of the santoor will float and undulate all over Vancouver and the Lower Mainland, the sound will fade and I will introduce myself again:

"You are listening to CiTR 101.9 FM Vancouver. This is Gitanjali . . ."

For twelve years of Sundays that radio show was my sanctuary and my balm. Slotted between *Queer FM* and *Radio Free America, Gitanjali* was a dislocation meme from the very beginning. And it was a needy, selfish one.

As a student in the '90s, I managed my life on a strict stipend. I did not own any audio equipment except for a Walkman I'd bought from London Drugs on West Broadway that first Christmas in Canada. A clock radio came with the basement I rented. When I'd saved enough money, it came down to adopting a cat or buying a stereo cassette player. I chose the cat. While my weekdays were busy with seminars and school work, the weekend nights were unforgiving stretches of loneliness, thick in a low-ceiling, single-bedroom shower-stall suite.

Gitanjali was my music room.

In that studio, for an hour on Sunday nights, I could sit in a quiet, sound-proofed space, top-quality headphones pressing against my ear, and listen to everything from Ravi Shankar to Sanskrit chants to Bollywood—and just about anything I could find from the grab-bag collection of tapes I'd brought with me from India. Marathi abhangs? Play them. Folk songs from Kerala? Why not? I knew the hour would fly and I'd be signing off soon. Walking down the corridors of the building, I knew I'd hear music from the underground pub, either Rod Stewart looking for somebody on a downtown train or Salt-N-Pepa hastily dragging me back to life, back to reality.

I had to soak it up for a week.

What I didn't know, had not given even a fleeting thought, was that my need for my music—the flute, the tabla, the cure for every malaise by Bollywood— would also become a celebration of memory and revival for so many in the city and the surrounding suburbs. Call it the upside of selfishness.

"Thank you-ji," said the cab driver waiting for a fare at the airport, calling from his car phone. "This song makes me miss my village in Punjab."

"A Meera bhajan on air in Vancouver!" a listener would exclaim every time I played a Hindu devotional. Another listener I'd nicknamed "Mr. Bedroom Voice" always wanted "a romantic song for my sweetie."

Last year, I found myself sitting in a roadside café in Chennai sipping sweet ginger tea. A transistor radio placed on a small shelf next to a framed photo of Gandhi was tuned to a station playing Tamil film hits, and suddenly I recognize a familiar refrain—

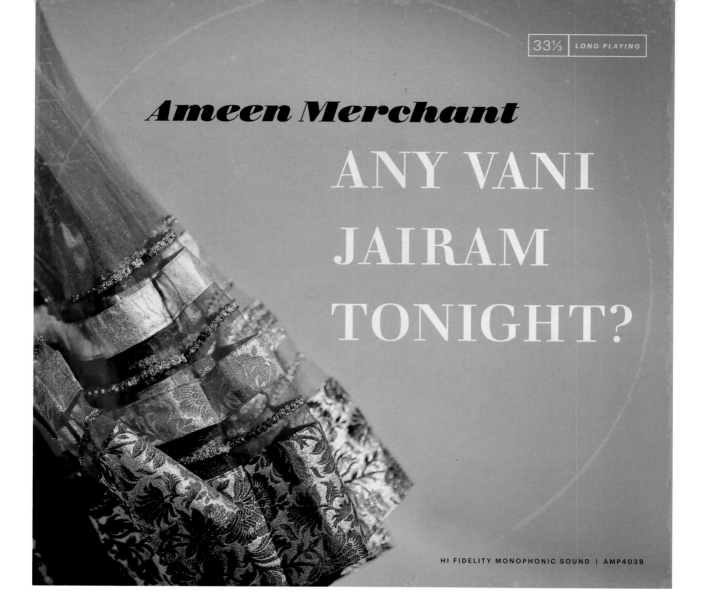

Ameen Merchant

ANY VANI JAIRAM TONIGHT?

HI FIDELITY MONOPHONIC SOUND | AMP403B

a song of the yearning within, both torment and delight . . . I say out loud: "I've played this for that listener from Burnaby!" I don't care if others in the café hear me talking to myself. I am time-travelling to Wesbrook Mall from Apoorva Tea Stall in Alwarpet.

My old music room at the university lights up. I've just announced the station ID and numbers on air. Square buttons on the phone flash red non-stop. I pick up the receiver.

"This is CiTR. . ." and before I can finish, the voice I've been expecting, an older man's, never any other question, asks:

"Any Vani Jairam tonight?"
 I see myself smiling, the song cued and ready to go. "I did not forget."

Ameen Merchant was born in Bombay and raised in Madras, India. His first novel, *The Silent Raga*, was published in Canada and India in 2007. He now lives in Vancouver, where he is working on his next novel and programming Bollywood and Indian classical music channels for CBC Music.

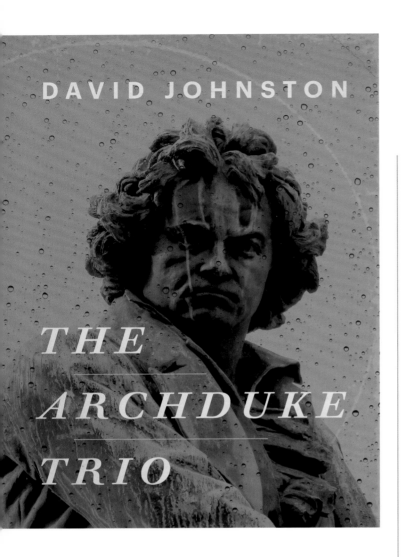

DAVID JOHNSTON

THE ARCHDUKE TRIO

At the age of eighteen I left my small Ontario town to go to Harvard, to study government and international relations. We had to do several courses outside our field, and for one I chose "Introduction to Classical Music," along with two of my football teammates, who were both great big guys. Every day we came and sat in the front row. I had sung in the school choir, but none of us know much about music. But we were keen.

The professor was Wallace Woodworth, but, unlike every other professor at Harvard, he told us to call him by his nickname: Woody. "You'll feel more comfortable that way," he said.

About a month in Woody announced, "Anyone who is uncomfortable seeing grown gentlemen cry shouldn't come to class tomorrow. I am going to play the third movement of Beethoven's Archduke Trio, a slow, really beautiful piano piece, and I can't get past ten bars without beginning to weep."

I came a little early the next day and sat quietly in the back row with my teammates. Sure enough, Professor Woody came on stage and began to play, and by the time he was ten bars in we all had tears flowing down our cheeks.

After that class we solemnly agreed to not say a word to the other players in the locker room, and we didn't. Those two were big, fierce guys on the football field, but not in music class. Not when they were face to face with the Archduke Trio.

That moment reminded me of playing ice hockey in Sault Ste. Marie. I was one of only three players on the under-seventeen team who wasn't Italian, including Tony Esposito, who was only fifteen and our backup goaltender, and his elder brother Phil; both were later NHL All Stars. Clemence Giovanatti, a defenceman, used to sing opera in the locker room.

That was my first introduction to tough guys who turned to jelly when the music got hold of them. Music does that!

David Johnston studied at Harvard, Cambridge, and Queen's universities, and was named to the All-American Hockey Team and elected to the Harvard Athletic Hall of Fame. He went on to a distinguished career as an academic and university administrator, including fifteen years as president of McGill University and twelve years as president of the University of Waterloo. He was Governor General of Canada from 2010 to 2017.

LONDON CALLING

Dave Gowans

I must have been fourteen the first time I used a Walkman. I'll never forget that day; it was also the first time I listened to the Clash.

It happened at Oak Bay High School in Victoria. The school had two buildings, east and west, and to get from one to the other you had to walk down this long path the length of a soccer field. It was a scene right out of one of those '80s movies: the jocks, the nerds, the different fashions, everyone trying to find their own place. I was a skateboarder, small for my age. Most of the time I just kept my head down and ran the gauntlet, trying not to be noticed.

On this day I saw a friend with this strange new device and asked him what it was. "It's a Sony Walkman," he replied. "You can borrow it if you want. It's great."

So I put it on and started walking down the path, with "London Calling" blasting into my eardrums. Listening to that song, I must have had the biggest grin on my face. I'd always been an obsessive music listener, and now, walking outside with headphones, I felt so alive. The look on my face was probably one of complete amazement.

"London Calling" is such a gutsy song. The way the guitars come pounding in, stomping out the beat.

And the voices, Joe Strummer and Mick Jones singing in unison, just belting it out. Hearing the fire in their voices, the strength. It's not an '80s love song, the stuff the radio was clogged with; it just came barrelling out of the headphones, the energy is so amazing. These guys don't care, they're just doing what they want to do. That really inspired me.

"What's so funny, Gowans?" some guy said, and I just looked at him and smiled. I'd never felt so powerful, like nothing could bother me. All the fear had evaporated.

From then on I always had a Walkman on: skateboarding to school, doing my paper route, I was completely lost in these artists. My parents were like, "Are you ever going to take those things off?" They were glued to my ears. Now I had a moving soundtrack for my life.

Dave Gowans played guitar, wrote songs, and toured with the Buttless Chaps for ten years and five albums, then spent another five years with Cloudsplitter. He now owns and runs Red Cat Records, a Vancouver indie store that opened a second location in 2016.

RODDY CAMPBELL

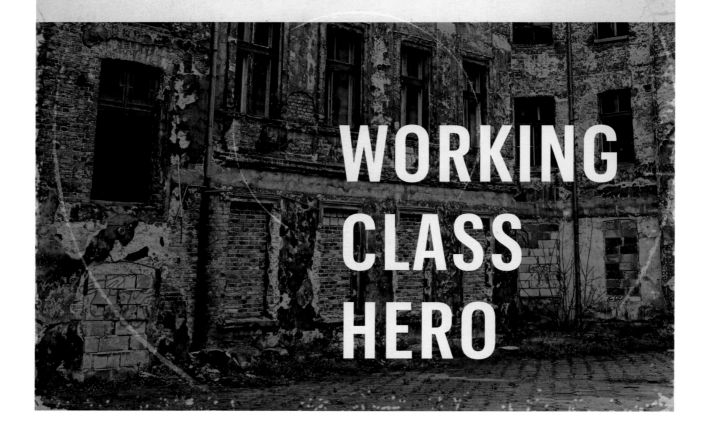

WORKING CLASS HERO

The LP cover consists of a stark, grim, grey photo of the remains of a dilapidated brick tenement slum. The title sits at the bottom of the right-hand side in white capital letters. *No More Forever* struck me instantly as a political statement rather than a record title. I had never heard of the Scottish folk singer Dick Gaughan, but I immediately bought his album, took it home, and proceeded to all but wear out the grooves.

Released in 1972, the record's eleven tracks draw largely from the folk tradition with one exception: "The John MacLean March" by Hamish Henderson.

Gaughan, twenty-three at the time, sings its four verses a cappella, powerfully and passionately annunciating the broad Scots words:

The jiners an hauders-on are merchin fae Clydebank
Come on nou an hear him he'll be owre thrang tae bide
Turn out Jock an Jimmie, leave yer cranes an yer
*   muckle gantries*
Great John MacLean's comin hame tae the Clyde

I absolutely loved that track from the first hearing. But who was this John MacLean? I had no idea. If he was worth a song it was worth finding out.

> **How reassuring to discover that the strength, integrity, and determination of one individual can motivate so many others to rise above oppression with dignity and conviction. One song instilled those beliefs in me.**

With clues from the sleeve notes I uncovered MacLean's remarkable history. He was born in Pollokshaws, now part of Glasgow, in 1879. Raised in dire poverty, he grew into a bright and industrious student who earned a master of arts from Glasgow University. He became a schoolteacher and delved into radical politics, convinced that the living standards of the working classes could only improve through social revolution. A fiery and charismatic orator, he taught industrial history, economics, and Marxist theory in his spare time to workers on the famous River Clyde.

When the First World War was declared in 1914, MacLean vehemently opposed the hostilities. The war brought inflation and landlords increased rents for Glasgow's destitute families bereft of their men fighting in France. MacLean led thirty thousand tenants in a successful rent strike. He also helped the powerful Clyde Workers' Committee renegotiate their galley-slave hours, meagre wages, and appalling working conditions.

The authorities took note of this firebrand and in 1916 he was sentenced to three years in jail for sedition and encouraging mutiny. Such was the outcry that a hundred thousand marched in Glasgow demanding his release. The government capitulated. His triumphant return to the city inspired Henderson's stirring song.

In July 1918 MacLean was again arrested and sentenced but released within months due to national and international pressure. He was granted a royal pardon by King George V for his last two prison sentences but refused it, telling the undersecretary of state for Scotland that the workers who had campaigned on his behalf had earned him his freedom, not the king.

After the war MacLean would go to jail twice more, latterly for encouraging the unemployed to take food rather than starve. He served both terms as a political prisoner. He died in 1923, aged forty-four, his health ruined by his political activity. Thousands lined Glasgow's streets for his funeral procession.

Now there's a history not taught in the Scottish schools I attended as a boy. How reassuring to discover that the strength, integrity, and unflagging determination of one individual can motivate, encourage, and inspire so many others to rise above oppression with dignity and conviction. One song—Dick Gaughan's passionate rendition of "John MacLean's March"—instilled those resolute beliefs in me.

The hail city's quiet nou, it kens that he's restin
At hame wi's Glesca freens, thair fame an thair pride
The red will be worn, ma lauds, an Scotlan will
*   merch again*
Nou great John MacLean has come hame tae
*   the Clyde*

Roddy Campbell is the editor and publisher of *Penguin Eggs*, Canada's folk, roots, and world music magazine. He emigrated from Scotland to Canada in 1975, and now lives in Edmonton.

RUNNING FASTER IN THE LAST VERSE

CHRIS BRANDT

We all go through breakups, and there are always songs that get us through them. "Moving Trucks" by Bob Mould was my anthem when I found myself going through a big one. The lyrics of the song carry the listener through, from the shock and awe of the initial breakup all the way through to a phoenix-like rebirth as a new person, stronger and ready to attack the world again. It is a whole journey of a love gone wrong, in three barnstorming minutes.

Many years later, the song still has the same effect on me—not because it takes me back to that breakup, but because its emotional arc drags me through whatever might be weighing me down that day, picks me up, and puts me right. It works perfectly through ear buds on a run, when everything hurts (because it has been far too long since my last run). And I run faster in the last verse, every time.

Chris Brandt has done most jobs in the music business, including ten years at Universal Music in sales and management and most recently as executive director of Music Heals, a Vancouver non-profit that works to help raise awareness of the healing powers of music. He now teaches music business at BCIT.

I'm a professional hockey player, and for me and my teammates, music is a powerful tool. When we're going to a game, we listen to music to pump ourselves up, to bring our energy levels up, so we're ready to play hockey. Sitting on the bus or going through the ritual in the locker room, I listen to up-tempo rock. Sometimes I'll find a rock song I haven't heard in a while and I'll literally get the chills. It's almost like a movie when you skate out onto the ice before the game starts, with your own soundtrack blasting in your head. It's such a powerful thing.

My dad is a musician, a guitarist who played in a band that did covers of '70s and '80s rock: AC/DC, Elton John. I was brought up listening to that sort of music, so it always reminds me of my family and of being home. It conjures up positive memories that make me happy. Country music, too, which isn't as big in New York as it is back home in Calgary.

After the game, it's really hard to sleep, you're so hyped. At these times, music does the opposite: it helps me come down from that high and get to sleep. After a game I mainly listen to acoustic music (I also play the acoustic guitar). On my phone I have playlists with slow, acoustic versions of some of my favourite songs, which help bring me down. You're so wound up after a game; sometimes you don't finish until after eleven at night, and it can be really hard to switch off the adrenaline. Music is a great way to control your energy level.

Playing in the NHL involves a lot of travel, and there are always ups and downs in the season, times when you're not doing well, losing games. We have sports psychologists on the team that help us to focus and stay calm, by reading, meditating, doing yoga. And listening to music.

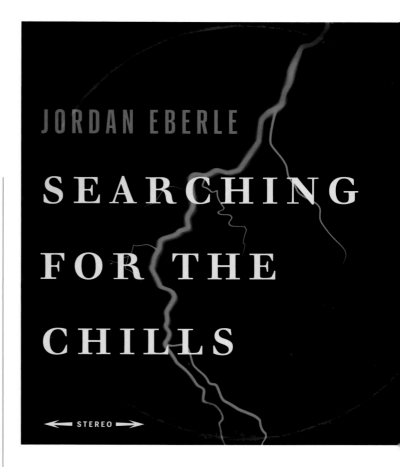

JORDAN EBERLE

SEARCHING FOR THE CHILLS

← STEREO →

It's the same if it's the Olympics, football, any event or sport—I've never met an athlete that wasn't a creature of habit, or one that didn't use music. If it's part of your routine, your body knows what's about to come, and starts getting ready for the rush. For me, it's rock and acoustic; the younger guys are listening to rap, EDM. We're all searching for the same thing: the pump up, that chill, to get you ready to play hard.

Jordan Eberle was born in Regina, Saskatchewan, and was drafted by the Edmonton Oilers in 2008. His first NHL goal, a short-handed backhand deke, was voted goal of the year by NHL fans. In 2011–12 he scored 34 goals and 76 points in 78 games, finishing second in voting for the Lady Byng Memorial Trophy. He was traded to the New York Islanders in June 2017.

MUSIC ENLARGES EVERYTHING

STEVE JORDAN

Music possesses me like nothing else. It freezes memories and feelings. People remind me of something I've said or done and it's fifty-fifty if I recall it. But ask me what year a song came out—it could be from three or thirteen or thirty years ago—and I can pin it to the year and the season. Songs transport me to the time and place. There I am in the back seat of the family station wagon, looking out the window, watching the countryside and imagining the harrowing scenes painted by "The Wreck of the *Edmund Fitzgerald*." Autumn 1976. It's startling how accurate these snapshots are. Music maps my life.

I grew up in the '70s and '80s. Like many people of my vintage, I romanticize the effect of the radio stations we relied on as our sole music source. As a kid lying in bed in suburban Kingston, the songs coming from that downtown radio station brought me the world far beyond my own. I learned about the Civil War ("The Night They Drove Old Dixie Down"), the existential effects of space travel ("Space Oddity"), prostitution in New Orleans ("Lady Marmalade"), alternate sexuality ("Walk on the Wild Side"), and whatever Steely Dan were on about. Radio also introduced me to cultures and energies that never touched my hometown. Reggae, southern soul, punk, rap, disco... all regional cultures delivered to me by radio years before they would manifest to me physically. That tiny, two-inch mono speaker enlarged everything.

Of course there was segregation. The musical monoculture of my hometown was mostly white. But the glory days of Top 40 still managed to bring all sorts of seemingly (but not really) incongruous treasures. You could hear Neil Young played next to Queen next to Sly and the Family Stone next to Charlie Rich next to Roberta Flack next to ABBA next to the Clash. The breadth of styles was wedged into that one all-service cultural space. The curated playlists and media silos of our current age bring their own thrills, but they miss the mass effect, the shared experience of radio that bound and brought people together. You'd hear a song debut on the radio and the next day at school everyone would be talking about it. Talking about what the words meant. Singing it in groups. Dancing to it.

As I grew older, music helped me understand and define complex emotions by expressing them for me and to me. I have a special affinity for soul music and its magical ability to express conflicting emotions simultaneously and beautifully, like sadness and joy. It helps me make sense of mixed feelings, and to live with the fact that we can be, and feel, many things at once. And that that's okay. I highly recommend soul music for these healing properties.

There's that question for those lucky enough to still have all of their senses: which one could you not live without? For me, without hesitation, it's hearing. Music is the most accessible and effective self-care. And I don't even want to fathom a world without the songs that help me not just get through, but celebrate life.

Steve Jordan grew up in Kingston, Ontario, where he started working in radio. After working in A&R for Warner Canada and True North Records, he founded the Polaris Music Prize, awarded annually for the best album by a Canadian artist; he is still executive director.

MULTI-DIRECTIONAL STEREO | AMP403B

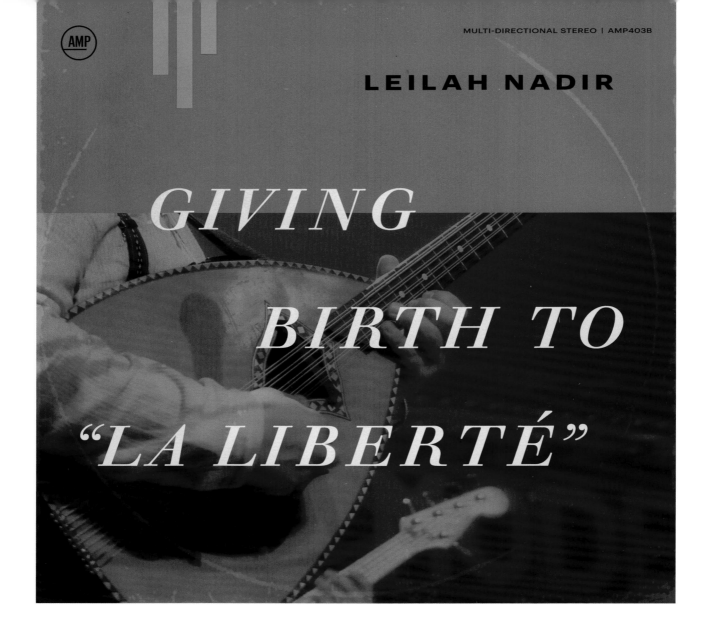

LEILAH NADIR

GIVING BIRTH TO "LA LIBERTÉ"

Opening yourself to let another life into this world, this existence, this earth is the most terrifying, electrifying, inexpressible experience there is. One moment a growing burden takes over your body, and the next, a child is here, whole, body and soul, an individual unlike any other. How to cross this threshold? How to trust your body to do the impossible? Bring in music and dance . . . My Iraqi great-grandmother and great-aunt were midwives in Baghdad, and I have to entice them, summon their ghosts to give me strength.

I want to birth my third child in the comfort of my home, with registered midwives, my husband, and a doula. Confident that my healthy pregnancy (though I am forty and taking insulin for gestational diabetes) will allow me to give birth safely, I know that in an emergency I can be at a hospital within ten minutes.

Those in the profession call third labours the wild cards that don't follow a pattern. The day before my due date, I am desperate to meet my baby. From my first two births, I know that having this baby is up to me. I expect acute pain at times, but when the baby is born there will be a joyful release. I'd forgotten my previous labour pain, but the ecstasy of allowing my baby through my body and into my arms is seared into me forever. I am still afraid—of pain, of unknown complications—but I know I have to let go, trust, and surrender.

In early labour, I bake a first birthday cake to distract myself and to give the midwives when the baby is born. As I lean on the kitchen counter and breathe through contractions, I measure and combine, stir, and whip the batter. The contractions deepen, and fear, excitement, and anticipation wash through me. The spicy, sweet aroma of baking fills the house, along with the lilting sounds of the Middle Eastern compilation we are listening to.

Then a sound pierces me. A grave, deep note announcing seriousness, demanding attention. The next low notes soar out from the strings, soulful, held and slowly releasing in rising anticipation. Tremulous, hesitating notes follow, a strained opening falling into relief. The melancholy minor key takes over and then the incredible, powerful, deep voice of Algerian rai singer Khaled overlays the strings, in Arabic, a language I don't understand. He sings of something earthy, yet otherworldly and profound. Then the percussion starts beating like my baby's heart, like my own heart pounding with excitement. It rises to a crescendo. Then the melody eases in and the French words "La Liberté" give over into a gentler rhythm. Excited, I sway, I move, I want to dance, I have to dance, I dance through pain. Uplifting rhythms give me confidence, the refrain of "La Liberté" is repeated, rising, and I want that. The liberty for my child to be born in comfort and hope, excitement and trust. The song goes on for five minutes and I have two contractions. I'm at the crescendo, when the contractions come like quick waves lapping at my body, bringing my baby through. Tears flow as this song unpeels me, bringing release.

> Excited, I sway, I move, I want to dance, I have to dance, I dance through pain. Uplifting rhythms give me confidence, the refrain of "La Liberté" is repeated, rising, and I want that.

But my baby is in the wrong position: face upward; the labour is jagged, not smooth. Irregular contractions make me work much harder. Then labour pauses, and my midwives suggest I rest until morning. They'll return. I'm shocked into action. Though apprehensive about what I know is approaching, I can't wait, I want to meet my child. The dancing joy chases down the fear. I muster my strength.

I climb stairs, dancing the baby out. The pain takes over, time slowing almost to a stop, I am hardly in the world. I slide in and out of my body, breathing through the pain, pushing and pulling, going to the brink of my endurance, like any athlete forcing their body to its limits. I cry out, I let go. Any inhibitions or shame of my nakedness is left behind as I put myself aside and make room for a new being.

All of a sudden, the baby is coming. I lie down, and within a few pushes she slides out. A perfect little girl is put on my chest. "There you are. You came. I knew you would," is all I say.

Leilah Nadir is a writer of fiction and non-fiction. Her memoir, *The Orange Trees of Baghdad,* was published in 2007 around the world. She lives in Vancouver and is working on a historical novel, *Sea of Gold and Clay.*

valerie fox

MOONDANCING

FULL SPECTRUM SOUND

In late 1971, at the age of seventeen, I reluctantly moved to Ottawa from Long Island, New York, with my parents, brother, and sister. I started attending Carleton University. A year went by and I was still having trouble adjusting to the culture.

Then one day, in early January 1973, I had an amazing dream about a guy with very long dark hair and a beard and the wings of a raven. In the dream he came through my bedroom window and scooped me up from my bed, and together we flew out into the world. It was breathtaking and exceptionally memorable, so I wrote it up in my journal.

A month or so later, to my surprise and delight, I was walking to a class at the university when I saw the very person from my dream, speaking to a group of his friends. I gathered up my courage and introduced myself to him, telling him all about my dream. That afternoon, I drove him and his friends to their house.

We saw each other the next day, and almost every day after that.

Gord lived in a house with six friends. When I visited him, his friends were usually there, too.

They would have music playing loudly on the turntable in the next room, and hockey blaring on at least three different TV sets (if there were that many games on). I wasn't a huge hockey fan so would likely be found in the next room, dancing away. I remember lighting a ton of candles and shadow dancing on the couches and chairs. My favourite song to dance to was "Moondance" by Van Morrison. I probably played that one a few too many times. I was lucky the games were on.

Gord and I got married a year later, in 1974, and after forty-four years of marriage with two wonderful kids and two gorgeous grandchildren, I still smile whenever I hear "Moondance."

Valerie Fox is a designer, creative director, and inventor. She is the co-founder of the DMZ at Ryerson University, and recently founded the Pivotal Point, a company that helps others grow innovation-rich environments that support a people-based economy. She is also a proud wife, mom, and grandmother.

maureen whittal | STEREO

walking on sunshine

The year was 1985. I was nineteen years old and living in Calgary. Since the age of ten, I had been into ten-pin bowling—not a cool sport, I know, but I really liked it and was good at it. I had been an Alberta girls provincial champion three times, and was heading into my last national tournament as a youth later that year, 1985. We had to raise money to pay our way to the tournament, which was in Montreal. I was also busy practicing, attending my first year of undergrad at the University of Calgary, and working part time at the local bowling alley. I recall the sadness as I parted with my complete set of Nancy Drew hardcover books, all to raise funds to go to Quebec.

That spring, I was skiing at Sunshine Mountain in the Rockies and doing nineteen-year-old things (read: things I had no business doing). As I landed a jump, my left elbow grazed the snow and I felt a jolt of pain shoot down my arm. At the emergency department in Calgary later that day, they couldn't determine the extent of the damage, but said I might have a break or a crack in the bones of my elbow. I am right-handed, but the other arm plays an important part in balancing when you bowl. If the damage was severe, I wouldn't be able to straighten my arm and would have to forfeit my position on the team.

After the requisite amount of time, I returned to the hospital for a follow-up X-ray. I was tense beyond belief as I sat in the waiting room. Going on this one last trip and representing my province meant so much to me. The X-ray showed that whatever was there had disappeared! There was still some rehabbing to do, but I was cleared to go.

I was so happy as I walked back to the parking lot. Alone in the car, I turned the radio on, and "Walking on Sunshine" by Katrina and the Waves blared out at me. That song, with its happy lyrics and bouncy melody, perfectly captured how I was feeling. It's so upbeat and so full of hope, just like me at that moment.

Hearing that song thirty-four years later brings me back to that spot as if it was yesterday. If I'm listening to the radio and "Walking on Sunshine" comes on, I smile and start singing along, and dancing, if the situation allows. It makes me feel nineteen again.

Maureen Whittal is a clinical psychologist who lives and works in Vancouver. She co-founded Anxiety Canada, a non-profit designed to provide evidence-based psychological information and treatment for people with anxiety disorders. The website receives over two million visits each year and the updated app, MindShift CBT, had 48,000 active users in the first month.

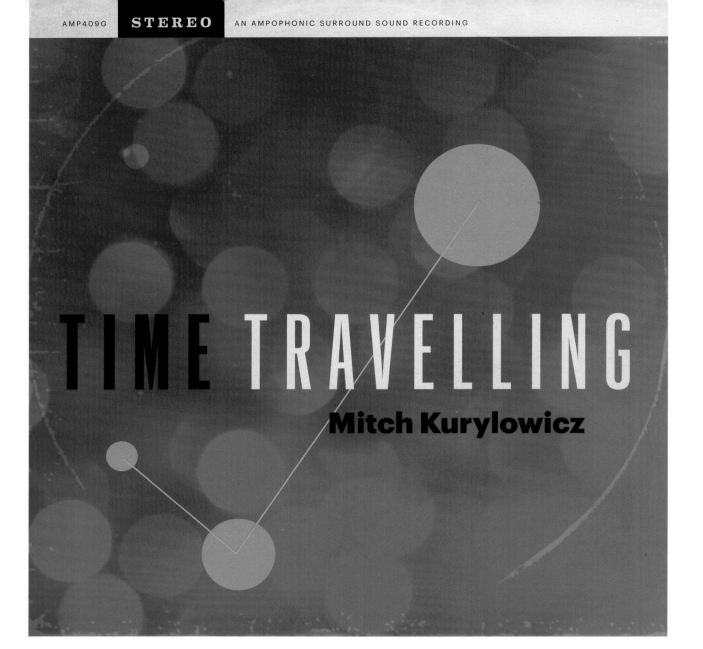

TIME TRAVELLING

Mitch Kurylowicz

Music allows me to time travel. I have songs on my iPhone that remind me of certain times and places in my life, often with no other connection than the fact that I was listening to that song at the time. I put one on and the sound just conjures up the memory—I'm instantly back in the Prius that I drove in high school, or a rustic hotel room in Tel Aviv, or a shipping-container-converted accommodation in Somalia.

In high school, for reasons I can't explain, my soundtrack was a Frank Sinatra compilation album from 2008: *Nothing but the Best*. Maybe it was the easy sound, the elegance, the alluring flow of it; even today I can sit down and listen to the whole thing, over an hour, and I'm back in that silver Prius winding through residential streets on the way to school.

Every song on Frank Ocean's *Channel Orange* takes me to Tel Aviv. I went there for a week-long

> **When I listen to *Zanaka* now, it reminds me of a place I love. And of optimism, in the sense that you can be in a place that is devastatingly underprivileged and war-torn, and still have moments of simple encouragement.**

conference on Israeli innovation at Tel Aviv University. What sticks out is having deeply thought-provoking academic discussions all day, then spending the evenings enjoying the vibrant Israeli culture and nightlife. Perhaps Ocean's mellow sound fused with the mellow vibe of Tel Aviv.

But my strongest musical memories are summoned up by *Zanaka*, an album by the French singer Jain. She spent her formative teenage years in the Congo, which she credits for her danceable melodies. Zanaka means "child" in Malagasy, the national language of Madagascar, and it's a perfect name for the album, which is very lively and optimistic.

I stumbled upon this album about a month before I departed for the UN's green zone in Mogadishu, Somalia. I was doing a market analysis for a company that ran the commercial operations, like grocery stores and restaurants, for aid workers and peacekeepers in war-torn areas. If I had been dropped off without knowing where I was, I surely would not have been able to place myself on a map. There were people in their fatigues representing countries from Africa, Europe, North America, and everywhere in between, all buying the same goods from the Italian company that ran the store. I was sitting behind the desk of one of our shops with the managers one day, discussing logistics, when I realized there was no music. So we put on *Zanaka*.

That album is just so upbeat, it encourages a sort of togetherness. Everyone who came into the store felt the power; it made them smile and step lighter, regardless of what was happening around them. When I listen to it now, it reminds me of the continent that inspired its lighthearted and sweet sound. It reminds me of a place I love. And of optimism, in the sense that you can be in a place that is devastatingly underprivileged and war-torn, and still have moments of simple encouragement.

That album stands the test of time, and not just because it still sounds good to me. The person who introduced me to it was my gram, who is now eighty years old. (I'm twenty-one.) That's how much it can bring people together—people from all over the world, and even within my own family.

Mitch Kurylowicz runs Make Luck History, a consulting firm that encourages social responsibility through profitable business opportunities and strategies. He is also the founder of Project Jenga, which has raised more than a million dollars for secondary education in Kenya, with the WE Movement. A public speaker, he has given two TEDx talks; he has also received the Governor General's Sovereign's Medal and the Mandela Legacy Award.

KICKING AT THE DARKNESS

Shekhar Gothi

I have always loved the Bruce Cockburn song "Lovers in a Dangerous Time," especially the slower Barenaked Ladies version, with its haunting bass interlude. The line "Kick at the darkness 'til it bleeds daylight" took on a whole new meaning when I was buried alive during the 2010 Haiti earthquake.

I deployed to Haiti in August 2009 as part of the Canadian military contingent in support of the United Nations stabilization mission. I was executive assistant to a Canadian colonel, who was military chief of staff for the UN mission and the third-highest military officer in the country.

The day of the quake, January 12, 2010, was like any other. I'd been in my office all afternoon. Around ten to five, I got up to get some fresh air.

We were on the ground floor of a six-storey building atop a hill. Our office door was a sliding glass panel, which I closed behind me as I stepped into the hallway. That's when everything started to shake. My vision blurred and my ears were pierced by a deafening roar. It's hard to describe the violent and unbelievable power of an earthquake. The whole building and everything within it was thrown side to side. The glass doors instantly evaporated into a million shards and everything went dark.

A local Haitian man was walking past me at that moment. He jumped on my back—I'm not sure if he meant to or was just propelled that way—and clung on to me. Within seconds we were both completely buried in debris and chunks of concrete, some the size of bowling balls. Luckily, where we were, the building crumbled into many fragmented pieces; in other places, like the neighbouring offices, whole slabs came down and crushed people to death, including some of our clerks.

We found ourselves in complete darkness, struggling to breathe. Debris and soot covered everything. There was no oxygen or sound, no power. We were essentially entombed in a semi-standing position; the only noise was this man screaming in Creole.

Military training kicked in and I went into crisis management mode. I don't know why, but "Lovers in a Dangerous Time" popped into my head. Not just symbolically—I actually kicked at the darkness so I could see daylight!

Time stood still. I may have been trapped for ten minutes or an hour, it was hard to tell. I got hit on the head by a lot of falling concrete, but didn't lose consciousness, thank God.

I struggled toward the front door but the exit there was completely sealed off. My injuries prevented me from walking, so I crawled back through my office and my boss's office. It was not easy; there were large steel filing cabinets squashed like pancakes everywhere. Concrete and mangled rebar cut my arms and legs. Somehow I made it out to the balcony and threw myself off. And again I was lucky, as some people below caught me. I had a contusion on my head the size of a kiwi, which I was unaware of until someone pointed it out to me.

When I was buried alive, the lyrics of Bruce Cockburn's song gave me inspiration as I struggled.

Six or seven hours later, I was put into a flatbed truck full of injured people and moved down to a makeshift casualty collection point near the airfield. That drive was an indescribable nightmare. I watched as the driver did his best to manoeuvre the massive truck around rubble and dead bodies in the darkness. That memory is forever burned into my mind.

The next morning I was medically evacuated on a UN transport helicopter to Santo Domingo in the Dominican Republic. A few days later I was on a plane back to Canada and, after one week, I returned to Port-au-Prince to rejoin the recovery effort.

I am fortunate that the post-traumatic struggles have not debilitated me as much as they have some of my comrades. I still rely on music every day. When I was buried alive, the lyrics of Bruce Cockburn's song gave me inspiration as I struggled: "One minute you're waiting for the sky to fall / The next you're dazzled by the beauty of it all." And "These fragile bodies of touch and taste / This fragrant skin, this hair like lace / Spirits open to the thrust of grace / Never a breath you can afford to waste."

When I think back on that fateful day, the lyric that resonates the loudest for me is "Nothing worth having comes without some kind of fight / Got to kick at the darkness 'til it bleeds daylight."

Lieutenant-Commander **Shekhar Gothi** is the innovation officer for Southern Ontario for Canadian Special Operations Forces Command (CANSOFCOM). He grew up in Thunder Bay, Ontario, and now lives in Toronto.

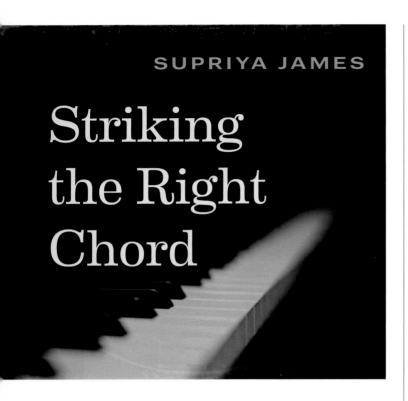

SUPRIYA JAMES

Striking the Right Chord

Music has always been an integral part of my life. In Georgetown, Guyana, where I was born and lived until I was thirteen years old, I was exposed to a musical mosaic of reggae, calypso, Bollywood, jazz, and Western pop. Our family home was often filled with throngs of guests, dancing and singing at the tops of their lungs at the elegant cocktail and dinner parties our parents hosted.

I quickly learned that music is everywhere: from the loud, harsh drops of the torrential Guyanese rainstorms hitting the loose stones on the ground to the swishing sounds made by the coconut palms in breezy weather.

I also learned that music is not just outside of us, it is also deeply within us.

A shy and lonely little girl, I would sometimes crouch down on my knees below our upright piano, put my tiny ear to its wooden case and listen to the loud vibrations produced while one of my sisters practiced. The muffled beats and sounds coming out of this huge, mysterious wooden box were inviting

and so comforting . . . which is not surprising, knowing that human life starts with the simplest of beats, our heartbeat.

As I got older, I too learned to play the classical piano, and soon felt a profound need to always have a piano close at hand, for enjoyment but also for peace of mind. To this day, after the children have finished their own piano practice and gone to bed and while my husband is hiding somewhere in the house watching hockey, if I still have the energy, I eagerly open the doors to our piano room and scurry onto the bench. My hands first take new and old sheets of music I am reading and greet them as if they are old friends, and then, with my fingers on black and white keys, my ears begin to tune into the musical sounds emanating from each piano key as they transport energy and light into my soul. A cleansing of sorts.

"To strike the right chord" is an expression I know only too well; those "right chords" can superbly lift my spirits or open the floodgates to an outpouring of frustrated tears. Both great spiritual releases.

When I am feeling overwhelmed or low in spirit, I head downstairs to our sauna, turn on the Bose speaker, and line up some music from my iPhone. In my isolation, in my naked, perspiring skin, I am humbled by the power and beauty of Beethoven's cello sonatas (No. 3 in A major is my favourite), Chopin's Nocturnes, or Rachmaninoff's Preludes. With its peaks and ebbs, this music breathes life into my every pore during this meditative state, and literally picks me up so that I can finish what I need to accomplish.

If I am feeling anxious or sad, to immediately switch to an upbeat mood I play my go-tos—more contemporary works with infectious beats, like The The's "This Is the Day" and "Uncertain Smile," with its exhilarating piano riff. This is when the dancing comes into play.

Supriya James is a communications consultant and music enthusiast who lives in Toronto. Her family, friends, piano, and art easel transport her to Heaven on Earth.

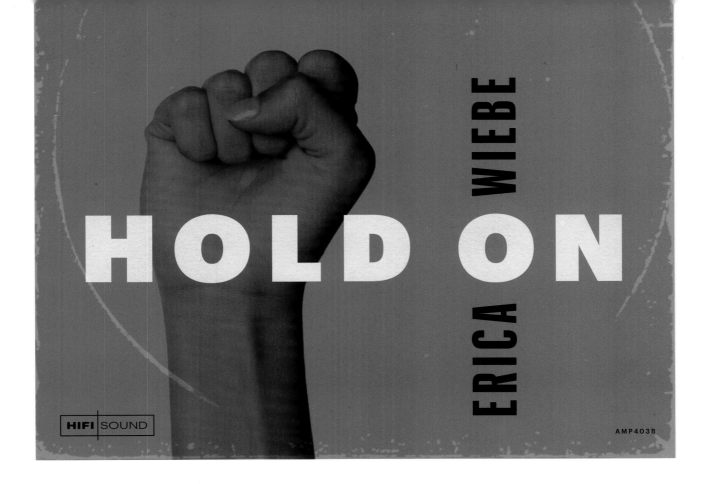

HOLD ON

ERICA WIEBE

HIFI|SOUND

AMP403B

Three weeks before I was set to step onto the mats at the Olympic Games, I couldn't even face myself in the mirror. Every time I looked into my own eyes I saw fear, uncertainty, doubt. I remember that day before practice so clearly. I felt something building inside me. How do you take one step deeper, beyond what you're capable of, physically, emotionally, mentally, each and every single day for a decade? How do you put it all on the line every one of those days with the almost overwhelming near-certainty of failure? I was pushing my body to its limits and feeling the weight of a nation's expectations on my shoulders.

What buoyed me through the darkest moments was music. One song captured the rawness of my emotions each day so beautifully, and lifted my spirits to step onto the mats at the Olympic Games and win a gold medal: "Hold On" by Sean Paul. That summer I had trained in Rio, and every day before practice,

I had walked into the building with the anthem of my journey blaring into my ears. It made me feel light and powerful, ten feet tall. The beat lifted me up and the lyrics gave me a pre-training pep talk every single day. I never tired of it.

When the day to compete at the Olympic Games finally came, I listened to the same song five times in a row on the bus ride to the arena. When I walked into the stadium, I already felt like a champion. All that was left was to enjoy the day as it unfolded.

Erica Wiebe is a wrestler from Stittsville, Ontario, who now lives and trains in Calgary. She is the reigning Olympic champion in women's 75 kg freestyle, having won gold at the 2016 Olympics. She is also the current Commonwealth Games champion in the same weight class, winning gold at both in 2014 and 2018.

mental health in canada by the numbers

1

35,500+

Patients who are treated for mental health issues in a single year at Toronto's Centre for Addiction and Mental Health. CAMH provides emergency care, inpatient, and outpatient treatment and specialized services for children, youth, families, adults, and seniors. It's also a leading centre for brain science research, focusing on genetics, molecular medicine, brain imaging, and new drug development.

source: CAMH

3

$29 billion

Prescription medications are the second most costly component of health care in Canada, accounting for almost 14 percent ($29 billion) of Canada's annual health care spending in 2013. For both men and women aged twenty-five to forty-nine, antidepressants are the number one prescribed medication.

source: Statistics Canada

2

4,000+

People who die by suicide in Canada annually—approximately eleven every day. Men are three times more vulnerable than women, and suicide is the second-leading cause of death for Canadians aged fifteen to thirty-four.

source: Government of Canada

MUSIC AND

MUSIC & THE BRAIN

**MICHAEL H. THAUT &
CORENE P. HURT-THAUT**

THE BRAIN

Biomedical researchers have found that music is a highly structured auditory language involving complex perception, cognition, and motor control in the brain.

The role of music in therapy and as therapy has gone through some dramatic shifts in the past twenty years, driven by new insights from research into music and brain function. These shifts are beginning to enter more and more into public awareness, and major health care providers are increasingly using music-based treatment techniques for neurorehabilitation and neurodevelopment.

Biomedical researchers have found that music is a highly structured auditory language involving complex perception, cognition, and motor control in the brain and thus can effectively be used to re-train and re-educate the injured brain. While the first data showing these results were met with skepticism and even some resistance, over time the consistent accumulation of scientific and clinical research evidence has removed this doubt.

While the notion that music has healing powers over mind and body has ancient origins, its formal use as therapy emerged in the middle of the twentieth century. At that time, music therapists thought of their work as rooted in social science: the art had value as therapy because it performed a variety of social and emotional roles in a society's culture. In this early therapy, music was used, as it had been down the ages, to foster emotional expression and support; help build personal relationships; create and facilitate positive group behaviours; represent symbolically beliefs and ideas; and support other forms of learning. In the clinic, patients listened to music or played it together with the therapists or other patients to build relationships, promote well-being, express feelings, and interact socially.

During the past two decades, new brain imaging and electrical recording techniques have come together to reshape our view of music in therapy and education. Techniques such as functional magnetic resonance imaging (fMRI), positron emission tomography (PET), electroencephalography (EEG), and magnetoencephalography (MEG) allowed us for the first time to watch the living human brain while people were doing complex cognitive and motor tasks. Now it was possible to perform brain studies of perception, cognition, and performance in music.

After years of such research, three findings now stand out as particularly important in regards to using music in rehabilitation and developmental therapy. First, the brain areas music activates are not unique to music; the networks that process music are generic control networks that also process other functions. Second, music learning changes the brain. Third, brain processes in music perception, cognition, and production can be translated to non-musical domains with clinical benefits.

The brain areas involved in music are also active in processing language, auditory perception, attention, memory, executive control, and motor control. Music efficiently accesses and activates these shared systems and can drive complex patterns of interaction among these systems. For example, an area near the front of the brain is activated when a person processes a problem in the syntax of a sentence or in a musical piece, such as a wrong note in a melody. This region, called Broca's area, after the French neurologist who described it in the nineteenth century, is also important in processing the sequencing of physical movement and in tracking musical rhythms, and is critical for converting thought into spoken words. Scientists propose, therefore, that Broca's area supports the appropriate timing, sequencing, and rule knowledge that are common and essential to music, speech, and movement.

A key example of the second finding, that music learning changes the brain, comes from research clearly showing that, through such learning, auditory and motor areas in the brain grow larger and interact more efficiently. After novice players have just a few weeks of piano training, the areas in their brain serving hand control become larger and more connected. Music—it quickly became clear—can drive plasticity in the human brain, shaping it through training and learning.

Third, brain processes underlying music perception, cognition, and production can not only shape musical responses but can also engage and shape responses that can change non-musical functions in motor control, language, and cognition, such as attention, memory, or executive function. Auditory rhythm can entrain movement and lead to better motor recovery. Musical cues can help retrain auditory attention. Melodic and rhythmic patterns can bootstrap non-musical information and become a mnemonic device to improve memory acquisition and retention (the "ABC song model").

These discoveries changed fundamentally how research, especially in neuroscience, could formulate and test new hypotheses about clinical applications and underlying neural mechanisms for music-based intervention systems. This new research area is often referred to as the study of the clinical neuroscience of music and the clinical translations of this research have been standardized in the evidence-based treatment system of neurologic music therapy.

This development can be illustrated in one of our most recent research studies, in which we decided to investigate the neural basis for potential preservation of musical memory and how triggering musical memories affects functional intra-brain network connectivity in Alzheimer's disease. Alzheimer's disease is a progressive neurodegenerative disorder estimated to affect almost thirty million people worldwide, a number projected to triple by 2050. In spite of substantial research to find a cure or effective treatment, existing treatments have been only modestly beneficial and newer experimental treatments have proven to date unsuccessful. It has long been understood that cognitive reserve capacity, generated by increased cortical development and higher cognitive demands throughout one's life, can result in resilience to neuropathological damage. Interestingly, behavioural evidence has shown that musical memories and associated autobiographical memories are often significantly longer preserved in Alzheimer's disease cases than non-musical memories. However, the brain mechanisms for this preservation effect are unknown. Without understanding underlying brain mechanisms, it is challenging to propose and apply music as a consistent therapeutic intervention.

Therefore, our study proceeded in two steps. First, we investigated via fMRI potential structural and functional differences between memory networks for long-known music (twenty-plus years) and music first heard only sixty minutes before brain scanning, which was newly composed. This step was meant to assess if there are specific brain network characteristics for long-known music that may explain why old musical memories are better preserved than other non-musical memories. This step would also serve as the foundation for the second step to test if interactive musical memory

Music can drive plasticity in the human brain, shaping it through training and learning.

exercises modulate brain function and thus could lead to the development of effective music-based memory interventions.

We found a significantly more extensive and widely distributed cortical and subcortical network for the long-known music, including cognitive, affective, auditory, language, and motor regions in both hemispheres. Briefly familiar music (known for sixty minutes) activated some of the same regions, but mostly only in one hemisphere, and showed only small activations in prefrontal executive and subcortical and non-motor regions. Interestingly, long-known music stimulated much stronger activations in both brain hemispheres than sixty-minute-old musical memories.

These preliminary findings provide strong first evidence why brain networks for long-term musical memories—by involving significantly more extended brain tissue and activating areas that are at least initially spared by the disease process, such as in subcortical regions—may be preserved in spite of the disease progression and thus may remain relatively intact and accessible for longer periods of time.

After three weeks of daily musical memory exercises to stimulate musical and associated autobiographical memories, fMRI imaging showed a significant increase in resting state connectivity between brain regions. Resting state network connectivity measures information flow between different brain regions, and reduced connectivity is an important indicator of brain pathology. Enhanced connectivity after musical engagement may suggest that the musical memory stimulation activated a neural mechanism to provide for—at least temporarily—cognitive boosts in those affected by Alzheimer's disease. Subjects were asked to listen for thirty minutes to playlists of their favourite long-known music and remember the music and life events associated with the music in interaction with family members or caregivers. These findings offer encouraging evidence that memory-based music interventions may modulate brain plasticity and boost cognitive functions in Alzheimer's disease.

To summarize, in the past twenty-five years, research in the basic and clinical neuroscience of music has discovered many transfer functions that show how music- and rhythm-based therapeutic exercises can assist in brain rehabilitation. Research has shown breakthrough results for motor recovery, speech, and language training, and cognitive-affective rehabilitation. By adapting a scientific theory model of studying the brain basis of music perception and cognition, these non-musical transfer functions of music have been well documented for many diagnoses, such as stroke, Parkinson's disease, traumatic brain injury, dementia, autism, and developmental disabilities. Research into other diagnoses, especially in mental health, shows encouraging beginnings. The clinical techniques have been standardized and codified since 1999 in neurologic music therapy, which operates on different scientific theory and clinical foundations than traditional music therapy and generic music and health practice.

Michael H. Thaut, PhD, and **Corene P. Hurt-Thaut**, PhD, are faculty of music in the Music and Health Research Collaboratory (MaHRC) at the University of Toronto.

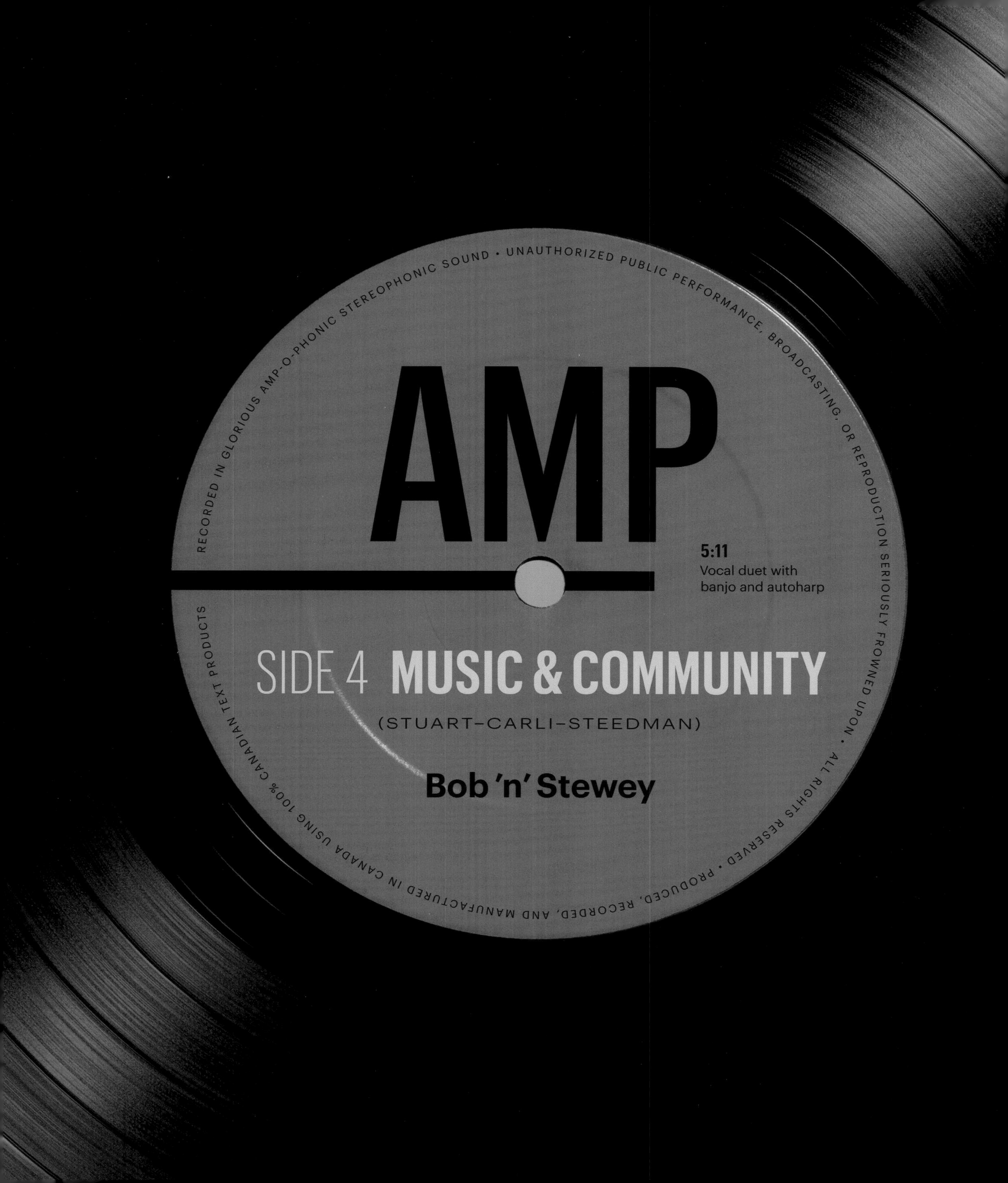

RECORDED IN GLORIOUS AMP-O-PHONIC STEREOPHONIC SOUND • UNAUTHORIZED PUBLIC PERFORMANCE, BROADCASTING, OR REPRODUCTION SERIOUSLY FROWNED UPON • ALL RIGHTS RESERVED • PRODUCED, RECORDED, AND MANUFACTURED IN CANADA USING 100% CANADIAN TEXT PRODUCTS
AMP
5:11
Vocal duet with
banjo and autoharp
SIDE 4 MUSIC & COMMUNITY
(STUART–CARLI–STEEDMAN)
Bob 'n' Stewey

LONG PLAYER LP

AMP9730 | BINAURAL MONO
RECORDED ON LOCATION IN FIJI

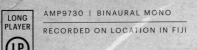

Tariq Hussain

SPINNING SONGS

Our new turntable arrived on the back of a moving truck, and it took two men to carry it into the house. I was barely in kindergarten so I was home when the men showed up and set it in place in our living room. Contained within a giant wooden cabinet, it looked more like a storage trunk than something to play music on, but that's how some home stereos looked back then, disguised to seem like furniture.

On weekends my mother would play her favourite records on the turntable while cooking supper. I'd relax whenever I saw the lid of the stereo propped open because I knew my father would cancel our lessons in Islam for the afternoon. Instead of reciting passages from the onion-skinned pages of his Koran, he'd join my mother in the kitchen and they'd cook together and sing along with the music. The house would fill up with the smell of fried onions and garlic and the sounds of Mohammed Rafi and Lata Mangeshkar—who sang on pretty much every one of those records—and I would be reminded that spontaneous celebration was still possible in our house and that the world didn't have to feel so weighty and serious all the time.

Most of the records belonged to my mother—hers was a modest collection of Indian movie soundtracks and singles. A few albums had been sent over by my grandmother "back home" in Fiji and had come in boxes along with packets of masalas and bottles of achaars. Sometimes, when no one was looking, I'd steal glances at the album sleeves my mother had left spread out on the carpet, pictures of curvy women and moustachioed men gazing into each other's eyes, lips close but never touching. Once my father caught me stepping over one of his Qawwali records—a sign of disrespect—and threatened me with a "good hiding" until my mother intervened and redirected his focus back to the music.

My mother had her favourite records and, with constant repetition, I learned to mumble along with a half dozen songs by imitating the sound of the Hindi words. For instance, one duet always sounded like: "*Kone a see hay woe cheese e Joe, ya han a hay mill tee.*" I couldn't speak Hindi but my mother would translate the lyrics of different songs for me in real time as they played. She'd hold up her hand for attention while listening and say something like: "The singer is singing about fate in this part," or "Here, he's reminding us that nothing is more important than love."

Sometimes my mother got so into the music she'd spin across the kitchen tiles in her knitted slippers with the elegance of an Olympic figure skater, gliding and stepping to the beat, pausing only to stir a pot on the stove. Once, she tied cloths to her slippered feet and began buffing the kitchen floor, swinging her hips back and forth, propelling herself wildly from one side of the kitchen to the other until she could no longer contain her own amusement and burst into a fit of giggles.

My mother had one album in her collection, *Isa Lei, Traditional Music of Fiji*, from which I learned

> **Sometimes my mother got so into the music she'd spin across the kitchen tiles in her knitted slippers with the elegance of an Olympic figure skater.**

about another style of music altogether. Ukuleles and slide guitars were the instruments of choice on this recording, or else the singers sang a cappella in either English or Fijian. One of the more poignant songs, the title track "Isa Lei," featured the multi-layered vocals of the Adi Cakobau Girls' Choir. On weekdays, if my father was at work, my mother would turn up the volume on the stereo, and while the rugs and copper plates rattled on their hooks on the walls, she'd close her eyes and join in with the choir, singing along as if she were summoning up the ocean to meet her at the front the porch of our small Quebec home, singing as if the carpet beneath her feet had been transformed into the warm, white sandy shores of her beloved South Pacific Island.

My mother's songs continued to play in my head long after the lid had gone down on the stereo on another weekend listening session. And even years later, after rock 'n' roll came into focus and I tried shedding pieces of my brown-ness bit by bit like a moulting animal, those songs remained in my cells, in my DNA, playing somewhere in the background, connecting me to something larger than myself.

Tariq Hussain is a Juno-nominated songwriter and guitarist. He grew up in Quebec and now lives in Vancouver, where he teaches creative writing at UBC and plays guitar with the band Brasstronaut.

ALAN TWIGG
MAPLE LEAF FOREVER

◄— STEREO —►

In recent years I broke up with Joni, but I remain faithful to Leonard. Leonard Cohen and I go way back. He was my musical best man in the eleventh grade. That was the year Tara came to our high school. We would sit on the floor of her parents' living room listening to Leonard Cohen droning on the hi-fi, smoking Old Port wine–tipped cigarillos. I would serenade her with barely passable renditions of "Suzanne" and "Hey, That's No Way to Say Goodbye." I still can't fingerpick properly. But I intend to be of enormous value in the nursing home when we're all on rocking chairs, trying desperately to recall the final verse of "One of Us Cannot Be Wrong."

Tara and I were married. I became a literary journalist. Leonard came to town for an interview. It was like meeting an old friend. I related to his Eeyore world view. He said many memorable things that day, my favourite being, "A book is a small thing in this world." I loved his sense of humour.

Afterward I called Tara and we all went for a walk in Stanley Park. We ate popcorn at English Bay. In retrospect, there was something ceremonial going on. Dressed in a dark suit, as always, Leonard was a ministerial figure. He posed obediently for pictures. Leonard and I were standing side by side when he picked up a large maple leaf. He twirled it, then slipped its stem under his belt. He became Adam. It was a spontaneous joke. He posed blank-faced. As Canadian as maple syrup.

I still have that photo. It's the only photo I keep on my office wall. There's my pal, Leonard Cohen, with a maple leaf covering his crotch. I'm the intrepid, shoddily dressed squinting young journalist who shouldn't be in the same picture.

Now my teenage son is at the same age I was at when I met his mother. From the basement, amid blasts of Pearl Jam and the Screaming Trees, I hear Leonard's voice. My son's friends like him, they dig the words. He is, apparently, still cool.

Thanks, Leonard. Our household thanks you. Our street thanks you. Our neighbourhood thanks you. You are in our hearts. You are in our basements. We're proud of you. You have given us much pleasure. (For a desert island classic, I'd probably pick "Song of Bernadette," Jennifer Warnes's version.) Now you're dead, we dangle icons of you from rear-view mirrors.

Alan Twigg is a writer, journalist, and biographer who lives in Vancouver. A member of the Order of Canada, he received the Lieutenant Governor's Award for Literary Excellence in 2016. Twigg founded and edits *BC BookWorld*, Canada's largest circulation publication on books.

ANNEKE BRUINSMA-FINDLAY

WEEKENDS

I'm nine years old and it's a snowy Sunday morning. The floury smell of hot pancakes wafts up the stairwell, ushered into my sleepy consciousness by the gay opening saxophones and rolling drums of "Rosalita (Come Out Tonight)," by Bruce Springsteen and the E Street Band. Downstairs, my father is busily whisking batter, sizzling butter, and flipping pancakes onto a warming stack in the oven, pausing only to play the occasional enthusiastic drum solo on the countertop, or boom out a lament about his dud of a machine stuck in the mud somewhere in the swamps of Jersey. As "Rosalita" builds, I am cut loose from sleep's reins. Joined by Little Dynamite and Little Gun, we three sisters jump a little lighter down the stairs.

Brimming with youthful energy, unbridled possibility, and colourful characters like Sloppy Sue and Weak Knees Willie, "Rosalita" weaves a heartwarming tale about staying true to yourself and following your dreams in the face of uncertainty and adversity. Through "Rosalita," I am fondly reminded of my father and how he still encourages my sisters and me to be guided by these cardinal principles as we live our lives.

Anneke Bruinsma-Findlay studied law at Queen's University, with one semester at Fudan University in Shanghai. After practicing corporate law in Toronto for some time, she returned to China to pursue further education.

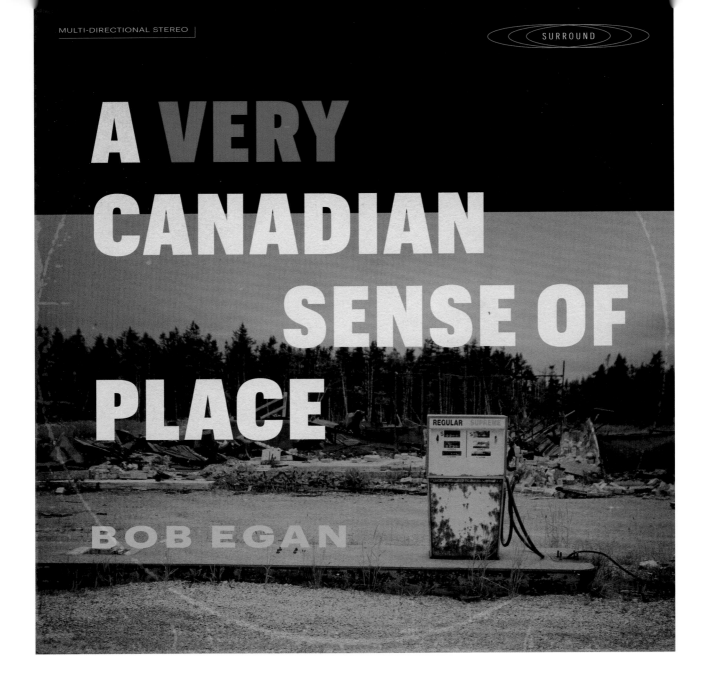

A VERY CANADIAN SENSE OF PLACE

BOB EGAN

When I was a pre-teen, my family moved a lot. I went to four different grade schools by the age of ten. I never fit in and was always the outsider... until I discovered music. At age twelve I received a twenty-nine-dollar guitar that changed my life forever. All of a sudden I had purpose: to learn and get better. I had connection: to other musicians and to listeners. I had belonging: people wanted to

hang out with me. I had identity: I was a musician now. I had comfort: music was a constant companion. And I had perspective: I was part of the fraternity of musicians that spanned history and the world. But most importantly, I had hope, as I saw the power of music to change lives and heal the world.

As a teen, music saved my life. When the depression set in hard, music was a lifeline that kept me from running away or harming myself or worse. I don't believe I would be here today without it. Music was the beacon in my bleakness.

As I aged and performed more frequently, I often saw the power of music in very stark terms. There was the call from Australia from a fellow who decided not to "take a header off the bridge" after hearing one of my songs that gave him hope. There was the night I had a peak musical experience in the recording studio, then stepped outside to gaze at the stars and cried tears of gratefulness that I was simply alive. There were the thousands of people who told me how the music of Blue Rodeo moved them, changed them, and even saved their lives.

Then there was "Bobcaygeon" by the Tragically Hip.

In 1999, the Hip flew me up from my home in Mississippi to their studio outside of Kingston, Ontario, to play on their *Phantom Power* record. I worked with them for a few days, then flew home and got back to my life as a starving (literally) solo artist. The memory of those sessions faded. The next year Blue Rodeo sent a van to Mississippi to move me to Toronto. After a long delay at the border I was finally allowed to enter Canada to begin my new life as a well-paid musician. When I got back in the van, "Bobcaygeon," a single from *Phantom Power*, came on the radio and at first I did not remember or recognize it. Then I heard the steel guitar I had recorded years ago and couldn't believe it—the first song I heard on Canadian soil was one I'd played on. When the DJ announced it as the Juno-award-winning single of the year I had a transformative experience; I felt like I was at home, that I had arrived, for the first time in my life.

What moves me about the song "Bobcaygeon"? Maybe it's the sense of place, from the Kawarthas to the Horseshoe Tavern, which still strikes me as being very Canadian. Or the name-checking of Willie Nelson.

I never fit in and was always the outsider... until I discovered music. At age twelve I received a twenty-nine-dollar guitar that changed my life forever.

Or the loping nature of the rhythm. It just feels so personal, which obviously connects to many, many people. That's what I like best—that it really resonated with Canadians.

Over the years I came to know Gord Downie a bit. He inspired me to treat others well and to help other musicians in any way that I could. Seventeen years later Gord would play the last show of his life in Kingston. On that very night in Toronto, I played my last show with Blue Rodeo and we paid tribute to Gord by performing "Bobcaygeon."

To this day "Bobcaygeon" serves as a constant reminder to live up to the example that Gord Downie set to make this world a better place for all.

Bob Egan is the manager of community development at the Kitchener Public Library in Kitchener, Ontario. Born in Chicago, he spent more than twenty years playing in bands, including Freakwater and Wilco, before moving to Canada to join Blue Rodeo in 2000.

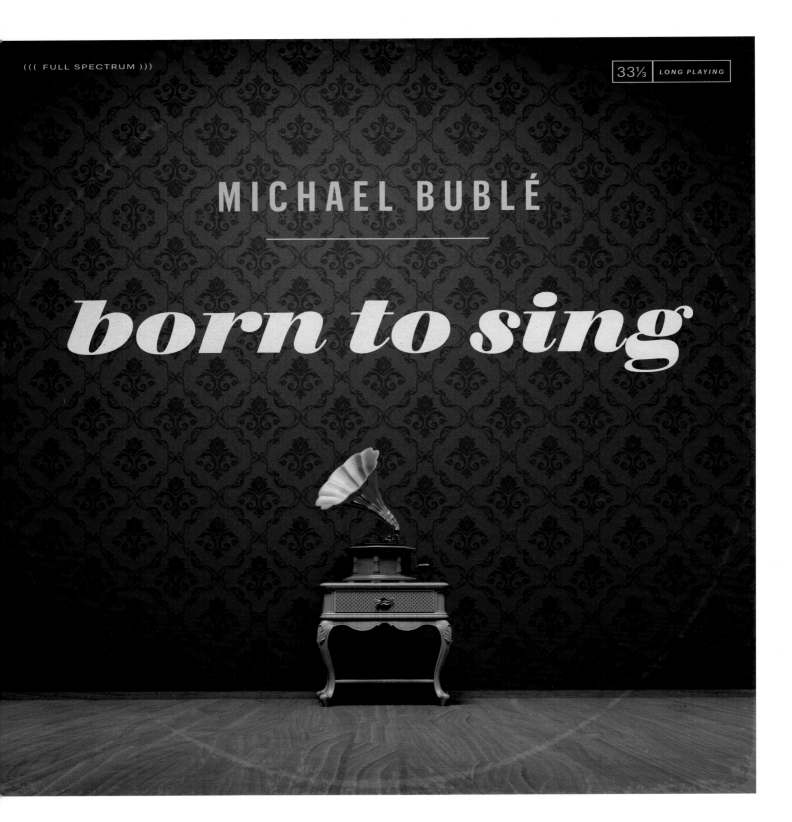

My maternal grandfather, Mitch Santaga, was responsible for introducing me to the old American standards, usually sung by Italian immigrants like my own family—crooners like Tony Bennett, Frank Sinatra, and Dean Martin. With Italian families, there is a genuine warmth and a lot of love, tactile, hands-on love. We love our family, our food, and our music. Grandpa Mitch loved those old singers, and he taught me to love them, too.

When I was little, I'd spend every day of my summer holidays with my grandpa Mitch. I'd go to his house and listen to old records on his 1970s-era RCA console, lying on the green carpet in his living room. He'd bring out his Mills Brothers or Brook Benton records, and we'd play them, old vinyl records that would hiss and skip. When I heard those golden voices, it was like I'd entered a place and time that made more sense to me than any of the contemporary songs my friends were listening to. Sure, I liked the bands that were big when I was a teenager, Guns N' Roses and Metallica, but I idolized the way the old-time singers could phrase a few poignant words so that they stayed with you long after the music had stopped playing. It was my first understanding of what it meant to make great art, which is to capture a feeling, be it the bitter pain of despair or the sweet bliss of being in love. And they did it with such style, too. This wasn't sloppy sentimentalism. This was straight-up delivery, and those guys could swing. My grandpa's passion for that music kick-started my own, and it has bonded us for life.

Unlike with a lot of performers, my career journey has not been solitary. My family has been with me every step of the way. It's basically been a joint project. For example, when I was recording *Crazy Love*, my fourth album, my grandpa Mitch, grandma Yolanda, mom, dad, two sisters, their husbands, and kids hung out for the day and watched me record multiple takes of the "Stardust" track. It was my niece Jade's birthday, so my mom brought along a big chocolate cake, my grandma Yolanda made her traditional lasagna, and my grandpa brought his homemade wine. Having them there, in Bryan Adams's Warehouse Studio in Vancouver, was like a typical Sunday in our household, filled with food and banter.

Every so often that day I'd look through the glass and see my grandpa Mitch sitting there, moving his lips to the lyrics he knew so well. "Stardust," recorded by Bing Crosby and everybody else back in the day, is one of his favourite old tunes. The pride on his face was unmistakable.

I come from a long line of fishermen, working-class men who worked hard and devoted themselves to family. They're macho Italian men, and they're proud of what they've earned. But they're not men who are afraid to show their emotions. As soon as I finished "Stardust," I rushed into the room and grabbed my grandpa's face between both hands. He put his arm around me and his eyes were moist: "This life you have, Michael, it's crazy. Crazy."

If I ever need a reminder of what I've accomplished, all I have to do is look at my grandpa's face when I'm singing. The only difference now is that we might not be sitting in his living room listening to the old RCA. Now, we're just as likely to be in a fancy recording studio or backstage at Madison Square Garden.

Michael Bublé is a Canadian singer, songwriter, actor, and record producer. He has won four Grammys and thirteen Junos, had three *Billboard*-topping albums, and sold more than fifty-five million albums worldwide.

QUADROPHONIC

"BLOW UP" AT THE EL MO

angeline ico

as studying, and sitting on the student association. Now I suddenly found myself in co-op housing in the centre of downtown Toronto with a whole bunch of friends. I was free to do all these things!

Discovering a whole new community, people I'd never hung out with before, was really exciting. So was really exploring the nightlife for the first time. The El Mo was comforting because they played great music I knew. It felt like a homecoming.

"The Passenger" is a thumping, simple song. It's very raw, like all the music at the El Mo. And so optimistic; it was all "made for you and me," Iggy sings. They always played it at peak time; we would all run onto the dance floor, you had to be in the centre of it all when that song came on. Everyone got happy.

On that packed dance floor, I once found myself thanking my parents for everything they'd done for me: moving to Canada from the Philippines three decades earlier as a young betrothed couple; bringing me up in a loving house in the suburbs of Toronto; and at that moment, playing '60s and '70s soul and rock music when I was a kid. I knew half the songs the DJ spun, all those early Rolling Stones hits and classic Motown numbers, because my dad owned the LPs.

"Blow Up" at the El Mo; I haven't found a like night that in the city since, but I'm grateful for all the experiences that magical place brought me.

Singin' la-la-la-la-la-la-la-la, la-la-la-la-la-la-la-la . . .

Whenever I hear Iggy Pop's "The Passenger," I can't help but be taken back to hot, sweaty Saturday nights at the El Mocambo club on Spadina in the early 2000s. "Blow Up" at the El Mo— as we called it—was Toronto's mod music night years before the Mod Club opened up on College Street. I'd frequent this second-floor oasis with my besties.

I was in my fourth year as an undergrad at Ryerson University then, and had finally saved up enough money and convinced my parents I should move out. I'd been commuting from the family home in Mississauga, spending two to three hours every day on the bus and the subway, working two jobs as well

Angeline Ico grew up in Mississauga, Ontario, and now lives in Toronto. She is the national innovation manager at Deloitte Canada.

MULTICHANNEL SOUND   AMPOPHONIC 178B

The prairie landscape of Southern Saskatchewan provided very few indicators of what a queer life would look like in the early '90s, or if it would ever be accepted at all. The only immediate references to anything "queer" were the playground taunts of "fag" and "homo" that would cause any young person questioning their sexual identity to skip a heartbeat or two, even if the jabs were not aimed directly at them. Burrowing myself deep into the closet and rationalizing my attraction to other boys as simple curiosity about how I might measure up (it's interesting what you can convince yourself of when you are young and terrified), I played my best straight man all through the theatre of adolescence.

Fortunately I had a brother five years older who, though I don't believe he suspected I was gay at the time, introduced me to a couple of things that I could quietly latch onto, and which helped me navigate these years.

Kids in the Hall was on well past my bedtime, but my brother would come up to my room draped in his duvet, hide me underneath it (me bear hugging him from behind, legs wrapped around his and standing on his feet) and sneak me past mom in the kitchen and down into the basement, where Scott Thompson and the other Kids would alter my perception of the

world with their unapologetic queer characters and outlandish skits.

The other small treasure he gave to me in 1992, when the Rheostatics released their album *Whale Music*. The fourth track, simply titled "Queer," is a letter from a boy to his older brother, after the elder sibling had been kicked out of the house by their father and had run away to another town, after dad discovered he was gay. Loyal, loving, and pissed at his dad, the boy writes a letter that is a touching gesture of acceptance; the line about how he wishes his brother had been there to see the day he scored a hat trick against the team that called him a "fucking queer" sends a shiver through me to this day.

While it would still be years before I would directly confront my sexuality, this song's overt handling of the subject and its fuck-you defiance in the face of that homophobic town elevated me, and the sentiment of brotherly love and loyalty was and is something I strongly hold on to.

Shaun Brodie is the artistic director of the Queer Songbook Orchestra, a Toronto-based twelve-piece chamber pop ensemble dedicated to exploring and uplifting queer narrative in pop music.

tian-yuan zhao

SPARKING MY ENTREPRENEURIAL SPIRIT

During my first year of university I founded a choir called Tales of Harmonia. I was studying industrial engineering and had been a musician since I was eight, playing the piano and the trombone and singing in various choirs. There were three major choirs at the University of Toronto, but they each focused on one genre of music: classical, jazz, or pop. I've always been an interdisciplinary thinker, so I decided that if there weren't any high-quality choirs that sang in more than one genre, I'd create my own. If you can beat them, then don't join them! I sort of reversed the age-old adage.

That summer back in Winnipeg, where I grew up from age five (I was born in China), I arranged my first songs for the choir. They were mostly from unconventional sources, like "Leaves from the Vine," from the cartoon *Avatar: The Last Airbender*, and "Fiat Lux," from the anime adaptation of *Tales of Symphonia*, a Japanese role-playing game. I was especially proud of that song because it satisfied a small dream of mine: it's a classical-type song but from my all-time favourite video game series, and it's from an obscure and underrated source. I also came up with an arrangement I called "The Meow Mix," a medley of songs about cats that included "The Cat Came Back," "Smelly Cat" from *Friends*, "Soft Kitty" from the sitcom *The Big Bang Theory* and "Everybody Wants to Be a Cat" from *The Aristocats*.

Every year our repertoire grew. We went from a cappella songs to ones accompanied by a piano, then to including a beat boxer, and we even ended up with our very own mini-orchestra. I was both managing and conducting; it was a massively rewarding and revealing experience. As I added people one by one, I ended up forming a dream team of executives, who I would eventually pass the direction on to.

My proudest moment was a concert a few months after I'd stepped down. There was an orchestra with thirty members, plus another thirty in the choir. It took place inside a beautiful venue called the Church of the Redeemer by Bloor Street and Avenue Road. Seeing all that come to fruition was a zenith in my life with the choir. It was breathtaking and awe-inspiring to watch it all from the sidelines.

One of its longtime members, Sarah Wensley, was incredibly introverted when she first joined the choir but through it was able to gain self-confidence. Imagine my face when her mother told me, "You've really brought her out of her shell." I was only twenty at the time and had never thought I'd be able to have that sort of profound impact on someone's life. I grew up an only child and for most of my early life was bullied, which didn't make me very confident, either.

This entire experience sparked my entrepreneurial spirit, as well as my curiosity about tech and innovation. Growing up I hated business, which I thought was full of greed, and was ambivalent about tech. Now I work in the blockchain industry. I've

> During my teenage years, I would often air-conduct the songs I listened to; I was dreaming of conducting a real-life group of musicians.

travelled the world, digital-nomaded around, participated in countless hackathons and fellowships, and am only one degree away from some of the most influential people in tech and entrepreneurship, thanks to my membership of the Thiel Foundation and the 1517 Fund community. I never thought that I'd end up pursuing all these things in the worlds of tech, startups, and entrepreneurship.

During my teenage years, I would often air-conduct the songs I listened to; I was dreaming of conducting a real-life group of musicians. Seeing Tales of Harmonia come to fruition was what led me into blockchain, design, and social impact, because it allowed me to realize my dream and learn that I want to create scalable, sustainable, and systemic impact. And because I saw how I was able to change people's lives with the simple vibrating of air between vocal chords. It's been nothing short of invigorating!

Tian-Yuan Zhao was born by the Yellow River, grew up by the Red River, and works in the blockchain industry by the Great Lakes. The choir he founded, Tales of Harmonia, was awarded the Outstanding Cultural Arts Award by the University of Toronto Students' Union.

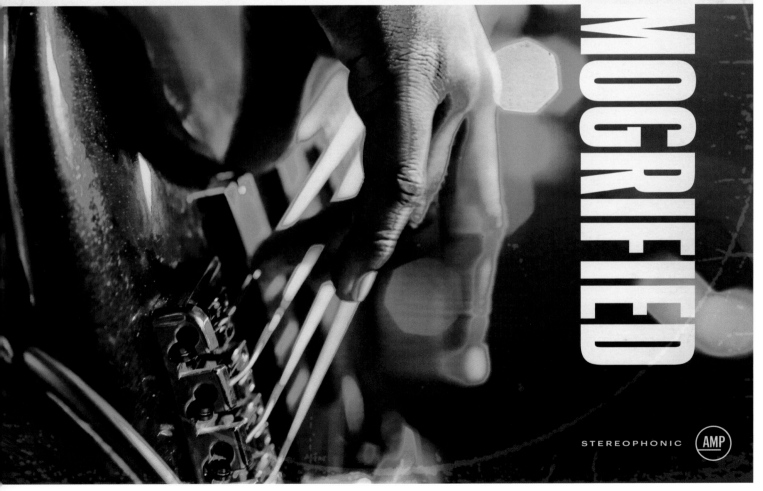

MARK MACARTHUR

TRANSMOGRIFIED

STEREOPHONIC AMP

I've been up here on stage at the Night Gallery for a torturous amount of time. It's winter, but despite the minus-thirty-degree Calgary temperature outside, the stage has been slow-cooking for hours under ferocious stage lights. It's already uncomfortable. A cheerfully expectant crowd have been milling about at the front, having ditched their winter coats and hoodies for T-shirts long ago. Most are now well warmed by their fourth drink. They're getting restless but it's nothing compared to how antsy I am, having enthusiastically and prematurely jumped on stage to tune my bass guitar, re-tie my shoelaces with mandatory double knots, and stretch in anticipation of high kicks and wildly errant jumps. Now all I can do is pace. I glance at my best friend, Aaron, who's grinning back at me at me wildly over his guitar, and Joel, who is calmly fiddling with his drumheads. We're still waiting for the house lights to go out. Still waiting for Andrew, our front man, to climb onto the stage.

This is the second-best part of the night.

At last. Andrew carelessly makes his way up. He coughs once into the mic. Everyone and everything pauses. People at the front look up expectantly. It is a brief moment of calm—the last one for the next forty minutes. The houselights dim. I scan the crowd, the community we have painstakingly drawn to us over the last decade—finally spotting the girl who has dutifully brought her camera to every show. Her presence is validation, evidence we're not dulling at the edges. Now we can begin. We launch, as always, into the piercing, thunderous, unruly "Transmogrifier." Notes charge out of the gate, stepping onto each other. Andrew's mouth becomes wider than anyone could have thought possible. Then people fly. The temperature in the room goes up five degrees.

As if on cue, sweat immediately starts to flow into my eyes and my fingers strain to hit every note. Bodies bounce.

This is what people have come for. The expectation of chaos; of being so close to a band teetering on the edge, near surrendering the whole show to sheer frantic energy; to thrill over not knowing till the last note if we, both band and audience, will make it through unscathed. Hungering to witness four individuals coming together and splitting apart, simultaneously.

That is the pact. The offering we make to this community of people who are willing to step outside, who agreed to leave the warmth of their apartments to trudge through snow and ice to spend their evening here, together. That's their end of the bargain; ours is to leave it all on the stage. No one expects us to hit every note square on the jaw tonight; they only want us to come out swinging.

We wrap it up. Andrew's voice holds the last yowl into the lights. Almost cracking the buildup of ice on the poorly insulated windows.

"Transmogrifier," the first song we wrote together as a band, the first song of any set worth a damn, the song that always lives up to the promise of its name, has transformed us again. The cold has been chased from the room. Every ear is warmly ringing, together.

Aaron is already counting in the second song.

Mark Macarthur played bass in the indie rock band Hot Little Rocket for more years than he can remember in the late '90s and through the 2000s. Today, he is executive producer of programming at CBC Music. Born in England and raised in Calgary, he now lives in Vancouver.

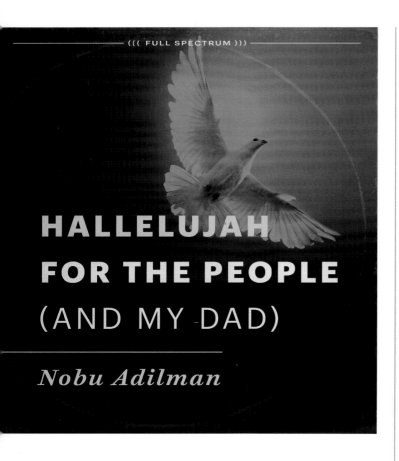

HALLELUJAH FOR THE PEOPLE (AND MY DAD)

Nobu Adilman

Music has always been a trusted companion. Each summer, the Beatles, the Weavers, and Queen were my family's soundtrack on the twenty-hour drive to Prince Edward Island; Portishead's *Dummy* saved me from self-destruction while tree-planting in the post-apocalyptic slash piles of deep Ontario; DJing radio shows at CKDU-FM introduced me to Halifax's incredible music scene, taught me how to create community and built life-long friendships. Music has saved my life more times than I can remember, and more recently, with Choir! Choir! Choir!, it's taken on new meanings time and time again as I've witnessed and experienced how songs help us celebrate the great times and comfort us through the sad.

In the summer of 2017 I did a lot of festival touring with Daveed Goldman, co-founder of C!C!C! The travel schedule was exhausting. Halfway through our tour, we landed at the Newport Folk Festival. The music that has been featured there over the years was my early education, but before we arrived, I had been too busy to think about what it meant to me.

The night before our show, Daveed and I were suddenly frozen into fear, silently freaking out about our 11 a.m. set the next morning, stuck in a tiny hotel room listening to R.E.M.'s *Automatic for the People*. Who would be there so early? Would anyone sing? Were we prepared to flop at one of the world's most storied music events?

The next morning, we were surprised to see a throng of people waiting to sing with us. We taught them our arrangement to Leonard Cohen's "Halle-lujah," and by the end of the last chorus we looked out at fifteen hundred people who were singing their hearts out and, beyond them, a beautiful, expansive harbour, dotted with boats, full of music fans enjoying the moment. We got off the stage and the staff told us it had brought them to tears. It was overwhelming.

I wanted to share the moment with my family, my loved ones. My mind drifted to my father, who had passed away more than ten years earlier. He intro-duced me to the arts, took me to concerts, and taught me the importance of music. He also loved Leonard Cohen. And that's when the tears started. A mix of relief that the show had gone so well, the love from the crowd, and the devastating need to share this with my dad sent me into emotional free fall. I couldn't control myself, and, pretty much cried tears of happi-ness and sadness for the rest of the day. Singing that one song in that special place made me feel both connected to my past and so grateful for where I was.

I don't care if anyone says that "Hallelujah" shouldn't be covered anymore. They're wrong!

Nobu Adilman is a television personality, filmmaker, and co-founder of Choir! Choir! Choir!, a drop-in sing-along that celebrates music and has held tributes to David Bowie, Prince, Leonard Cohen, and Gord Downie. In 2016, they established the Choir! Choir! Choir! Foundation, and they now tour the world to bring people together and sing.

THE BRIGHT SIDE

Aqsa Zubair

STEREO

CAT NO. 322B

That **Toronto** morning, I stumbled into an Uber. My antisocial self settled into the back seat, opening the *Financial Post* to keep my mind off work and my destination.

"Do you mind if I turn on some music?" I asked the middle-aged driver. I never got his name, but he had kind eyes and a thick accent. I guessed he was Middle Eastern, but didn't feel relaxed enough to ask.

"Sure, go for it," I replied without thinking twice. Another distraction from a conversation I wouldn't know how to carry. That is, until I heard myself humming a familiar tune. I looked up, and yes, without a doubt, the Killers' "Mr. Brightside" was playing.

"Oh my God, I LOVE this song!!" I yelled, startling the driver. The roaring guitars and tumbling, delirious lyrics had snapped me out of my stupor.

"Really?" he replied. "It's my favourite, too. Do you know all the words?"

"YES!" I answered. So he cranked up the volume and we proceeded down Front Street West, music blaring, singing along at the tops of our lungs a song we both knew all too well. The driver's singing was horribly out of tune, but mine wasn't any better. It really didn't matter.

Sometimes it's moments like these that take you out of the shell we feel so safe in. Sometimes it takes songs like "Mr. Brightside" to unlock a carefree version of ourselves. Sometimes, all we need is a reminder that we are social beings.

Aqsa Zubair is a senior officer with the Bermuda Monetary Authority, where she specializes in fintech and blockchain strategy. A graduate of the University of Waterloo and the Saïd Business School in Oxford, UK, she grew up in Markham, Ontario, and now lives in Toronto.

AMAZING GRACE

The great guitar lick from the Smiths' "How Soon Is Now?" cuts through the air and people flood the Luv-A-Fair dance floor. From the DJ booth up above I see punks with mohawks, goths in hoodies, New Wavers and gay people in outrageous outfits, all dancing with pure abandon. The bravest, the exhibitionists, get up on the speakers and do their thing as the heaving mass cheers and sings along: we are human, we need to be loved, just like everybody else does.

It was the late '80s, and I was doing my undergrad degree in literature at UBC. I had started DJing at CiTR, the university radio station, and had worked my way up to Luv-A-Fair, this huge barn of a place in a sleazy part of downtown Vancouver, where the red-light and the gay districts met. It had been a gay disco club, then started attracting a more alternative crowd. The old DJs told me about the night it went New Wave; the patrons sat down on the dance floor and demanded *their* music. The first song of the new era was Lou Reed's "Walk on the Wild Side." The club never looked back, becoming the outré place to go out in Vancouver. Going there was like walking into a Fellini movie.

One of the servers was a hetero guy who liked to wear high heels and stockings. Another whirled around on roller skates. Everything was accepted. Straight, gay, goth, punk, as long as you weren't a dick, anyone could walk onto the floor and dance. Nobody questioned it, nobody judged. There was a level of acceptance that predates the era we live in by decades. It was an amazing zone of tolerance. It was a community, a place to go, where being yourself wasn't just allowed, it was celebrated.

It was a special thing DJing at Luv-A-Fair. The crowd trusted us to deliver what they wanted to hear, in the way you trust a sommelier in a restaurant. Before digital, great alternative music was hard to find, and we were the source. We played the latest, coolest sounds and they danced: the Cure, Iggy Pop, New Order, the Cramps, Depeche Mode . . .

One of the DJs worked at Nettwerk Records, who produced great local bands like Skinny Puppy and Moev. They'd cut a new single, press the vinyl, then take it down to the club and spin it. Some great songs got their first airing at Luv-A-Fair. It was an incubator, a womb for creative people or anyone who just wanted to be different.

I'll never forget my last night DJing there. It was the summer of 1994; I had quit everything and was going off to Scotland to pursue academia. The last song I put on was "Amazing Grace," a bagpipe version. Everyone stormed the floor, just a pillar of people. One of the huge doormen (the place had these really tough bouncers, to keep out tourists and troublemakers) came up to the DJ booth on the second floor, grabbed me, and carried me down.

I found myself floating above this mass of people loving me, whirling around the dance floor, during "Amazing Grace"!

So I found myself floating above this mass of people loving me, whirling around the dance floor, during "Amazing Grace"! Then someone in the booth threw on Nirvana's "Smells like Teen Spirit," an amazing juxtaposition, and the crowd just started jumping. There I was in a mosh pit of insanity for my last song.

And that was it. My last moment at Luv-A-Fair.

Well, not quite. After close to three decades, the club announced it was closing in 2003. On September 1, I went down to pay my respects and dance with the throngs at the closing party. We let it all hang out one last time. They even played "How Soon Is Now?"

Now a condo tower with a Starbucks has replaced the Luv-A-Fair at the corner of Seymour and Drake. How Vancouver is that?

Darren Reiter has an MA from Edinburgh University. He is CEO of eMedia Networks International, a music company, and a producer with Purple Productions, an independent film company responsible for such features as *Random Acts of Romance* (2012). He was born and still lives in Vancouver.

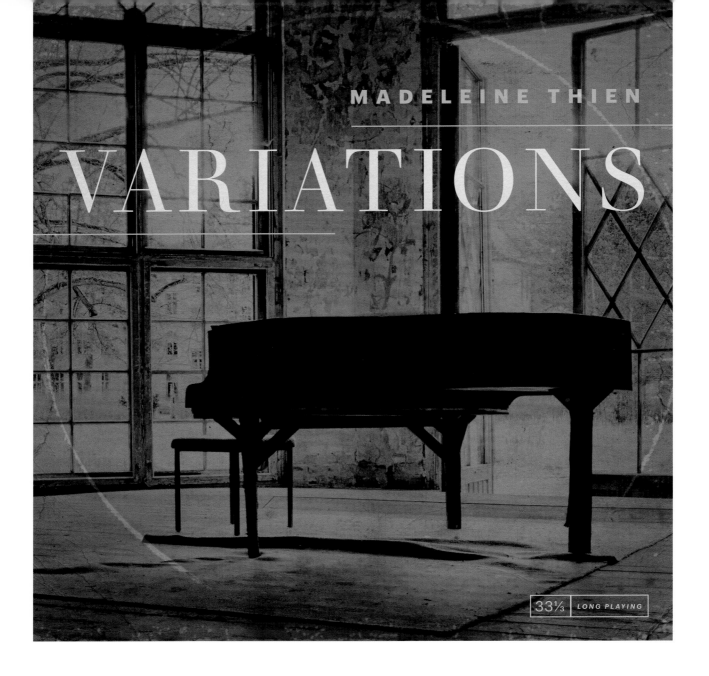

33⅓ | *LONG PLAYING*

MADELEINE THIEN

VARIATIONS

In 2011, I lived in Berlin for a year, accompanying my partner who had a fellowship in the city. For the previous three years, I had been experiencing what felt like a continuous sorrow, which the doctors called depression. For months at a time, I had found it difficult to move, rise from bed, and think clearly. Perhaps the reasons for this state were many and old. I had been working on a novel that troubled me. That work, *Dogs at the Perimeter*, had brought me to Cambodia over months and years to research the Cambodian Civil War and genocide. After five years of thinking and re-thinking, returning often to this country that I loved, the novel was published that spring.

But I could not lift myself from the things I had learned. One morning, worried that I was falling back into illness, I took my music player and went for a long walk. I found myself in a neighbouring area

These unfolding variations elicit joy, playfulness, grief, lightness, devastation, wonder, and more: a universe of feelings for which we have no names.

where thirty-three viaducts, the Yorckstrasse bridges, span a busy thoroughfare. The vast majority of these bridges, supported by numerous cast iron columns, lead nowhere, or are obsolete; their destinations— warehouses and yards—were destroyed during the Second World War. It felt like walking through a light and dark corridor, ruined, disturbing, and full of memory. The structures still in use rumble as trains arrive and depart, or as the traffic at street level grows heavy.

As I came to the bridges, Glenn Gould's 1955 recording of Bach's *Goldberg Variations* began playing through my headphones. I passed beneath these bridges that led to nowhere. The opening aria, haunting and simple, passed through me. From this aria, Bach builds his variations. A handful of notes, initially played by the left hand, are reworked into a series of thirty variations and canons, as if a strand of DNA is living out its permutations. These unfolding variations elicit joy, playfulness, grief, lightness, devastation, wonder, and more: a universe of feelings for which we have no names. I wept as I passed under the Yorckstrasse bridges, through the endless movement, changes and histories around me and into those thirty minutes of music. So many things of life seemed tied together, unwilling to be separated, shading into the next and the next.

Over the next five years, I listened to the *Goldberg Variations* again and again as I worked on another book. This one would be about music, revolution, and time. This novel became *Do Not Say We Have Nothing*, published in 2016. The *Goldberg Variations* provided a structure to this five-hundred-page work; it provided hope in the form of beauty, continuity, and the re-experiencing of time itself, time which grows ever more dense and complex as the wheel turns, as history rises, overwhelms, recedes, and returns around us.

Even now, years later, when I re-listen to Glenn Gould's recording, I'm brought back to the world that seemed to open around me back in 2011. Lately, I've fallen in love with Beethoven's last three piano sonatas. People say that, through these compositions, Beethoven, who by then had lost his hearing, found a way to bring together old forms and present dichotomies; he found a further way to exist. Like the *Goldberg Variations*, these three sonatas continue to confound, move, and enchant me even after countless listenings; they create an ever-shifting landscape. The recordings that move me greatly are those by Claude Frank, who passed away in 2014.

Madeleine Thien has published three novels and a short story collection. Her most recent novel, *Do Not Say We Have Nothing*, won the Governor General's Award and the Giller Prize and was shortlisted for the Booker Prize. Born in Vancouver, she lives in Montreal and is a professor of English at the City University of New York.

KEN MACLEOD

HYMN OF JOY

Starting a new social service program from a blank page is a slog.

Introducing a completely new idea—using after-school orchestra music classes to inspire and transform the lives of marginalized children—required me to explain it hundreds of times.

And then there was the insistent cajoling, enticing, promising, and pleading to government, school officials, teachers, and donors to get the initial pilot project going.

It was exciting, and I was passionately convinced this would change the lives of kids. But I don't play music. I don't teach music. My part is done on the computer, on the phone, over coffee, in countless meetings and so many "what if?" conversations.

So, on a warm day in June, ten months into the launch, I was expecting a good event, but was in my manager and promotor mindset. This was the public benchmark of success for the first year, and we would leverage it to build support for more.

> Faces lit by the joy inside them, the young singers and musicians brought us to tears with their commitment to the moment.

As always, I was thinking of how I would report it to various people.

The basement room was set. Concrete floor. Steel chairs in rows. Sunlight filtering through high windows. The space was packed with parents, grandparents, siblings, aunts, uncles, all vibrating with anticipation.

Seated before them, ready to play, was the string orchestra. For three hours each day, five days a week after school, for ten months, these grade schoolers had studied how to play music and perform as part of an orchestra. The musicians were six and seven years old, fidgeting, poking their neighbours, waving to mums and dads and grandparents.

The conductor stepped into place. The children stood, instruments ready, now completely serious. Heads held high with pride. Behind them, a children's choir.

The conductor signalled. The children threw themselves into the performance. Instantly transformed, no longer children from poverty but orchestra musicians, they owned the room.

The pleasure was exquisite. We were dazzled. The room was awash in sheer joy.

We were all transported to a new place, where the future is bright and everything is possible. They made visible the nurturing impact of playing music together and the incredible power of feeling their own accomplishments.

The song was "The Hymn of Joy," a poem written by Henry van Dyke in 1907, sung to the rousing and triumphant melody of the final movement of Beethoven's Symphony No. 9. The children sang of light, the challenge to the darkness that can overwhelm us. They sang of the beauty of nature, of human creation, and the brotherhood of humanity.

Faces lit by the joy inside them, the young singers and musicians brought us to tears with their commitment to the moment. They beautifully delivered the hymn's call for all of us to "join this mighty chorus" and to learn how to love each other, for it is this joyful music that will lead us "sunward."

My soul was flooded with joy. My agenda disappeared. The weight of our struggles and setbacks dropped away. All that was left was the music, the children, and the blinding brilliance of their potential.

Sistema NB was created to provide opportunity for children who would otherwise be left out in society. Ten years later, it operates ten centres in New Brunswick, where more than twelve hundred children and youth sing and play music each day.

All the musicians and singers and teachers have extraordinary memories of their time with Sistema NB. But I often return to that basement. The scene is vivid. I conjure up the sight and sound and, again, feel that joy.

I emerge every time refreshed, and think, *Who would not want* that *for more children?*

Ken MacLeod, a former university teacher, owner of a fundraising consulting company, and provincial MLA, is now CEO of the New Brunswick Youth Orchestra. He has led NBYO to international recognition for the quality of its musicians and its diverse and innovative programming, including the Sistema NB program.

MULTI-DIRECTIONAL STEREO | AMP403B

Rilee ManyBears

MOTHER EARTH'S HEARTBEAT

LONG PLAYER LP

Music plays a huge role in my life, as it does in many people's lives. The emotions it stirs up, whether it's a happy song or a sad song, inspires me or gets me going. As an athlete, I love to slap on my headphones and jam out. It helps me face so many challenges.

It's an old one, but "Going the Distance" by Bill Conti, from the film *Rocky*, is one song I love to put on in my vehicle. It gets me pumped up, inspires me when I'm on the way to a competition. I listen to it pretty much every day.

Indigenous music, powwow music, is different. It calms my emotions, brings peace to my soul. The beat of the drums reminds me of Mother Earth's heartbeat. I get chills and goosebumps when I think of all the Indigenous people, the ancestors, who came before us. Their presence flows through the drumbeat and gives me strength. Every year I go to the powwow, I love hearing the drumming and seeing the dancers.

Another song that gets me pumped up is "Electric Pow Wow" by A Tribe Called Red. I run long distance— on some workouts I run twenty-plus kilometres— and I often listen to music like that to get me going.

I just came back from several months in Kenya, where I was doing high-altitude training. Now I am working out on the reserve where I live, which is the second-largest by area in Canada. It inspires my connection to the land, knowing that my ancestors have lived here for generations, and that I'm leaving my footprints on the nation.

Rilee ManyBears is a long-distance runner from Siksika Nation, a Blackfoot settlement an hour east of Calgary. He won one gold and two bronze medals at the 2014 North American Indigenous Games, and gold in the 8 km race at the 2015 World Indigenous Games. In 2016, he became the first member of Siksika Nation to complete the Boston Marathon.

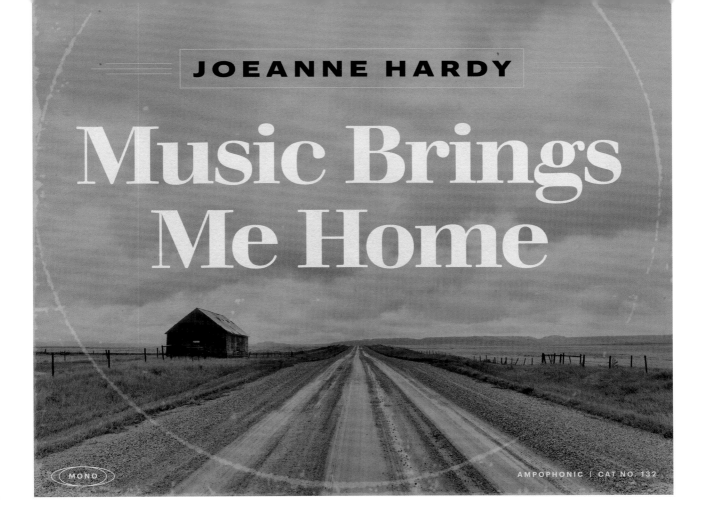

JOEANNE HARDY

Music Brings Me Home

MONO

AMPOPHONIC | CAT NO. 132

My story of music starts, as I imagine many stories do, in my childhood, in rural Saskatchewan. I grew up on an acreage in a ranching community called Maple Creek. My parents had a great record player in the living room—one that looked like a beautiful piece of furniture—and an old portable 8-track player. They played old-school country music in the house and in the barn, and when we travelled to rodeo competitions, that old portable 8-track came with us.

There weren't a lot of albums—Charley Pride, Kenny Rogers, Ned Miller—so I got to know them all well. But the favourite was Don Williams. It wasn't possible to put on his album *You're My Best Friend* without my mom breaking into song.

Those feelings and those memories make me feel like home. I live in the city now and the life we had in the country is a faraway memory. That is, until I start playing Don Williams's title song "You're My Best Friend" and I'm instantly back there, feeling connected to my roots. My body feels a little lighter and my heart just beats a little stronger somehow.

For some people it's photos or physical things that connect them to their home. But for me it's simple. It's that song.

JoeAnne Hardy is president of WBM Technologies and lives in Saskatoon with her husband and family. An entrepreneur and industry advocate, she is also grandma to a curious and fearless little boy who is the apple of her eye.

States of Mind

THEO FLEURY

It's wild how a song comes together, when you're with those really smart, creative people who can take a thought or a word or an idea and turn it into this magical thing.

Métis people are very musical; it's in our DNA. My fondest memories of being a kid are of sitting by my grandfather, listening to him play the fiddle. My dad and my uncle were entertainers and there was always music happening at all of our family gatherings, lots of great singers. My first cousin Amber finished top ten on *Canadian Idol* one year.

When I played hockey, we used dance music to get pumped up before a game, the kind they play in clubs. I still love that stuff. I listen to a lot of '80s and '90s music, and old country. Funny how you end up liking what your parents liked: Charley Pride, Hank Snow. I was country back before it was cool.

About fifteen years ago I started dealing with my addiction, which was rooted in trauma. I listened to a lot of sacred songs in sweat lodges. The drums and rattles put you in a meditative state of mind; it's a cool experience. The thing about healing is, you're never really in a bad place. Healing is forever, there's no end to it, you just continue. We're always looking for the cure, but when it comes to healing from trauma, it's just a continuum of self-reflection and self-knowledge and self-relationship, to get to a place of forgiveness. To do that you have to learn compassion, empathy, vulnerability; you can't learn those in one sitting, you have to feel them. It's a state of mind. And music can change the way you feel. There's a Clint Black song about that, "State of Mind," that I really like.

I'm a left-handed person—writing books or songs or making documentary films taps into the creative part of my brain. Hockey was no different; it's a very creative sport. I've always been a creative guy. Five years ago I turned to making music: writing songs and singing them.

I'm really proud of the first album I put out, *I Am Who I Am*. It's basically my book, *Playing with Fire*, turned into music. Putting together an album is a really awesome process: the drum and bass start it, then you put all the filling instruments in, then I show up and sing my vocals, then you add the harmonies. Hearing it after it's been mastered is amazing.

It's wild how a song comes together, when you're with those really smart, creative people who can take a thought or a word or an idea and turn it into this magical thing. Not a lot of people can do that—not well, anyway. There's a lot of dopamine and serotonin happening when you're in the zone. For somebody like me, who struggles with mental health issues, I can use all the dopamine and serotonin I can get. It puts me in that really great space.

Theo Fleury played more than a thousand NHL games between 1989 and 2003 for the Calgary Flames, Colorado Avalanche, New York Rangers, and Chicago Blackhawks, helping Calgary win the Stanley Cup in 1989. He represented Canada twice at the Olympics, winning a gold medal in 2002. His bestselling autobiography, *Playing with Fire*, was made into a play and a documentary film. His many awards include an honorary doctorate from the University of Guelph-Humber for outstanding contributions to the mental health of Canadians.

ZAYNAH BHANJI

your eyes

AMPORAMA 927 | BOLLYWOOD CLASSIC SERIES

My grandmother turned eighty last year. At the birthday party, I got up and sang a song for her: "Teri Aankhon Ke Siva." I started to learn Indian classical singing when I was four years old, and it's the first song I ever learned to sing. Now I'm sixteen and it's still my favourite. Hearing me sing it made my grandmother cry a bit. It was a beautiful way to mark this important milestone in her life. She was born in Tanzania in Africa, but her grandparents came from India.

"Teri Aankhon Ke Siva" is from *Chirag*, a classic black-and-white Bollywood movie from 1969. The first line translates as "What else is there in the world, apart from your eyes?" It's a long song, and all the words are a guy singing to a girl about her eyes. On the surface level it is just about her eyes, but it's really about love, not just romantic love, but love in general. I sang it in Panorama, a competition for Bollywood singing, when I was eleven. I won first prize.

Even to this day I still sing that song. I sing it pretty much anywhere, when I'm doing my homework or at home doing chores. If I'm feeling sad it cheers me up. My mum sings it, too; she joins in sometimes. It really means a lot to me and my family.

Zaynah Bhanji is in grade 10 at Woodlands School in Mississauga.

196 THE AWESOME

STEPHEN DABOUS

IF YOU WERE THE ONLY GIRL IN THE WORLD

My father passed away from Alzheimer's and Parkinson's dementia. He had a long good-bye, spending the last five years of his life in the Veterans Centre at Sunnybrook Hospital in Toronto. There he—and I, and all the rest of the family—were exposed to music therapy. Toward the end of his life, when Dad wasn't quite who he had been, one of the few times he seemed to have any real comfort was when he was engaged in his music therapy.

The day he passed away, Candy, the Sunnybrook music therapist, did something remarkable. She came into his room with her guitar in her hands and sang to him in his last moments. The song she played was one she knew he loved: "If You Were the Only Girl in the World." My mom and dad had danced to Perry Como's hit version of this old standard at their wedding in 1947. My mom, my aunt, and I were at my dad's bedside as Candy played guitar and sang, and it was beautiful.

Eleven years later, when my mom passed, we played the same song for her as she took her last breaths. And we told ourselves that Mom was dancing her way into Dad's arms, and being greeted by my brother (who had passed away at forty-one) and all her family and friends who had passed before her, all singing her into her new world.

The remarkable thing was that Mom had been in a comatose state for about twenty hours. Then, just as she took her last breath, she lifted her right hand, looked me in the eye and made a sign that she and Dad had done together all of their married life: an "It's beautiful" sign with her thumb and forefinger.

Whenever I hear "Only Girl," either because I've selected it or because it just randomly pops up, I'm hit with a rainbow of emotions—inspiration, love, hope, images of my parents and my brother reuniting in a "special" place . . . and the awesome feeling of being washed with happiness.

Stephen Dabous played semi-professional hockey in Europe, then returned to Toronto to enter the corporate ranks, build his own business, and raise his family. Blessed with positive DNA, he is inspired by the energy of youth.

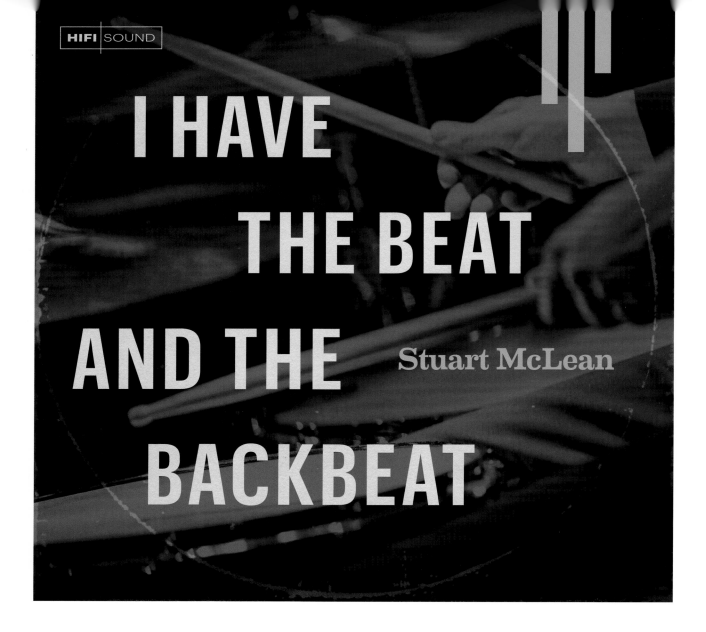

I HAVE THE BEAT AND THE BACKBEAT

Stuart McLean

For more than a decade, I produced a radio and live show called The Vinyl Cafe, which was created, hosted, and written by the late Stuart McLean. Stuart wrote fictional stories about a guy named Dave who owned a record store called, you guessed it, the Vinyl Cafe. Music played a big role in Dave's life and, as a result, on our show.

When The Awesome Music Project reached out and asked us if Stuart had ever written anything about music, I immediately thought of this story. It captures what Stuart loved about music: it connects us to others, reminds us to have fun, and helps us feel things deeply.

This is a short excerpt from a story we call "The Lost Chords." Stuart wrote it for a live concert that we recorded at the Hillside Festival in Guelph, Ontario. As always, I was sitting backstage at that show, in the shadows, out of view of the audience but within eyeshot of Stuart.

He was reading the story for the first time. Sometimes he would look over at me during a story or a song . . . especially when he was feeling what he

> **I have the beat and the backbeat. I have the Beatles and I have the Rolling Stones. I have Leonard Cohen singing "I'm Your Man" and Bob Dylan singing "Positively 4th Street" and, God bless her, I have Aretha Franklin.**

would call "big feelings." When he got to the last few lines, he looked over at me and—just like Dave in the story—he beamed. I did, too. I beamed because I knew what Stuart was feeling, as I was feeling the same thing. It was happiness. It was love. It was gratitude. It was the recognition that music—like all great art—makes life a little bit better, a little bit clearer, a little bit more meaningful.

Jess Milton, longtime producer of *The Vinyl Cafe*.

Dave went to the show, of course. This time he stayed till the end. He stood on the edge of the stage like the old days.

As Scamp walked on, Dave grabbed him by the arm and said, "This is nice."

Scamp laughed. Standing there on the edge of the stage with his guitar on his shoulder. "Yeah," he said. "It's nice."

Then he said, "I've been writing, eh. I've got a record coming. In the fall. New songs."

It was one of those shows Dave knew he would always remember. Dennis on bass, *not* playing so many notes. And the drummer, all snapping and syncopated and all over the off beats. Keith? Keith rocked as always. But Scamp took a lot of the vocals. Scamp at the mic. Singing his new songs.

There was a moment halfway through the set, when they were doing a bluesy kind of thing, but up-tempo and rocky . . . locked in a groove and the guy on drums did this totally joyful thing which caught Dennis by surprise and he laughed out loud and Scamp turned and they all smiled at each other. Scamp looked into the wings right then and beamed at Dave and Dave thought, it will never get any better than this. Some people have God, and some people have money, and some people don't have anything at all. I have this. I have the beat and the backbeat. I have the Beatles and I have the Rolling Stones. I have Leonard Cohen singing "I'm Your Man" and Bob Dylan singing "Positively 4th Street" and, God bless her, I have Aretha Franklin. That's when he started dancing.

Stuart McLean was a radio broadcaster, humourist, and author, best known for the CBC Radio program *The Vinyl Cafe*, which he hosted from 1994 to 2015. This is an excerpt from "The Lost Chords," a *Vinyl Cafe* story written by McLean. He wrote seventeen books and won many awards, including three Stephen Leacock Memorial Medals for Humour and the Order of Canada. He died in 2017.

A SENSE OF CONNECTION

Jennifer Stephen

The first time I felt how powerfully music can bring people together was in high school, at Sir John Franklin in Yellowknife. Our meagre school band, all ten or so of us, had a trip planned to the community of Łutselk'e, population three hundred, on the east arm of Great Slave Lake. We boarded a plane on Yellowknife Bay in the middle of winter and took a very bumpy ride along with our band director and instruments: a few saxophones and trumpets, flutes, drums, and my tuba. As we neared our destination all we could see was the frozen lake and a few trees, behind which stood the buildings that made up Łutselk'e.

We landed on the frozen lake and were greeted by a welcoming committee of men and women with snowmobiles. We all piled onto snowmobiles and rode through the snow to the local school. There we played a concert in the gym with what felt like the entire community in attendance. As a young adult I couldn't believe how generous our hosts were with their time and how much they appreciated what we

were bringing to them. For those few hours I felt I was a part of their community as well as my own.

Fast-forward a couple of years and the roles were reversed. I attended my first orchestral concert as a teenager. The touring orchestra had planned to perform at our local arts and culture centre, but it was too small to accommodate their numbers. Instead, the gym was draped with black fabric, the bleachers were pulled out, and we concertgoers piled in to witness what for us was a rare and extremely welcome experience. I have no recollection of what music the orchestra played, but I do remember being in awe of the sound of so many instruments together, and the power of the sound the ensemble produced. Once again, I was struck at how people will come together around music, to experience it not only as individuals but also together, as a community. It was an incredibly powerful experience, and one that I have carried with me ever since.

Growing up in a fairly isolated city, these two experiences helped give me a sense of connection to those outside, as we shared in the impact of the musical experiences together. For those few hours, not only did our paths cross, we were also on the same journey. Today, when I sit in the audience of a concert, or when I am on stage myself playing, I am still struck by that sharing of the journey. It's a big reason why I ended up choosing the career and path that I did.

Jennifer Stephen is originally from Yellowknife and now lives in Toronto, where she teaches and plays the tuba with groups such as the Toronto Symphony Orchestra, the Canadian Opera Company Orchestra, the National Ballet Orchestra, the Hannaford Street Silver Band, Esprit Orchestra, and the Hamilton Philharmonic. She is on faculty at the National Music Camp of Canada and the Royal Conservatory of Music.

EVERYTHING IS AWESOME!!!!

ROSE STEEDMAN

I like really happy and lively songs, like "It's Going Down" from *Descendants 2* and "High Hopes" by Panic! at the Disco. When I'm bored, they're fun to listen to. It makes me feel cheerful-er and more comfortable. I forget the things that are worrying me and want to sing along. I do dance class and play the piano, but I like just listening to music more.

I love the song "Everything Is Awesome!!!" by Tegan and Sara, from *The LEGO Movie*. It's about sticking together and doing things in a team. It's the favourite song of Emmet, the movie's hero—he listens to it all the time! I'd like to do that, too, if I could. I'd feel better about life.

And the exclamation mark is my favourite character! It makes everything happy.

Rose Steedman is just starting grade 3. She lives in Vancouver with her brother, Sami, and Puzzle, a tortoiseshell rescue cat who is awesome.

music, the universal language

The Oldest Art

- Neanderthals made music, as does every known human culture, past and present.

- Archeological evidence shows that music is older than agriculture or cave painting.

- Flutes 43,000 years old made from bird bone and mammoth ivory were found in a cave in southern Germany. These were used by early *Homo sapiens*.

- There are many references to classical Indian music in the Vedas, the Hindu scripture, the oldest known religious text, created between 1700 and 500 BCE.

Medicine for the Soul

- Ancient Egyptian priest physicians called music "medicine for the soul" and often used chant therapies to help cure illness.

- In Ancient Babylon, healing rites often included music.

- In Ancient Greece, music was prescribed for emotionally disturbed individuals.

- Patients in manic states were told to listen to the calming music of the flute, while those suffering from depression were prescribed dulcimer music.

A Positive Vehicle

- Plato described music as medicine, and "an art imbued with power to penetrate into the very depths of the soul."

- In the Bible, King Saul's depressive symptoms were alleviated by the skillful harp playing of David, "the sweet psalmist of Israel."

- The Roman philosopher Boethius believed that music either improved or degraded human morals.

- Saint Basil the Great recommended music as a positive vehicle for sacred emotion.

- The United States' Bureau of Indian Affairs contains 1,500 songs used for healing purposes by Native Americans.

A Remedy for Melancholy

- Italian Renaissance composer Gioseffo Zarlino thought that music could be used to relieve pain, and to treat depression, mania, and the plague.

- In *The Anatomy of Melancholy*, written in 1621, Robert Burton wrote, "Besides that excellent power [music] hath to expel many other diseases, it is a sovereign remedy against Despair and Melancholy, and will drive away the Devil himself."

- The Italian castrato Farinelli was said to have cured King Philip V of Spain's depression by singing for him in the 1730s; the high-pitched singer was rewarded with a salary for life.

sources: BBC.com, History of Music and Art Therapy blog, Claire Growney

HEALING CLINICAL DEPRESSION THROUGH MUSIC

One of the primary goals of The Awesome Music Project is to fund research that studies the links between music and mental health. Below is an overview of a special research initiative between the Centre for Addiction and Mental Health (CAMH) and the Music and Health Research Collaboratory (MaHRC) of the University of Toronto. The Awesome Music Project is proud to have identified this project as its initial benefactor.

Music has long been known to stimulate emotions, change mood, and revive memories. A growing body of research shows evidence that music can have a positive effect on behavioural issues, mood disorders, chronic pain, and neurological conditions like Parkinson's disease.

A new joint research project between CAMH and MaHRC explores the power of music to treat clinical depression. Depression is a leading cause of disability globally, and this project offers both an opportunity to understand more about its cause, and to develop a novel, non-pharmacological approach to treating depression and healing damaged neural functions.

Patients in this project will participate in a four-week, twelve-session neurologic music therapy program focusing on selective attention, executive function, and movement exercises. Cognitive testing for different domains of function will be carried out repeatedly, and neuroimaging of nerve connection density will be completed both before and after the therapy program.

Using positron emission tomography (PET)–based brain imaging techniques, researchers will study the effects of neurologic music therapy on brain systems—specifically those that control attention, memory, and movement. People suffering from depression often experience difficulties with these functions, and this study will examine how music can be applied to help re-train the brain in these areas. The researchers are particularly interested in the ability of music to form new neurological connections to improve mood, concentration, and coordination of thought and movement. This will help identify how effectively music can be used as a treatment for this common and disabling mental illness.

These imaging techniques will also allow researchers to gain a better understanding of the biological factors associated with cognitive impairment in depression. Of particular interest is discovering the relationship between the density of the nerve connections and the performance of brain systems impaired by depression. Researchers will also explore the potential of developing a new diagnostic tool for depression—specifically, a blood test to identify biomarkers reflecting nerve connection density. This could identify patients with depression who would benefit from neurologic music therapy.

The project will be led by a team of three researchers, including members of CAMH's Campbell Family Mental Health Research Institute. Each scientist is a distinguished Canada Research Chair in his field.

CAMH/MaHRC Joint Music Therapy Research Project Team

Jeffrey Meyer Head of the Neurochemical Imaging Program (Mood and Anxiety Disorders) at the Research Imaging Centre, Campbell Family Mental Health Research Institute

Michael H. Thaut Director of the Music and Health Research Collaboratory at the University of Toronto

Neil Vasdev Director of the Azrieli Centre for Neuro-Radiochemistry at the Centre for Addiction and Mental Health

acknowledgments

The Hollywood movie producer Samuel Goldwyn once said, "The harder I work, the luckier I get." Mr. Goldwyn was right about a lot of things, but he was wrong about that. No amount of effort would have made this project possible without the amazing good fortune of working with many great people along the way. We feel extremely lucky for the ideas, passion, and support offered by so many organizations and individuals.

Our publisher, Page Two in Vancouver, has distinguished itself as a unique force in Canadian book publishing, for good reason. Jesse Finkelstein and Trena White have created a company that combines the robust framework of a big publisher with the compassion and personalization of an indie record label. They work with an incredible team, including Rony Ganon, Mary Trentadue, Lorraine Toor, Annemarie Tempelman-Kluit, Deanna Roney, Melissa Edwards, and Alison Strobel.

Scott Steedman served as writer and editor for this project. He helped collect the stories, wonderfully capturing the voice of each storyteller through interviews, email transcripts, and conversations. Without him, there would be no words.

Peter Cocking, Page Two's incredible designer, somehow managed to create not only the design and feel for the book, but also 111 beautiful album covers. His talents have brought these stories to life in ways we could not have imagined.

The Awesome Music Project is not just a book; it's a campaign to establish a global community that will accelerate solutions to mental health issues through the healing power of music. A small army of people have been essential in making this happen. Carrie Penner and Kristjan Bergey offered daily support, as did the entire Deloitte Digital team, including Sarah Lovering, Derek Derouin, Adiela Aviram, Christopher Page, Aqsa Zubair, and Shaunna Conway.

For their advice and ideas, thanks also to Tom Fishburne, Paul McNulty, Mike Kray, Chris Brandt, Maegan McConnell, Danny Michel, Carol-Ann Granatstein, Steve Dabous, and professor Nouman Ashraf and the MBA Social Innovation students from the Rotman School of Business at the University of Toronto. And for their expertise: Jennifer Buchanan, Eric Windeler, Melanie Lovering, and Eric Alper.

Our neighbour and project manager, Derek Vigar, has been vital to keeping us organized, dedicating countless hours of his free time. His Ultimate Frisbee game has suffered as a result.

Our families have been incredibly supportive. Our deepest thanks to Lilla, Nikki, Michael, Bridget, Jane, and Thomas. We have full-time jobs and have relied on our loved ones to be understanding and forgiving when we weren't doing what we were supposed to be doing while we were launching The Awesome Music Project.

Finally, the 111 contributors. It is the stories that make this project what it is. Every single contributor volunteered time and energy to take part in this idea. We are eternally grateful.

Movements are created one tiny step (or song) at a time, and this is no different. We are honoured and grateful for everyone's participation, support, ideas, and words of encouragement along the way.

Enjoy the crescendo,
Rob and Terry

People have always felt that music heals and soothes, and that it connects us to other people—and to the divine. Now, there is a growing body of scientific and clinical research to show that music therapy can help people facing all sorts of mental health challenges. The Awesome Music Project believes that, in an ideal world, every health care facility, employee assistance program, and learning centre would have a certified music therapist who could work with anyone and everyone who needed help.

Finding a Music Therapist

Call a music therapist if you or a loved one is suffering from a mental health issue. When selecting your music therapist, look for someone who:

- **is certified**
  Many countries have national certification programs for music therapists who have graduated with the prescribed educational requirements, including supervised clinical work. Try these professional associations to find a certified therapist in your region:

  CANADA
  Canadian Association of Music Therapists
  musictherapy.ca

  UNITED STATES
  American Music Therapy Association
  musictherapy.org

  WORLDWIDE
  World Federation of Music Therapy
  wfmt.info

- **participates in ongoing education**
  A commitment to continuing education and training indicates that a therapist has initiative and a passion for their profession. Their choice of training areas will also help you identify where their interests lie. Look at what they study, and decide if their continuing education is related to the goals you have for yourself.

- **is someone you can get along with**
  Your relationship with your therapist is essential to the healing process, so it is important to find someone you can connect with, and who makes you feel safe. A good therapist will take the time to get to know you, and to understand your goals.

Music therapists work with some of society's most vulnerable, including youth at risk; people with brain injuries, mental health issues, or learning challenges; and people in palliative care, long-term care, or dementia care. They also work with professionals, educators, and corporations to make sure that people experiencing stress can access this valuable and unique service when they need it.

A good music therapist will get to know the individual they are treating, and will use music—almost always live music—to develop a relationship. Together, the therapist and the patient will work toward improvements in mood, motivation, and memory.

Cataloguing in publication information
is available from Library and Archives Canada
ISBN 978-1-989025-29-1 (hardcover)
ISBN 978-1-989025-30-7 (ebook)

Page Two
www.pagetwo.com

Edited by Scott Steedman
Design and illustrations by Peter Cocking
Music consulting by Mark Macarthur
Printed and bound in Canada by Friesens
Distributed in Canada by Raincoast Books

19 20 21 22 23   5 4 3 2 1

Every reasonable effort has been made to contact the
copyright holders for work reproduced in this book.

This book is not intended as a substitute for the medical
advice of physicians. The reader should regularly consult
a physician in matters relating to his/her health and
particularly with respect to any symptoms that may
require diagnosis or medical attention.

Earlier versions of "Suzanne" and "Maple Leaf
Forever" appeared in *Take This Waltz: A Celebration
of Leonard Cohen*, edited by Michael Fournier and
Ken Norris (Muses, 1995).

An earlier version of "Skating to the Oldies" appeared
in the *Vancouver Courier* on March 5, 2012.

"A Voice That Touches My Heart" was adapted from
a post on Ron McDougall's blog *My Four Ladies*;
see myfourladiesblog.wordpress.com.

"Here Come the Drums" by Robert Wiersema was
adapted from his book *Walk like a Man: Coming of
Age with the Music of Bruce Springsteen*
(Greystone Books, 2011).

"The John MacLean March" by Hamish Henderson
quoted in Roddy Campbell's "Working-Class Hero"
© the Estate of Hamish Henderson.

"Born to Sing" by Michael Bublé is adapted from his
book *Onstage Offstage* (Doubleday Canada, 2011).

AMP   www.theawesomemusicproject.com